Solomon – Wise and Foolish

Solomon – Wise and Foolish

Tecwyn Morgan

THE CHRISTADELPHIAN
404 SHAFTMOOR LANE,
BIRMINGHAM, B28 8SZ

2007

First Published 2007

© 2007 Christadelphian Magazine and Publishing Association

ISBN 978-085189180-4

ACKNOWLEDGEMENTS

Cover
istockphotos

Bible Quotations
Scripture quotations are from the *The King James Version* of the Bible

Illustrations
Redrawn illustrations are based on the following publications (where only the author's name is given, details are included in the Bibliography):

pages – 29,143,145: *"Wilmington's Guide to the Bible"* (1987), Tyndale; 90, *"Macmillan Bible Atlas"* (1993), Carta; 118a,128, Leen Ritmeyer (with kind permission); 118b,119 *"Israel's Laws and Legal Precedents"* , C F Kent (1907), Hodder and Stoughton; 120, *"The Symbolism of the Biblical World"*, O Keel (1978), SPCK; 121, 173a, Shaw Caldecott; 131, 199a, Conner; 173b, Kitchen; 144, 199b,c, *"Interpreters' Dictionary of the Bible"*, Abingdon Press; 207, *"Bible Mapbook"*, Jenkins (1985), Lion.

Printed in England by:
The Cromwell Press Limited
Trowbridge
Wiltshire

Contents

MAPS, DRAWINGS AND CHARTS

vi

Preface

KING Solomon is renowned as someone who reigned in style, surrounded by luxury, pomp and ceremony. People came from far and near to behold his magnificence, including his outstanding public works and the splendour of his court, and to listen to his wise counsel. At a time in the ancient world when people loved pithy sayings and deep proverbs, he outdid everyone. But how wise was he really? Did his wisdom save him from sin; was he wise enough to secure eternal life in God's Coming Kingdom, when a greater than Solomon will sit upon David's throne in Jerusalem?

These are questions that intrigue people the world over. I once belonged to a small ecclesia on the South Coast of England which regularly considered this question. If there was an awkward silence during the discussion of the daily readings, an elderly brother had the habit of asking "Do you think Solomon will be in the Kingdom?" Once on a visit to Alayi ecclesia, in Eastern Nigeria, I was quite taken aback, having invited questions, to hear that very same question coming from the rear of the ecclesial hall. It is the sort of question you are left with when you finish reading about the exploits of the great king and there is a good reason why Scripture leaves you wondering about it.

This book began as a series of twenty articles in *The Christadelphian* in 1998-9 and has now been substantially enlarged and rewritten. A deliberate choice has been made to include references to other publications, where different points of view or further information can be obtained, to encourage readers to follow these things up for themselves. These have been relegated to notes at the end of each chapter so as not to disturb those readers who prefer not to be troubled by extraneous details. A bibliography has been provided for the same reason.

This is not a critique of Solomon's life, written to highlight his successes and failures. It is an attempt to pinpoint those things that we can learn from his experience so that we can be wiser in our own lives. We too are sometimes wise and sometimes foolish, but the same God who worked with Solomon, in an attempt to bring him to perfection, is also working with us and in our lives. May that long continue, to His praise and glory.

Tecwyn Morgan

Hampton-in-Arden, October 2007

Abbreviations

ABD   Anchor Bible Dictionary

BAR   Biblical Archaeological Review: bi-monthly publication of the Biblical Archaeology Society

EBDB   Enhanced Brown-Driver-Briggs-Gesenius Hebrew Lexicon

HBD   Hastings Bible Dictionary (1902)

LXX   The Old Testament in Greek (The Septuagint) 3rd Century BC

SBD   Smith's Bible Dictionary (3 Volume Edition; 1863)

Bibliography

Commentaries

Anderson, A A: *2 Samuel* (Word Biblical Commentary, 1989)

Auld, A G: *Kings* (The Daily Study Bible, St Andrew Press, 1986)

Baldwin, Joyce: *1 & 2 Samuel* (Tyndale Old Testament Commentaries, IVP, 1988)

Braun, R L: *1 Chronicles* (Word Biblical Commentary, 1989)

DeVries, S J: *1 Kings* (Word Biblical Commentary, 1989)

Farrar, F W: *Commentary on The Book of Kings* (The Expositor's Bible, Baker, 1982 Reprint)

Keil & Delitzsch: *Commentary on Kings & Chronicles* (Eerdmans, Reprinted 1976)

Kirkpatrick, A F: *2 Samuel* (Cambridge Bible for Schools & Colleges, 1903)

Lumby, J R: *1 Kings* (Cambridge Bible for Schools & Colleges, 1898)

McConville, J G: *Chronicles* (The Daily Study Bible, St Andrew Press, 1984)

Rawlinson, G: *Kings & Chronicles* (Speaker's Commentary, John Murray, 1872)

Selman, Martin: *1 Chronicles* (Tyndale Old Testament Commentaries, IVP, 1994) (1)

Selman, Martin: *2 Chronicles* (Tyndale Old Testament Commentaries, IVP, 1994) (2)

Willcock, M: *The Message of Chronicles* (The Bible Speaks Today series, IVP, 1987)

Williamson, H G M: *1 & 2 Chronicles* (The New Century Bible Commentary, Eerdmans, 1982)

Wiseman, D J: *1 & 2 Kings* (Tyndale Old Testament Commentaries, IVP, 1993)

Wordsworth, Christopher: *Samuel, Kings & Chronicles Commentary* (Rivingtons, 1873)

Other Works

Ashton, Bro. M J: *Chronicles of the Kings* (CMPA, 2003)

Bright, J: *A History of Israel* (SCM, 1980)

Bruce, F F: *Israel and the Nations* (Paternoster, 1963)

Crockett, W D: *A Harmony of Samuel, Kings & Chronicles* (Baker, 1974)

Davies, John J & Whitcomb, J C: *Israel from Conquest to Exile* (Baker, 1989)

De Vaux, R: *Ancient Israel – Its Life and Institutions* (Darton, Longman, Todd, 1961)

Edersheim, Alfred: *Old Testament Bible History* (Eerdmans, Reprinted 1986)

Farrar, F W: *Solomon – His Life & Times* (Men of the Bible, James Nisbet)

Fausset, A R: *Fausset's Bible Dictionary* (Regency Reference Library)

Fereday, W W: *Solomon and his Temple* (Ritchie, 1993)

Garstang John: *The Heritage of Solomon* (Williams & Norgate, London)

Heaton, E W: *Solomon's New Men* (Pica Press, 1974)

Islip, Bro. Peter: *Solomon the King* (Printland Publishers, 2002)

Kaiser, W C Jnr: *A History of Israel* (Broadman & Holman, 1998)

Kitchen, K A: *On the Reliability of the Old Testament* (Eerdmans, 2003)

Merrill, E H: *Kingdom of Priests* (Baker, 1987)

Standeven, Bro. Roy: *The Warrior Tamed* (Roelian Books, 2003)

Stanley, A P: *Lectures on the Jewish Church* (John Murray, 1866)

Tennant, Bro. Harry: *The Man David* (CMPA, 1969)

Thieberger, F: *King Solomon* (East & West Library, 1947)

Whittaker, Bro. Harry A: *Samuel, Saul & David* (McDonald Publishing Services, 1984)

Wood, Leon: *A Survey of Israel's History* (Zondervan, 1979)

Wood, Leon: *Israel's United Monarchy* (Baker, 1979)

Solomon's Temple

Ariel, I & Richman, C: *Encyclopaedia of the Holy Temple in Jerusalem* (Carta, 2005)

Bannister, J T: *The Temples of the Hebrews* (Blackwood, 1861)

Conner, K J: *The Temple of Solomon* (KJC Publications, 1988)

Ritmeyer, Bro. Leen: *The Quest* (Carta, 2006)

Ritmeyer, Bro. Leen & Sis. Kathleen: *Secrets of Jerusalem's Temple Mount* (Biblical Archaeological Society, 2006)

Shaw Caldecott, W: *Solomon's Temple, Its History and its Structure* (Religious Tract Soc., 1907)

1
"I am with Child"

WHEN David heard those words for the first time they must have sent his mind into a spin. Brought to him by a messenger from Bathsheba, they conveyed the most serious implications. He was the King of Israel, God's anointed monarch, ruling over God's people and sitting upon *"the throne of the LORD"* over Israel (1 Chronicles 29:23). Unlike pagan monarchs, he was a civil *and* religious leader; both functions combined in one post, in one person. God had called him to shepherd His people and both Jew and Gentile had now come to trust in his protection.

Yet, while David's army of mighty men had been away from Jerusalem, fighting against the Ammonite city of Rabbah, David had committed adultery with the wife of one of his soldiers, and not just any one of them. Uriah, Bathsheba's husband, was a Hittite who had come to Israel to serve David, and had been such a valiant and loyal servant that, despite his nationality, he had risen through the ranks to become a member of the King's personal bodyguard (2 Samuel 23:39). How badly he had been treated by the king he loved. And worse was in store.

David – The Deceiver
This is not the place to describe what happened next, for those details are well known. Suffice to say that David's conduct proved the truth of the poetic stanza:

"O, what a tangled web we weave,
When first we practise to deceive".[1]

1

SOLOMON – WISE AND FOOLISH

Uriah could not be persuaded to sleep with Bathsheba, even when he was drunk, so no cover-up proved possible. It followed that Bathsheba's message – that she was pregnant – triggered desperate action on David's part. Faithful Uriah returned to the battlefield carrying his own death sentence in the king's letter that he passed to Joab. For him it was to be the forefront of the hottest battle,[2] and certain death.

Bathsheba's warning – *"I am with child"* (11:5) – thus caused David to compound his original sin. Now, a few weeks later, he was also a deceiver, a murderer and a sinner separated from his God. For the next nine months or so, David became a recluse, apparently not daring to attend at the Tabernacle services in Gibeon, near to Jerusalem.[3] It was the prophet Nathan who broke through David's defences, with that sublimely subtle parable of the rich man and the poor lamb – a story calculated to arouse all David's shepherd instincts, as well as his innate sense of fair play. His indignant sentence, *"the man that hath done this thing shall surely die"*, was met with Nathan's inspired coup de grace – *"Thou art the man"* [4] – and David knew he was in deep trouble with his God.[5]

His Psalms from this period [6] give us a profound insight into David's feelings of deep repentance and contrition over a prolonged period. In the 2 Samuel 12 account, those feelings are expressed in just 6 words – *"I have sinned against the LORD"* – and the Divine response, which appears to come instantaneously, comprises just 12 gracious words – *"The LORD also hath put away thy sin; thou shalt not die"* (12:13). Neither the confession nor the forgiveness came easily, but the Scriptural narrative is compressed for a very important reason. Presented in this way it demonstrates a truth that is vital for all of us: *"If we confess our sins, he is faithful and just to forgive us our sins, and to cleanse us from all unrighteousness"* (1 John 1:9).

But does it really mean what it says – forgiveness for *"all unrighteousness"*? Could a man who was an adulterer, who had conspired another man's murder, and who had lied and deceived his fellows, really be forgiven? He could!

2

In time, David came to understand that, to accept it, and to marvel at it, just as we should.

The Forgiven Sinner

His words speak to forgiven sinners in all ages, whatever their sin, as the apostle Paul makes clear. *"Blessed is he"*, David wrote in his Psalm, *"whose transgression is forgiven, whose sin is covered. Blessed is the man unto whom the LORD imputeth not iniquity"*, and the apostle Paul endorsed and amplified that understanding in his careful exposition about "justification" by faith, given us in his Letter to the Romans.[7] Paul explains that God's forgiveness is full and free; for it is the product of His abounding grace – "unearned, unmerited ... indeed, demerited (favour) ... his free grace and gift, displayed in the forgiveness of sins, extended to men as they are guilty".[8]

No wonder Paul referred to, and quoted from, David's writings. The king was the perfect exemplar of the grace of God in action. As Nathan had said, David would not die, despite the letter of the law that stood against him. Instead he was a forgiven sinner. Not that he would escape the consequences of his actions, any more than we do when we commit acts of folly and stupidity. Nathan made that quite clear, too, cataloguing the things that inescapably would follow – the sword would never depart from his household, and David's *"neighbour"* (who turned out to be his son, Absalom), would pay him back in kind.[9] But David was forgiven and his dynasty would continue as God had promised, and according to the oath He had sworn to the King.[10]

That Davidic covenant is of vital importance to all of us, too, because of the eventual connection with the coming of the Lord Jesus Christ, who was so clearly anticipated in the promise of the One who would uniquely fulfil the words *"I will be his father, and he shall be my son"* (2 Samuel 7:14). Those who came before could only be fore-runners; their relationship to God could only be that of adopted sons, and that by faith.[11] When Jesus was born, nearly 1000 years later, he alone would be the literal fulfilment of the promise. So where was the first *"son"* to come from the house of David? Would he be one of the members

3

of the existing family, or was it to be someone who was still to be born?

Spoilt for Choice

David had been married early on, to Saul's daughter Michal, and had continued to enlarge his family, both in the wilderness and after his establishment as king, first in Hebron and then at Jerusalem. 1 Chronicles 3 lists the six sons born at Hebron (Amnon, Daniel, Absalom, Adonijah, Shephatiah and Ithream – to six of David's wives) before listing thirteen[12] born later in Jerusalem – in the last 33 years of David's life. In addition, there were *"the sons of the concubines and Tamar"* (verse 9). It was just as well David had a palace, with all those wives and children to look after!

The sons we know best, apart from Solomon – Amnon, Absalom and Adonijah – were able and influential in their own way. Absalom, in particular, came of kingly stock from both father and mother. Two of the lads certainly thought themselves worthy successors to their father and would have both been very distressed and angry if they had known the full details of what Nathan had said to David. Quite when he said it is difficult to know, because the actual prophecy was only made public when David was dying. But it seems that it was part of the set of covenant promises made at the time of 2 Samuel chapter 7 – what we know as 'The promises to David'. This, then, is what Nathan told David about his immediate successor:

> *"Behold, a son shall be born to thee, who shall be a man of rest; and I will give him rest from all his enemies round about: for his name shall be Solomon, and I will give peace and quietness unto Israel in his days. He shall build an house for my name; and he shall be my son, and I will be his father; and I will establish the throne of his kingdom over Israel for ever"* (1 Chronicles 22:9,10).

There are many indications that David did not make this prophecy public until near the end of his reign and we can understand why. To have done so could have sparked open rebellion on the part of the older sons of David, those born in Hebron years before Nathan spoke. But David now knew that the promised son was yet to be born, and when he was born he was to be named *"Solomon"* (peaceable). Given David's evident affection for Absalom in particular, that promise must have put David in something of a dilemma.

It is impossible to know which of the nine sons born to David in Jerusalem had been born before the prophetic promise – Ibhar, Elishama, Eliphelet, Nogah, Nepheg, Japhia, Elishama, Eliada, and Eliphelet. But, because it is clear that David's act of adultery with Bathsheba came after the gracious covenant God made with him, we do know that at least four sons were born after that, because they were all Bathsheba's children – *"These were born unto him in Jerusalem; Shimea, and Shobab, and Nathan, and Solomon, four, of Bathshua (or Bathsheba) the daughter of Ammiel"* (1 Chronicles 3:5). Just imagine the predicament for David and Bathsheba every time one of their sons was born. What were they to call the new-born? Could this conceivably be the child who was to be called *"Solomon"*?

They called the first one *"Shimea"* (rumour) and that probably speaks volumes for the public attention that was coming their way at the time,[13] and what they felt that people were saying about them behind their backs! The second they named *"Shobab"* (falling away, rebellious), perhaps because they were only too aware of the potential for rebellion if any of their other sons got to find out about God's arrangements for a successor. The third, they called *"Nathan"* (whom God gave), which was a nice way of showing that they bore God's prophet no ill will.

A "Solomon" – At Last

None had been named *"Solomon"*, perhaps because David and his new wife thought it impossible that God would accept a King from their union. But there must have been some indication of God's will in the matter, for the fourth and last son born to them was so named, and it pleased God:

> *"David comforted Bathsheba his wife, and went in unto her, and lay with her: and she bare a son, and he*[14]

5

called his name Solomon: and the LORD *loved him. And he sent by the hand of Nathan the prophet; and he called his name Jedidiah, because of the* LORD" (2 Samuel 12:24,25).

Notice again how compressed the narrative is. It reads as if Solomon had been born as an immediate replacement for the baby who had died.[15] Discreetly, the 1 Chronicles 3 account sets the record straight, but the compression shows that:

(a) God forgave the sin of David and Bathsheba;

(b) He accepted the relationship, and

(c) The promised successor was born to that couple – despite the wide choice available of David's other wives and concubines, as well as the sons who were already born.

In that way the grace of God, in all its splendour and magnificence, is seen displayed, and forgiveness is seen to be just that – a wiping clean of all the offences that had previously stood against the King and a total acceptance of his new wife, despite all that had happened. To this day we may have some difficulty coming to terms with things like this, but it is evident that God does not.

To confirm His acceptance of the new-born child, God sent Nathan who *"called [Solomon's] name Jedidiah, because of the* LORD" (2 Samuel 12:25). *"Jedidiah"* means *"beloved of Yah"* and that declaration was His way of confirming the choice as an acceptable one.[16] This was indeed the promised, and God-blessed, child. Now David knew for sure that he had been restored to fellowship. As he later said about all this: *"Of all my sons, (for the* LORD *hath given me many sons,) he hath chosen Solomon my son to sit upon the throne of the kingdom of the* LORD *over Israel"* (1 Chronicles 28:5). What made this confirmation especially significant for David was the linkage between his own name and that of his new-born son.

"Jedidiah" was a new name – coined for the purpose – and a very fitting one at that. For *"Jedid"* and *"David"*

come from the same Hebrew root, or from two very closely related ones.[17] *"Jedid"* combined David's own name with that of *"Yahweh"*, thus assuring him beyond doubt that he and his God were now entirely at one, through the birth of the child. In just the same way, the birth of the long-awaited Son of God assures us of Divine favour.

Because of the prophecies about him,[18] it was also known about the new-born babe that he would grow up to be –

- a man of rest, who would have rest from all his enemies round about;

- a Temple builder, for the name of the LORD;

- God's chosen 'son';

- God's appointed king, to rule over a Divine kingdom that would last forever.[19]

That was Solomon's destiny and, as David later made clear to his son, it placed demands upon him of the highest order, if he was to live up to God's great expectations. Like us, Solomon had to make his *"calling and election sure"* (2 Peter 1:10). He was born to greatness; just as we have been reborn into that same state – *"chosen ... before the foundation of the world, that we should be holy and without blame before him in love; having predestinated us unto the adoption of children"* (Ephesians 1:4,5). So whilst, at first glance, we may appear to be very different from Solomon, there are important parallels and we should learn from his life experiences, not just about Jesus but also about ourselves.

NOTES

[1] Sir Walter Scott: *"Marmion"* vi, xvii.

[2] 2 Samuel 11:15.

[3] 1 Chronicles 21:30.

[4] 2 Samuel 12:1-7.

SOLOMON – WISE AND FOOLISH

5 There appears to be general agreement that Nathan came
to challenge David about a year after the adultery had first
occurred (Davies & Whitcomb, pg.304; 2 Samuel 11:27 compared with 12:14-15).

6 Psalms 32 and 51 (see Bro. Whittaker, pgs.217-233, for
more details of this unhappy time in David's life).

7 Psalm 32:1,2 cited in Romans 4:6-8. Bear in mind that
David's "works" at this time merit death by stoning: this adds
weight to Paul's conclusion that we are not justified by works,
but by faith. Bro. Standeven, pg.299, makes the observation
that by his actions David had broken the 6th, 7th, 9th and
10th Commandments. Baldwin pg.244: *"... there is a way
back into fellowship with God even from the depths of evil".*

8 Trench, *"Synonyms of the New Testament"*, 9th Edition,
pages 153-161.

9 2 Samuel 12:10-12: *"I will take thy wives before thine eyes,
and give them unto thy neighbour, and he shall lie with thy
wives in the sight of this sun".*

10 2 Samuel 7:10-17; Psalm 89:33-35.

11 This was made clear in later Psalms, where the enigmatic
reference in 2 Samuel 7:14: *"If he commit iniquity, I will chas-
ten him with the rod of men, and with the stripes of the children of men",* is seen to have reference to those immediate
descendants of David who reigned as kings (see Psalm 89:30
and 132:12).

12 The 13 are separated into 4 and 9 (1 Chronicles 3:5-9), for
reasons that will become clear.

13 It is difficult to know for sure if this was the son who died
as a punishment from God (2 Samuel 12:19); the rumours
would have carried on for a long time, if today's interest in
media gossip is any indication of public interest in a
monarch's love life. There is nothing to indicate that the first
child died immediately after it was born – it may have been
2-3 months old. If so, he could have been named *"Shimea".*

14 It may be that Bathsheba named him *"Solomon"* as some
Hebrew manuscripts suggest; or it could have been Nathan
(see Keil & Delitzsch, who see this as explaining the expression *"because of the LORD",* i.e. on God's behalf). But it reads

as if the parents called him by that name (perhaps tentat..
ly) and Nathan confirmed that this was indeed the promise
child when he then declared him Jedidiah: *"beloved of the*
LORD".

[15] If Solomon had not been the last of Bathsheba's sons, there
is no sensible way of accounting for the record in 1 Chronicles
3:5. Farrar, pg.8, does his best to support the view that
Solomon was the next child to be born by suggesting that possibly his name is placed last for emphasis. He cites Josephus
in his favour (Antiquities vii.7.4); but the historian does little
more than paraphrase the 2 Samuel account.

[16] God never expresses Himself nominally; he really loved
Solomon, and was saying so at the outset (Nehemiah 13:26).

[17] SBD, article *"Jedidiah"* and Kirkpatrick, pg.132.

[18] 1 Chronicles 22:8-10 and 28:4-7.

[19] The Kingdom would last forever (or for an age), although
not the mortal king. As Wordsworth says (ii, pg.98): *"Solomon*
pre-figured Christ as Prince of Peace; and as the Well-Beloved
of God; and as the builder of the Temple; and as excelling in
Wisdom and Knowledge".

Child"
-ive-
d

2

The Silent Years

WHAT was it like for young Solomon as he grew up in the palace, perhaps the youngest of all David's children? Busy and noisy for sure; for he was a member of a very large family, and they all lived together.[1] If it is indeed the case that David and Bathsheba chose not to make Nathan's prophecy known – that the child named *"Solomon"* was to succeed David as king (1 Chronicles 22:9,10), they would have had a tricky problem to solve. They would have wanted to bring him up as the future king without making that obvious to his siblings and their mothers. On the other hand, if they made it known early on, Solomon could have been the target for a lot of unpleasantness, to say the least. The way things worked out later, his life might well have been in danger.

David as Father

David had seven sons, born during his wanderings or at Hebron, who would have reckoned themselves likely successors: two of whom – Absalom and Adonijah – actually tried to get the kingship. So, whilst David now knew whom God had appointed to succeed him, it is likely that he would have been afraid to reveal Solomon's appointed destiny any earlier than it needed to be known. No doubt he would have wanted to train Solomon for his forthcoming role as king, but he would have to do it in a way that raised no suspicions, and he had much else to do in consolidating his victories and getting the kingdom on to a sound economic and administrative basis.

There are indications that David did not look after his

children's spiritual education that well, and he paid the price for that neglect. Adonijah was David's fourth son, born to David's wife Haggith (2 Samuel 3:4), yet it said of him that: *"his father had not displeased him at any time in saying, Why hast thou done so?"* (1 Kings 1:6).[2] Being brought up in a palace as part of a king's household can easily give children the impression that they are "royalty" and that ordinary people are "commoners". Even though these were early days in terms of Israel's monarchy, it seems that the boys at least were becoming accustomed to a life of self-indulgence and privilege.[3]

These things are written for our instruction and guidance, of course, not to enable us to gloat over David's inattention or inability as a parent. He was a very busy man with huge responsibilities and his children had to share his time with many others. But recognising, as he did, that children are a gift from God[4] and knowing, as he certainly would, that his children would have an important part to play in the future rulership of God's kingdom, either as king or as a member of that king's household, it is clear that David, and his various wives, could have done better in bringing up their children. That challenge now falls to those of us who are parents, who seek to bring up our own children or grandchildren in a godly way. For we too know that children are a gift from God, for the family and the ecclesia alike, and the effort we expend in bringing them up, and preparing them for the coming Kingdom, is time and love well spent.

Solomon's Education

Solomon would have been formally educated, of course, as were the other sons (if not the daughters). We are told that Jehiel was the tutor to whom David entrusted them: *"Jonathan David's uncle was a counsellor, a wise man, and a scribe: and Jehiel the son of Hachmoni was with the king's sons"* (1 Chronicles 27:32). He is listed here among the members of David's inner cabinet – together with Ahithophel, Hushai, Jehoiada, Abiathar and Joab – so Jehiel the Levite, about whom we know nothing more, was clearly a much trusted man.[5]

There is a possibility that Solomon was also tutored by

SOLOMON – WISE AND FOOLISH

Nathan the prophet. The record says that:

> *"David comforted Bathsheba his wife, and went in unto her, and lay with her: and she bare a son, and he called his name Solomon: and the LORD loved him. And he sent by the hand of Nathan the prophet; and he called his name Jedidiah, because of the LORD"* (2 Samuel 12:24,25).

The Hebrew text may indicate that David entrusted the lad into the care of Nathan, who then called him *"Jedidiah"*, but we cannot be certain of that.[6] Plumptre catalogues the sort of things Nathan could have taught Solomon, had he been appointed, and what he could have done for him.[7] The prophet wrote up the annals of David's reign (1 Chronicles 29:29), so he had an intimate knowledge of the kingdom; and his sons could have been Solomon's teenage companions, as they later came to be numbered among his advisers (1 Kings 4:5). Such things would have been helpful to Solomon, whether or not Nathan was involved directly with his education.

Even if David spent little time with his other children, the busy father did find some time to tutor and counsel this chosen successor, and so did his mother, as Solomon later remembers:

> *"For I was my father's son, tender and only beloved in the sight of my mother.[8] He taught me also, and said unto me, Let thine heart retain my words: keep my commandments, and live. Get wisdom, get understanding: forget it not; neither decline from the words of my mouth"* (Proverbs 4:3-5).[9]

Clearly Solomon remembered that lesson at least and it would seem that David recognised him as an apt and responsive pupil for, much later, he would acknowledge him as *"a wise man"* (1 Kings 2:9). But the teaching that Solomon received wasn't just by word of mouth; there was a lot to learn from David's own experience, and the years during which Solomon was growing up were full of significance to someone who was keen to learn. For the father that Solomon got to know was not the carefree and confident man he had once been. By the time Solomon was

12

born, he was both older and wiser. As F W Farrar comments:

> *"His father was a king who, in many respects, had fallen from his high estate. The golden dawn and glorious noonday of his reign were over. He was no longer the pride and the idol of Israel and Judah. Not only had his administration ceased to be so vigorous as once it was, but the dark story of his relations to Bathsheba and Uriah was but an imperfect secret, and in proportion as it became known David lost ground in the affections of his people. There was, indeed, no concealment in the intensity of his remorse, and God forgave him, and restored to him the clean heart and the free spirit. But the forgiveness of sins is not the same thing as the remission of consequences, and the consequences of sin are moral and spiritual as well as physical. They leave their scars upon a man's character".*[10]

Solomon's Family

Far from concealing what had happened with Bathsheba, David had in fact publicised his expressions of deep remorse, and his appeal for forgiveness, in two Psalms which would probably have become part of Israel's worship during his lifetime.[11] Solomon would thus have been only too aware of the skeletons in his family closet and that could have affected him as he was growing up. Perhaps Solomon got to know a father who was struggling with the consequences of all that had happened and who was seeing his family slip away from him as he proved increasingly unwilling or unable to intervene to put things right.[12] And he may have had a beautiful mother whose conduct was despised by many other mothers, and who may have suffered as a consequence.[13]

On the assumption that the sequence in Samuel and Chronicles is more or less chronological, except for an Appendix which details such matters as the Census, the purchase of the Temple site, and the list of David's mighty men (2 Samuel chapters 23 and 24), Solomon would have been born into a family which was beginning to go out of control.[14]

Impeded by his conscience and the lingering sense of guilt, unworthiness and unfitness to perform judicial acts, especially against his family, David took no action even when urgent action was desperately needed. The rape of Tamar, Absalom's summary justice, the subsequent estrangement of father and beloved son, and the eventual attempt at seizing the throne, took place over some eleven years, a third of the time that David was king in Jerusalem. It is intriguing to surmise that the rebellion might have been sparked off by a growing suspicion that Solomon was David's appointed heir. And it is equally fascinating to wonder if Solomon, still only a young lad, was with David, or in the company, when the king and his household (2 Samuel 15:16) left Jerusalem for Mahanaim, as Absalom mounted his coup attempt.[15]

- Did he see his father weeping as he ascended up the Mount of Olives, leaving Jerusalem behind, a grief that was made worse by the news that Ahithophel, his chief adviser, had defected? [16]

- Did he see Shimei the Benjamite throwing stones at the departing king, reminding him that he should have been stoned to death under the Law?

- Did he personally benefit from the kindness of Shobi, Machir and Barzillai (2 Samuel 17:27-29), kindness that he was later asked to reward (1 Kings 2:7)?

- Was Solomon there when David lamented so fervently after the death of Absalom?

If so, how did he react and what did he think when he heard his father declaim with such passion: *"O my son Absalom, my son, my son Absalom! would God I had died for thee, O Absalom, my son, my son!"* (2 Samuel 18:33)? The unavoidable inference was that David would personally have preferred to see Absalom as the next king, rather than Solomon.[17]

Still Waiting

After Absalom's rebellion, David may have considered it even more important to keep the news from his family that Solomon was to be his successor. For if Absalom had such ambitions, and was prepared to openly rebel against his father, what about the other sons? The monarchy was only a recent institution in Israel and, as yet, no king had succeeded to the throne other than by seizing it, a precedent David had set by establishing a rival kingdom in Hebron and then challenging the claim of Ishbosheth, Saul's surviving heir.

No king had yet appointed his successor and then announced his choice to the people for, up to that point, they had made the choice – both of Saul (the peoples' choice) and of David. Thus they welcomed him back as king on his victorious return to Jerusalem after Absalom's attempted coup (2 Samuel 19:8-15,40), even if some of them were a little slow to come and offer their congratulations. But if they had not done so, he would have had no obvious mandate to continue to rule.

The reaction of the people of Israel (as opposed to the men of Judah) when Sheba the Benjamite revolted (2 Samuel 20), shows what a tenuous hold David had on the throne, and how imperative it was that his trained soldiers and personal bodyguard should deal with that rebellion speedily, something that Joab understood only too well. And Joab was equally concerned when David ordered a census of all Israel (2 Samuel 24), for he seems to have understood that it would be unpopular, perhaps because it should be accompanied by the payment of a half-shekel tax, per person.[18]

So there were plenty of reasons why David made no announcement about his successor, leaving the door open for an enterprising son to stake his claim, which is exactly what happened when the king was on his deathbed and apparently about to expire. By now Adonijah was next in line according to human reckoning and it was he who made the claim, mustering formidable support from among some of David's courtiers. That led to a swift counter-claim on Solomon's behalf, for he was still only young at the time. Bathsheba and Nathan went to speak to the ailing king.

Significantly, they were unable to ask for action according to a published statement about succession. Their plea was based implicitly upon the prophecy and explicitly upon a private promise made at some unspecified time by David to Bathsheba, so he had at least told her about Nathan's prophecy. Entering his chamber, David's favourite wife told him what Adonijah had done, before reminding David of something that had passed between them some time before:

> *"My lord, thou swarest by the LORD thy God unto thine handmaid, saying, Assuredly Solomon thy son shall reign after me, and he shall sit upon my throne. And now, behold, Adonijah reigneth; and now, my lord the king, thou knowest it not ... And thou, my lord, O king, the eyes of all Israel are upon thee, that thou shouldest tell them who shall sit on the throne of my lord the king after him"* (1 Kings 1:17,18, 20).

Nathan followed on in similar terms. So, David had sworn privately, by the LORD, that Solomon should succeed him, as the prophetic word had declared, but he had not announced that publicly. Was it just his fear of even more family feuding? Or was there a more significant reason?

NOTES

[1] Farrar, pg.6, calculates that David had at least 20 sons from named wives as well as others from unnamed concubines.

[2] 1 Kings 1:6 then adds *"... and he also was a very goodly man; and his mother bare him after Absalom"*. His mother was Haggith, whilst Absalom's mother was Maachah (1 Chronicles 3:2), so the point being made is that Adonijah was some way down the pecking order, but he still got his own way. This is a clear indication that David's children got their own way about everything. David's attitude when Amnon wanted to get Tamar by herself (2 Samuel 13:6,7) is another indication that the children were used to getting their own way.

[3] Bro.Tennant, pg.122: *"...it becomes clear that the royal upbringing in godliness and righteousness was not attended with unqualified success"* – a nice touch of understatement!

[4] *"Lo, children are an heritage of the LORD and the fruit of the*

womb is his reward" (Psalm 127:3), where the heading reads "A song of Degrees for (or "of") Solomon".

[5] That Jehiel was a Levite can be inferred from the appearance of the same name in 1 Chronicles 15:18,20 and 16:4, and the likelihood that David would have wanted the boys to be taught about God's law, not just about secular things.

[6] See Kirkpatrick pg.132: "Some commentators would alter (the text) slightly in accordance with the Vulgate, and render he (David) committed him to the hand of Nathan, that he might take charge of his education. But the explanation is doubtful and there is no further trace of the fact, though it has been very generally supposed that Nathan was Solomon's tutor". So, HDB, IV, pg.560.

[7] SBD, pg.1343.

[8] The expression *"only beloved"* seems to indicate that Solomon was especially cherished by Bathsheba. The same Hebrew word, *yahid*, is used about Isaac in Genesis 22:2,12,16.

[9] Solomon does not say that Bathsheba instructed him, although there is a tradition that she was the writer of Proverbs chapter 31 ("the mother of King Lemuel"). Farrar comments wryly that "if she were, those exhortations to chastity would have come with more weight from other lips" (pg.7).

[10] Farrar, pg.5.

[11] If you accept the intriguing suggestions made by Mrs A M Waller in *"The History Behind the Psalms"* (1907), Psalm 32 would have been in the Service Book for the worship taking place before the Ark at Jerusalem and Psalm 51 would have been sung at the Tabernacle in Gibeon.

[12] The latter part of David's life is characterised by an unwillingness to intervene, perhaps because he thought that he was unfit to take action because of what he had done. For example, he took no action when Amnon molested Tamar, perhaps because he had done the same himself to Bathsheba. The result was that David ceased to administer justice as he was meant to (see 2 Samuel 15:1-6) and also lost control over his family, notably his sons. They soon realised that they could do exactly what they wanted and that their father would take

no action, which proved to be right. This is a terrible example of the debilitating effect of sin.

[13] Adam Clarke says, in respect of Bathsheba's willingness to come at David's bidding (in his commentary on 2 Samuel 11:26): *"The whole of her conduct indicates that she observed the form without feeling the power of sorrow. She lost a captain and got a king for her spouse; this must have been deep affliction indeed: and therefore, 'She shed reluctant tears and forced out groans from a joyful heart' "*. Others take a rather more generous view of her behaviour.

[14] There are some difficulties with the chronology of David's reign and different opinions exist about quite when Solomon was born, and how old he was when he succeeded to the throne. These ideas are considered later.

[15] Plumptre (SBD 1344) thinks that Solomon might have been ten or eleven at the time of Absalom's rebellion, and all the indications suggest that Solomon was among the exiled household. David could not have risked leaving him behind knowing, as he did, that *he* was God's appointed heir.

[16] This is another pointer to the fact that no public announcement had been made about Solomon, for would Ahithophel have defected to Absalom if he knew that David's successor was to be his great grandson?

[17] In the same way, Joab was quick to point out to David that the men in the king's army would conclude that David would have preferred them dead and Absalom alive, unless he said something to the contrary (2 Samuel 19:1-7). Note the reference to the king's *"sons and daughters"* in verse 5.

[18] The half-shekel tax was prescribed by Exodus 30:11-16, although opinions differ as to whether or not this was requested when Joab's men (rather than the Levites) did this partial count of the able-bodied fighting men.

3
Adonijah makes his Move

DAVID had been brought up the hard way, having to fend for himself. If he wanted something done he had to do it or it didn't get done; that taught him independence and made him self-reliant, in the best meaning of that term. For his early responsibility as a shepherd, with helpless dependants,[1] had also taught him that he must trust absolutely in God. He became self-reliant but God-dependent, the best possible combination. First, that attitude of mind gave him the confidence to tackle a lion and a bear that came after his sheep; then it encouraged him to go out against Goliath, when he came to ravage the flock of God.

Boyhood Skills

Remember David's words in the valley of Elah? *"Thy servant slew both the lion and the bear: and this uncircumcised Philistine shall be as one of them, seeing he hath defied the armies of the living God ... The LORD that delivered me out of the paw of the lion, and out of the paw of the bear, he will deliver me out of the hand of this Philistine"* (1 Samuel 17:34-37). The lessons David learned as a youngster stood him in good stead: they were skills for life. So his experience reminds us that the sooner we start to practise living by faith, the better it will be for us. Solomon might have been thinking of his own father's experience when later he wrote: *"Train up a child in the way he should go: and when he is old, he will not depart from it"* (Proverbs 22:6).

But life for Solomon was very different. He was born in

Jerusalem at a time when David was a settled monarch with an established and privileged family. Solomon's education would have been within the palace; probably that was where Jehiel instructed him and those of his brothers who were still under tuition.[2] As he grew up, apart from the occasion when he had fled the city at the time of Absalom's rebellion, he would probably not have enjoyed the freedom and responsibility enjoyed by his father, who was then only a shepherd boy in a large farming family in Bethlehem. If Solomon got a glimpse of the world outside it may have been as a courtier, or perhaps sitting in at some of the judicial enquiries that came the way of a king who had been appointed by God as the final arbiter.

There are some indications that when he was old enough he made up for this lack of hands-on experience, perhaps because he wanted better to appreciate what life was like for the ordinary man and woman in Israel.[3] Meanwhile back at the palace, if the young prince wanted something done there was always someone there to assist; help would always have been close at hand. In that sheltered environment it must have been difficult to learn how best to cope with the challenges of life.

You may feel that this aspect of Solomon's life has little to teach us, for we are not palace-born. But many of us, or our children, can be sheltered from the harsher aspects of the world, with its challenges and temptations. Those educated at home, or in Christadelphian or small private schools, have eventually to face the world without further assistance, and it can be difficult. Some react in an extreme way when exposed to opportunities that have been denied them hitherto; some cope by remaining withdrawn and becoming introverted. Others manage the transition more successfully. Whatever our early experiences – and we must all at least face the challenge of moving away from home and learning to cope by ourselves, sooner or later – what happened to Solomon indicates a good way of making the change. He had to make his own way in life, but he was supported and advised whenever guidance was needed, and he was wise enough to listen and learn.

The Plot Thickens

With Amnon and Absalom dead, Adonijah appears to have been the next of David's sons in line for the throne, humanly speaking.[4] Knowing that his father was nearing the end, and perhaps suspecting that he was not David's chosen successor, he now took his chance. First, *"he prepared him chariots and horsemen, and fifty men to run before him"* (1 Kings 1:5), exactly as Absalom had done.[5] Perhaps it was a declaration of intent, to let his father see what he thought should happen, and give the old man a chance to come out on his side.

But David did nothing. By now he was *"old and stricken in years"* (1 Kings 1:1)[6] and it must have seemed to Adonijah that David would continue his policy of non-intervention, for that had characterised much of his life after the affair with Bathsheba. As David had always indulged him and had never denied him anything (1:6), why should he deny him the kingdom? So Adonijah summoned his supporters, who included Joab and Abiathar,[7] *"all the men of Judah, the king's servants"*,[8] and he invited all his brothers, except Solomon.[9] They were to meet him at the *"the stone of Zoheleth, which is by Enrogel"* (1:9) and, like Absalom before him, he began the meeting with a feast which may have been sacrificial in character (see 2 Samuel 15:12).

There is a good deal of uncertainty about the precise location of *"the stone of Zoleleth"* which is variously translated *"serpent's stone"* (RSV) and the *"rolling stone"*, apparently because it was a large stone which young men tried to roll to show their strength. Both those meanings would have relevance in this context. But where exactly was it? *"Enrogel"* appears to be a location to the south of the city, right on the border between Judah and Benjamin, where that tribe's boundary touched Jerusalem.[10]

This was the very spot where Jonathan and Ahimaaz had stayed during Absalom's rebellion, when they spied for their exiled King,[11] so it must have been near to the city, but sheltered from it. Now it was just the place for the insurrectionists to gather, out of sight but easily accessible to the city. Josephus says that Enrogel had become

21

part of the royal gardens or park lands.[12] F. F. Bruce suggests that the site may have been "the spot where kings of Jerusalem had been installed in the Jebusite era".[13] Whether it had any such associations or not, Adonijah now sought to confer upon it some religious association of his own.

Solomon's Response

We know nothing about Solomon's reaction to all this. He was still a young man and was used to others seeing to his every need. The record doesn't say that, but it is implicit in what happened next. The events at Enrogel did not go unnoticed; how could they, when all Solomon's brothers had been summoned to a party and he had been left off the guest list? The happening would have been known about all over the palace, even if its significance was not understood. And news about it reached Nathan the prophet, wherever he was then living, prompting his reappearance into the Biblical account, the first time for many years.

Nathan was the prophet who had told David about God's choice of a successor and he evidently felt responsible for that prophecy and its proper fulfilment. First he conferred with Bathsheba, to tell her what was really afoot, to warn her of the danger and to seek her assistance. He outlined his plan and explained what she must do. It was imperative that they tell the king of the danger now facing the kingdom, not merely the personal danger to Solomon and Bathsheba – though that was anticipated.[14] The real danger was that the purpose of God, which included Solomon's reign of peace, might be thwarted. That was what they warned David about and that was why David was urged to take the necessary action. So Bathsheba went first into David's bedroom and Nathan came next to reinforce the message, the key point being that God had chosen Solomon to sit upon His throne and now Adonijah was trying to take it instead. Once again it becomes apparent that no formal announcement had been made by David about a successor, but now was the time to put that right:

> "She said unto him, My lord, thou swarest by the LORD thy God unto thine handmaid, saying, Assuredly

Solomon thy son shall reign after me, and he shall sit upon my throne. And now, behold, Adonijah reigneth; and now, my lord the king, thou knowest it not ... And thou, my lord, O king, the eyes of all Israel are upon thee, that thou shouldest tell them who shall sit on the throne of my lord the king after him" (1 Kings 1:17-20).

While all this was going on Solomon did nothing, or so it would seem. He just waited for others to give a lead and, when he was told what to do, he willingly obliged.

Why had David waited so long?

We have already considered some of the reasons why David had said nothing to his family, or to the nation, about God's choice of Solomon as the next King of Israel. Quite likely, David feared the reaction of his elder sons as one family upset followed another, for Solomon was still quite young. But now that upset had occurred anyway, there was no reason to wait any longer and the danger was now pressing.

So often David was capable of the unexpected and this was no exception. He shed his tiredness in order, once again, to become a man of action. First, he recalled Bathsheba to assure her that he was a man of his word. Then, summoning Zadok, Nathan and Benaiah into his presence, he issued precise orders. They were to fetch the royal mule,[15] seat Solomon thereon, take him to Gihon and there anoint, trumpet and proclaim him king in David's place – Solomon would thus become the true and anointed successor over both Israel and Judah. Then they were to process back to Jerusalem. It was as if David had contingency plans all worked out; it only needed the occasion to bring them into action. Now the occasion had come, and could not be avoided.

But why should David have wanted to avoid anointing Solomon as his successor, to share power with him during the next few weeks or months? Perhaps it was that he had been hoping for someone better than Solomon, and had been waiting for that promised heaven-sent successor. We are not left to conjecture what dominated David's thoughts as he came towards the end of his life; he tells us that in his closing words. In the Psalm he wrote for, or to, Solomon – which is declared to be his last – he was thinking about the Coming King who could reign over a Kingdom that would last forever before God:

> *"Give the king thy judgments, O God, and thy righteousness unto the king's son. He shall judge thy people with righteousness, and thy poor with judgment ... His name shall endure for ever: his name shall be continued as long as the sun: and men shall be blessed in him: all nations shall call him blessed. Blessed be the* LORD *God, the God of Israel, who only doeth wondrous things. And blessed be his glorious name for ever: and let the whole earth be filled with his glory; Amen, and Amen. The prayers of David the son of Jesse are ended"* (Psalm 72).

In his very last words, he returned to the same theme, declaring this to be *"all my salvation, and all my desire";* for David looked for one who would be: *"just, ruling in the fear of God. And he shall be as the light of the morning, when the sun riseth, even a morning without clouds; as the tender grass springing out of the earth by clear shining after rain"* (2 Samuel 23:3,4). David knew that no-one from his house could be like that, without Divine assistance. He was only too aware of his own acts of darkness, and of the lurking injustice in every human heart. So he added: *"Although my house be not so with God; yet he hath made with me an everlasting covenant, ordered in all things, and sure".*

God would provide a way and David would have preferred it sooner rather than later. Had not the prophetic covenant declared to him by Nathan said that:

> *"When thy days be fulfilled, and thou shalt sleep with thy fathers,*[16] *I will set up thy seed after thee, which shall proceed out of thy bowels, and I will establish his kingdom. He shall build an house for my name, and I will stablish the throne of his kingdom for ever"* (2 Samuel 7:12,13).

If only David could have held out, and held his kingdom

together a little longer, then the next king would have come when his days were fulfilled, when he slept with his fathers. But it was not to be; so David yielded once again to the Divine will and his action plan was put into effect. Once again David's focus and desire, upon the coming Kingdom and the promised King, challenges us to consider whether we have made that our heart's desire.

NOTES

[1] Psalm 78:70-72 makes the express connection between David's education in the sheepfold and God's choice of him to feed God's flock: *"From following the ewes great with young (God) brought him to feed Jacob his people, and Israel his inheritance. So he fed them according to the integrity of his heart; and guided them by the skilfulness of his hands"*.

[2] 1 Chronicles 27:32.

[3] Indications that Solomon yearned after life outside the palace come from the Book of Ecclesiastes (where he catalogues all those things that he experimented with) and the Song of Songs (where Solomon did some shepherding himself and developed a love of the outdoors and the beauties of the natural world).

[4] Chileab, 2 Samuel 3:3 (also known as Daniel, in 1 Chronicles 3:1), who was Abigail's son, is not otherwise mentioned and may have died young.

[5] 2 Samuel 15:1.

[6] It is recorded of Abraham and Sarah that they were *"old and well stricken in age"* (Genesis 18:11) as they awaited the birth of Isaac; and God said that of Joshua (Joshua 13:1) when he reminded him that there was still much that needed to be done. God works with and through old people in just the same way as he does with those of us who are younger. What matters is our willingness to respond to the opportunities and challenges of life in God's service.

[7] We shall consider in due course why these erstwhile loyal supporters of David deserted on this occasion.

SOLOMON – WISE AND FOOLISH

⁸ It seems unlikely that *"all the men of Judah, the king's servants"* is to be taken literally, for that would mean all those from David's tribe who served in the court in any capacity, which could have made this a very large gathering. In 1:25 these same invitees are described as *"the captains of the host"* which explains that it was key members of the tribe of Judah who were invited. This is a further reminder of the need to rule by a measure of consensus, with members of your tribe in support.

⁹ It seems that not all of David's brothers accepted the invitation. Farrar singles out Shimei and Rei as brothers who did not attend and who later supported Solomon (pg.27).

¹⁰ See Joshua 15:7 and 18:16. Wiseman, pg.69, gives other suggestions, as do other commentators. Yigael Yadin, *"Jerusalem Revealed"* (1976), pg.75, describes En-Rogel as a well (Siloam being the only spring supplying Jerusalem), some 150 metres south of the confluence of the Kidron and Hinnom valleys.

¹¹ 2 Samuel 17:17

¹² Josephus: *Antiquities* vii.14. 4: *"Now Adonijah had prepared a supper out of the city, near the fountain that was in the king's paradise (garden), and had invited all his brethren, except Solomon"*.

¹³ Bruce, pg.34.

¹⁴ 1 Kings 1:21.

¹⁵ The first reference to mules in Israel is during the time of David (see also 2 Samuel 13:29; 18:9). Earlier governors had ridden on she-asses (Judges 5:10) but horses were prohibited (Deuteronomy 17:16). Whilst Absalom and Adonijah had both horses and chariots (1 Kings 1:5), David only had a mule on which to ride.

¹⁶ Can it be coincidental that Bathsheba deliberately quotes those words in her plea for action: *"Otherwise it shall come to pass, when my lord the king shall 'sleep with his fathers', that I and my son Solomon shall be counted offenders"* (1 Kings 1:21)? Perhaps David had explained to her why he had delayed announcing Solomon as his successor: that he wanted God's appointed king to succeed him after his death and thus fulfil the covenant promises (of 2 Samuel 7) straight away.

26

4

"God Save the King"

DAVID was far from well and he was now an old man. In Bible times people did not live as long as we do today and few of the kings lived to seventy years old. David was nearing that age now, having been thirty when he was appointed king at Hebron and having reigned there for 7 years and in Jerusalem for the last 33 years (2 Samuel 5:4). Just how poorly he was can be reckoned by two things:

He could no longer maintain his bodily heat and needed Abishag to keep him warm in bed; and now he appeared to be bed-ridden, with Abishag as his nurse,[1] Adonijah, who must have known his father's physical condition, had judged it opportune to announce his kingship in the sure expectation that David could, or would, do nothing about it. But he was seriously wrong about that.

Man of Action

Many times in the past David had sprung into action when something had to be done and such old habits die hard. Poorly though he had been he was far from spent and this crisis brought out the best in him. First he summoned Bathsheba again and confirmed that Solomon was indeed the successor that God had appointed:

> "As the LORD liveth, that hath redeemed my soul out of all distress,[2] even as I sware unto thee by the LORD God of Israel, saying, Assuredly Solomon thy son shall reign after me, and he shall sit upon my throne in my stead; even so will I certainly do this day" (1 Kings 1:29,30).

27

He would have preferred a King who was heaven-sent, immediately to fulfil the covenant promises but now he recognised it was not to be and knew instinctively that his own family line could not achieve what was needed without Divine intervention.[3] They must have spoken together about these things and Bathsheba clearly recognised his disappointment, for what she now said, to the ailing king, looks forward to the time when a future Messianic king would sit on David's throne, with David there as well, raised from the dead.[4] For her words were much more than a conventional flattering phrase, the sort of thing that was said to pagan kings:

> *"Bathsheba bowed with her face to the earth, and did reverence to the king, and said,* **Let my lord king David live for ever***"* (1:31).

Nathan had already told the King who had, and who had not been summoned to Adonijah's coronation feast and those were the people David now summoned into his presence – *"Zadok the priest, and Nathan the prophet, and Benaiah the son of Jehoiada"*. Notice the order. This was not a military counter-coup but a priestly procession, with military support; for Solomon was to be accompanied by David's servants,[5] and that certainly included those mighty men of the King's bodyguard – the Cherethites and Pelethites (1:38) – who had stuck by David through thick and thin.

Solomon was to ride upon the king's mule, which hitherto only the king would have ridden, and they were to go to Gihon (1:33). Just as there is uncertainty about the precise location of the *"the stone of Zoheleth, which is by Enrogel"* (1 Kings 1:9), so now there is uncertainty about the exact location to which Solomon was to be taken.

David gives a geographical clue,[6] when he said *"bring him down to Gihon"*, and *"then ye shall come up after him, that he may come and sit upon my throne" (1:35)*. It seems very likely that this was the Virgin's Spring – to the east of the city and down in the Kidron valley – the ancient water supply to the city.

So, both Adonijah and Solomon were being declared king near water, which suggests that water was an integral part of the ritual or a vital symbolic element.[7] But there the similarities end. At Enrogel it was a private party, perhaps within the palace ground, or in a place set apart for the rich and privileged. The group included two disaffected elder statesmen (Joab and Abiathar) and some other dignitaries, and it quite failed to catch the public imagination. By contrast, the procession David had master-minded was a grand and public affair – a coronation for the people of Jerusalem – and they loved it.

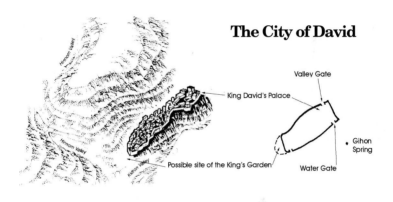

The City of David

Just as a ceremonial procession attracts tourists today, it seems that this one was soon spotted and a crowd followed as they wound their way down towards Gihon. With Solomon seated on David's mule it would have been obvious what was about to happen and you can imagine the excitement this aroused. In UK terms, it would have been the equivalent of Prince Charles attending at the Trooping of the Colour[8] in place of the Queen, and sitting astride her horse.

Zadok, who was destined to become the new High Priest, and Nathan the trusty prophet both anointed Solomon with sacred oil.[9] There they were together – prophet, priest and king – at the dawn of a new era for the nation: the long awaited reign of peace.

A King in Jerusalem

Now the blast of trumpets rent the air, which guaranteed an even larger crowd for the return journey, as they slowly climbed back into the city, than there had been on the way down. All the people at Gihon shouted *"God save King Solomon"*[10] and then followed the procession, with some people piping on pipes and everyone rejoicing greatly. There was such a commotion that *"the earth rent with the sound of them", the city was in "an uproar", and "the city rang again"* with rejoicing, having previously been somewhat restrained, it would seem, whilst the people of Jerusalem awaited news of David's further decline (1:40,41,45). The Septuagint has a slight variation, for it reads: *"And all the people went up after him, and they danced in choirs, and rejoiced with great joy, and the earth quaked with their voice."* Whether they were piping or dancing, it's clear that those present were very excited by the proceedings.

It was Joab's trained ear that first heard the trumpet blast, though they had all heard the general commotion, and he was wondering what it meant. Perhaps their first thought was that there had been an announcement of David's death, but they were soon disabused of that notion. Jonathan, Abiathar's son, came to tell them that:

● David had made Solomon king;

● Solomon was already enthroned in the palace – *"Solomon sitteth on the throne of the kingdom"* (1:46); and that,

● the king had himself sealed the appointment with a dedicatory prayer to God.

Jonathan must have been there himself judging from the eye-witness account, including David's very posture as he prayed: that he *"bowed himself upon the bed"*. Adonijah's followers knew at once that they had lost the initiative – for timing is all important in any coup attempt – and that they were all in serious trouble. Like mist in the early morning when the sun begins to shine, they dissolved: *"all the guests that were with Adonijah were afraid, and rose up, and went every man his way. And Adonijah feared ..." (1:49,50).* He headed for the nearest altar, either the one David had built on what had once been the threshing floor of Araunah the Jebusite, or one in front of the tent David had pitched for the Ark, which was probably within the palace grounds. The would-be king now grasped its horns, pleading for sanctuary and refuge.

First Political Decision

When news was brought to Solomon that Adonijah was pleading for mercy the young king was faced with his first political decision, and that very early on in his reign. He had only just sat down on the throne! What was he now to say? Was Adonijah best executed; so that his followers would have no focal point for any future resistance? That had certainly been David's attitude when Sheba revolted.[11] These are the first recorded words of Solomon. They may have followed a quick consultation with Nathan, Zadok or even his father, but it fell to the young king to send the message, as follows:

> *"If he will shew himself a worthy man, there shall not an hair of him fall to the earth: but if wickedness shall be found in him, he shall die"* (1:52).

And when Adonijah was brought to the palace to pay obeisance to the new monarch, his young half-brother, Solomon, again showed his maturity. For he merely said: *"Go to thine house".* No more needed to be said; but a less confident man might well have said more. Solomon showed a calmness and generosity of spirit that boded well for the future, an attitude that was in marked contrast to how Adonijah would have behaved had he succeeded with his attempt, when both Solomon and Bathsheba might have been killed without a second thought. Solomon's attitude and actions enabled this coronation day to continue as one of joy and rejoicing. There were longer term matters that needed to be resolved from all that had happened, but they could wait. Solomon had to make the most of the opportunity which now presented itself. As David's successor, indeed his co-regent while his father still lived, Solomon needed all the help and advice he could get.

David's Last Chance

David did not die straight away, in the mercy of God. He had things to do and final duties to discharge so that the young king could be given the best possible start. He had been wasting away but now he enjoyed a brief revival of his powers. He had been given enough energy to raise himself up in bed, when the coronation procession had returned from Gihon, and had made that telling prayer – *"Blessed be the LORD God of Israel, which hath given one to sit on my throne this day, mine eyes even seeing it"* (1:48). And how telling it was! He knew that Solomon was not the promised One who will reign in Jerusalem: the covenant God had made with him made that quite clear.

So David needed to counsel and prepare Solomon for the work ahead; to warn him about immediate problems and talk seriously to him about covenant responsibilities. For it was Solomon who was now to carry forward David's hopes, and it was he who would be allowed to fulfil what David had longed to accomplish. Do we have that sense of responsibility, as we are privileged to see the things our forebears longed to see, and stand on the brink of the building of a glorious temple ourselves? We can be sure that the counsel David now gave to Solomon will stand us in good stead, too, when we are asked to undertake the Lord's work.

Perhaps David had not been able to prepare Solomon for the kingship in the way he would have liked, because he had feared what open disclosure of the succession would have produced. But now he was given strength to assist Solomon and to achieve a managed handover. For a while they would reign together[12] and then the young man would take Israel forward towards a better and happier future. But he would never go alone; God would always be with him, and he needed to know that. And so do we, in all the circumstances of our lives, as we prepare for the coming kingdom centred in Jerusalem.

NOTES

[1] When Bathsheba went in to see the king, and Nathan likewise, it was into his bedchamber that they went (1 Kings 1:15). Although the record has already said that David *"was old"* (1:1), that point is now repeated (1:15).

[2] Note the similarity with Jacob's expression of faith and his confidence in God's oversight all his life long (Genesis 48:16).

[3] Thus his last words included the comment *"Although my house be not so with God; yet he hath made with me an everlasting covenant, ordered in all things, and sure"* (2 Samuel 23:5).

[4] The kingdom promise to David included the assurance that these things would happen *"before thee"* (2 Samuel 7:16).

[5] The expression *"king's servants"* often refers to courtiers.

[6] This geographic indication is confirmed by the narrator when he adds that the participants, swollen by a large crowd, *"went down, and caused Solomon to ride upon king David's mule, and brought him to Gihon ... and all the people said, God save king Solomon. And all the people came up after him ..."* (1 Kings 1:38-40).

[7] Hershel Shanks, *"Jerusalem"*, 1995, pg. 47. Farrar, pg.29, note 3, says that, according to the Talmud, kings ought always to be anointed near a fountain.

[8] Trooping the Colour is a grand ceremonial occasion in London when the Queen reviews the Guard regiments who exchange their regimental colours as they march past her.

[9] Whether the oil was obtained from the *"tabernacle"* at Gibeon, or the *"tent"* David had constructed for the ark in Jerusalem, is hard to say. If the former, then contingency plans had already been made, for there would not have been time to visit Gibeon now because of the urgent situation. Or the oil might have been brought into the city in anticipation of David's death. Zadok was the priest in charge of the tabernacle at Gibeon (1 Chronicles 16:39-42), so that would point in the direction of the oil having been brought from there in advance, for whatever purpose.

[10] Notice the designed contrast within the chapter where

"God save the King" rings out twice. Once it was in respect of Adonijah (1:25), and then for Solomon (1:39), the second shout being so much louder than the first!

[11] 2 Samuel 20:6.

[12] Kings and Chronicles make it clear that Solomon and David reigned together for at least the time it took for the convening of a National Assembly and another Coronation – this time one that involved representatives of the entire nation. Merrill, pgs.243-248, has a suggested chronology of David's reign in which he reckons that the co-regency was from 973-971 BC (up to 2 years in duration); and Kaiser agrees, pgs.248-250. If that is so, David's recovery took a little while to achieve and the pace of the handover would have been slower than the record appears to suggest.

5

Preparing his Successor

THERE were bound to be difficult times ahead: change is unsettling and disturbing in all ages – stimulating for some, disorientating for others. The Kingdom of God on earth was still in its developing stage. This was the first time *"the throne of the LORD"*[1] over Israel had passed from father to son,[2] and that simple happening showed that a settled dynasty had now begun, just as God had promised David: *"the LORD telleth thee that he will make thee an house ... thine house and thy kingdom shall be established for ever before thee: thy throne shall be established for ever"*. David had understood that to mean that he was to be the founder of a dynasty of many kings (2 Samuel 7:11,16,18-19), and that was now beginning to happen.

Time Passing

Solomon was the successor whom God had chosen and it seems that David had anticipated trouble once that became public. Now he could see exactly what trouble there was to deal with. Adonijah had just shown his hand, and both Joab and Abiathar had supported him in his bid for the throne as, it would appear, had many of David's other sons. How was the position to be managed? What should David do, if anything? There might have been a huge desire on David's part to leave it all to God and just get on with the slow process of dying, snuggled up to Abishag! But men of God are made of sterner stuff than that, and David was a man who had always lived according to an active faith. He was not going to throw it all away at the last minute – all the waiting, fighting, preparing, planning, hoping, desiring. If the purpose of God was to go forward with his family, and he had a vested interest in its success, because of the covenant God had made with him, he still had work to do. So, aged though he was and infirm, he roused himself to do it.

There is a powerful precedent for us in all of this, just as David had examples he could look back on. Abraham had evidently counselled Isaac and Jacob about his under-standing of God and His gracious promises.[3] Moses had apprenticed Joshua with great care from early on, and still he took enormous trouble to encourage his young and seemingly timid successor on the plains of Moab just before his death. It has been suggested that the advice *"be strong and of a good courage"* was repeated 16 times to Joshua,[4] not always by Moses. If that *phrase* captured Joshua's need, it was just *one word* which encapsulated David's main concern for his youthful successor, and for all Israel's kings who would come after Solomon.

Joshua's example was instructive in other ways too. He had been an old man when God asked him to get on with the work of conquest: *"The LORD said unto him, Thou art old and stricken in years,[5] and there remaineth yet very much land to be possessed"* (Joshua 13:1). People lived longer in those times, for Joshua died aged 110, but the message was clear. Time was passing and he still had much to do. We are not expected to retire in the Lord's service. While there is still something to do, and while God enables us to do it, we must continue to exercise ourselves in the Lord's service.[6]

The Divine Condition

God had said to David that descendants would sit upon his throne for as long as one condition was met. When first declared, the covenant that God made with David merely anticipated the fuller statement that was to follow, and the key word – *"if"* – appeared just once:

> *"**If** he commit iniquity, I will chasten him with the rod of men, and with the stripes of the children of men: but my mercy shall not depart away from him ..."* (2 Samuel 7:14,15).

But when that covenant clause was repeated and amplified, it explained the sentence that sometimes causes us difficulty in relation to the sinless life of our Lord. For then the conditional nature of the Divine treaty became evident. David was told quite clearly that his descendants must be faithful if they were to continue to reign on his throne in Jerusalem. If they were not faithful, David's dynasty would end, until some other arrangement came about:[7]

> "*The* LORD *hath sworn in truth unto David; he will not turn from it; of the fruit of thy body will I set upon thy throne. **If** thy children will keep my covenant and my testimony that I shall teach them, their children shall also sit upon thy throne for evermore*" (Psalm 132:11,12).

> "***If** his children forsake my law, and walk not in my judgments; **if** they break my statutes, and keep not my commandments; then will I visit their transgression with the rod, and their iniquity with stripes. Nevertheless my lovingkindness will I not utterly take from him, nor suffer my faithfulness to fail. My covenant will I not break, nor alter the thing that is gone out of my lips. Once have I sworn by my holiness that I will not lie unto David*" (Psalm 89:30-35).

To remain as God's appointed and anointed King, every occupant of David's throne had to remain faithful and obedient. If disobedient, he could expect to be chastened in order that he might be brought back into line with God. If the disobedience was prolonged or unabated, then the entire kingdom would be forfeit. Now David took enormous care to stress that point to Solomon, time and again, and it is clear from Solomon's subsequent reference to it, in his own prayers and statements, that the lesson really went home.[8]

It mattered to David and it should matter just as much to us for we, too, want our children and the young people in our ecclesias to reign as kings and serve as priests. So if the aged and infirm David could rouse himself to action when he saw the end drawing near, we must be able to do the same. If the Lord delays his coming, the next generation has got to carry on with the work older believers have begun. It is incumbent upon all those who are young to take their responsibilities seriously, just as Solomon now proceeded to do. But it is also the responsibility of those who are more practised in the Lord's work to help, encourage, foster and develop the talents of the next generation.

For the generation which is privileged to be alive when the Lord returns – as we hope to be – it will be a work which is equally valuable. In fostering and developing the abilities of our younger people we will be developing the skills and aptitudes of fellow believers, who will thus have enhanced talents to put at the disposal of our King when he reigns from Jerusalem. But, however things are to work out for us with God's blessing, the charge lies upon us just as clearly as it did upon David and men and women of faith in every age.[9] So David prepared again for action.

Private and Public

David's strategy was to attack the problem from two directions. It is impossible to be sure which came first – the private talks he had with Solomon or the public address he delivered to a large assembly of specially invited representatives. In all probability the two went on side-by-side. If you want to convey an important truth to your children, every parent knows the necessity for repetition – they need to be told over and over; and it is the same for each of us with regard to spiritual matters. We are not naturally responsive to the things of God and the Word has to be allowed to make its impact gradually if the spiritual mind is to be developed.[10]

It must have been like that with Solomon. Now that he had emerged from the palace into the public spotlight, and now that it was evident that he was the man with a future, there would have been plenty of advice coming his way. David's voice would have been one of many voices, and a feeble one at that. Perhaps David involved his son in the preparations for the National Assembly he was about to convene; maybe he even talked through with him the speech he wrote and, no doubt, rehearsed beforehand. He may have asked Solomon's advice, and taken it. In all probability, they would have worked together in the weeks or months it took to get everything ready for David's departure, and talked as they worked. For David was determined to leave his house in good order.

1. Private

However it was done, David gave Solomon some very valuable personal advice and spiritual guidance. It is recorded for us, too, who now stand on the verge of entering into God's kingdom. Some of David's advice was specific and some of the actions they discussed – especially about Joab[11] and Shimei – might have been put into immediate effect. David's request about Barzillai's sons anticipated a longer period of time, and a more settled regime, and showed that David wished to remain true to the promise he had made to his faithful friend.

Much of David's counsel was of general application for people in every age. Privately, he said to Solomon that:[12] *"I go the way of all the earth"*. David was ready to die and faced that prospect without concern; he would die as he had lived, in faith. Long ago, in the wilderness, he had learned to stare death in the face without fear: it is a testimony to his faith that he had lost none of his confidence in the mercy and faithfulness of God.

> *"Be thou strong therefore, and shew thyself a man ... Be strong and of good courage, and do it: fear not, nor be dismayed".*

Just like Joshua, Solomon needed encouragement and exhortation to take his chances and act boldly. Although he would be a man of peace, he must be a man of courage and conviction, ready to seize whatever opportunity for service and praise came his way.

> *"For the LORD God, even my God, will be with thee; he will not fail thee, nor forsake thee,[13] until thou hast finished all the work for the service of the house of the LORD".*

Solomon must never forget that he was working with God, as well as for God. The God who had been with David all through his adventuresome life would now be Solomon's God also: He was a God of peace as well as a God of war. He is with us, too.

> *"And, behold, the courses of the priests and the Levites, even they shall be with thee for all the service of the house of God: and there shall be with thee for all manner of workmanship every willing skilful man, for any manner of service: also the princes and all the people will be wholly at thy commandment"* (1 Chronicles 28:21).

Solomon would not be alone in all this. A community of people would be keen to work with him and their mutual enthusiasm and support would be vitally important, to keep the project alive in many hearts. God would make the talent available and they would want to join in, providing Solomon encouraged them and made full use of that voluntary resource. He could not do it without their help, nor they without him: it had to be a spiritual partnership. And it remains the case that the building of the house of God requires all our God-given talents if the work is to glorify God, as it must.

> *"And keep the charge of the LORD thy God, to walk in his ways, to keep his statutes, and his commandments, and his judgments, and his testimonies, as it is written in the law of Moses, that thou mayest prosper in all that thou doest, and whithersoever thou turnest thyself."*

Solomon must play his part if he was to prosper with God. He was the heir of God's precious promises and his was a solemn responsibility, as the Davidic covenant made clear. If he was faithful and obedient he could expect to prosper in all his ways. So for us; we have to do our part if the communal effort is to be what it should be – the fruit of lives that exist at all times to glorify God.

> *"That the LORD may continue his word which he spake concerning me, saying, If thy children take heed to their way, to walk before me in truth with all their heart and with all their soul,*[14] *there shall not fail thee (said he) a man on the throne of Israel"* (1 Kings 2:1-4).

God never forgets the faithful service rendered by His servants, but amply rewards it both in this life and in the age to come, when there will indeed be a wonderful man sitting on David's throne throughout the glorious Kingdom Age.

2. Public

When we first come to understand God's will as it affects our lives, we have to do a lot of private thinking as we weigh up Bible truth and decide how it affects the direction of our own lives. But when we decide that we want to follow the Master, he has asked that we make a public declaration of our faith, including confessing it and then being baptised into the saving name of the Lord Jesus. There was something similar in these inaugural events. For, having spoken privately to his son, David now went public with what he had to say.

He convened one or two assemblies in Jerusalem. The first might have comprised Levites and Temple officials, the second the secular leaders of the nation. Only 1 Chronicles records this event, as you might expect,[15] the Book of Kings focusing instead on the private words that passed between father and son.[16] Chronicles devotes seven chapters (1 Chronicles 23-29) to a detailed account of who was there and what was said, bringing the First Book to a close with the thought that King David: *"died in a good old age, full of days, riches, and honour: and Solomon his son reigned in his stead"* (29:28).

These were much more than ceremonial occasions to present Solomon to the nation. The Conventions served that function, of course, but David wanted a spiritual renewal of the nation, an act of communal fellowship, a joining of hands together to pledge dedicated service in pursuit of the task God had now graciously allowed them to perform. For, after his death, they were the people who were being allowed to build a House for God in Jerusalem, and they must do it together. Every one of us has some part to play in the Lord's work and we are richly blessed when we come together in earnest to serve God and to strengthen one another in the faith.

The National Assembly (or Assemblies)

David summoned the leaders of the nation, both spiritual and secular. It is difficult to be sure from the record whether there was just the one assembly; there might have been two.[17] If so, 1 Chronicles chapter 22 might comprise the first address – to the princes, priests and Levites; and chapters 28-29 could be the substance of the second address.

The parallel with Moses who addressed Israel on the plains of Moab before his death – his three Deuteronomy addresses – should not be overlooked. The inspired author appears to have made a deliberate connection, to point out that this was another Exodus experience. God was again calling out a people for Himself, not now to build a Tabernacle but a Temple; not in the wilderness but in Jerusalem – the place He had chosen where He would set His name, in the midst of a people who were at rest in the Land.

Whether in one Assembly or in two, the people who were summoned to join the king and his son – the spiritual, civil and military leaders of Israel – were about to be told something very important indeed, something that matters to us as well.

NOTES

[1] 1 Chronicles 29:23.

[2] When Saul died, it was Abner who made Ishbosheth king in his father's place. It was neither a planned nor a managed succession, and appears to have been made possible only after the gradual conquest of parts of the land from the Philistines, and a process of gradual persuasion as, tribe by tribe, Gilead, Asher, Jezreel, Ephraim, Benjamin and all the rest of Israel accepted Ishbosheth as their king (2 Samuel 11:8-10). The result was civil war, as David was now the chosen king of Judah, at Hebron.

[3] See Genesis 18:19 and Hebrews 11:9.

[4] See Bro. Harry Whittaker, *"Israel in the Wilderness"*,

pg.180, for a list of the passages.

5 If Caleb's age was similar to Joshua's, we know that he was 85 at about this time (Joshua 14:10).

6 This is a New Testament injunction as well (see Titus 2:2).

7 *"... it shall be no more, until he come whose right it is; and I will give it him"* (Ezekiel 21:27).

8 Bro. Whittaker, pg.295, lists the following passages: 1 Chronicles 28:2; 2 Chronicles 7:17; 1 Kings 3:14; 6:12; 9:4; Psalm 132:12, and makes a very interesting comparison with those later passages that predict the coming of the Lord Jesus to sit on David's throne, when no such conditionality appears.

9 Consider how, later, our Lord prepared his disciples to continue his great work, and how Paul prepared and then charged Timothy to keep up the fight of faith.

10 See the original preface to the Bible Companion in which Bro. Roberts wrote that acquiring the Divine likeness is *"a work of slow development (which) can only be acquired by the industrious application of the individual to ... the expression of His mind in the Scriptures of truth"*.

11 *"Thou knowest also what Joab the son of Zeruiah did to me ... do therefore according to thy wisdom, and let not his hoar head go down to the grave in peace"* (1 Kings 2:5,6).

12 The following Scriptures are conflated from the accounts in 1 Kings 2:2-4 and 1 Chronicles 28:20,21.

13 The promise that God will be with His people, and that he will never forsake them, goes right back to Jacob (Genesis 28:15) and Joshua (1:5), and is repeated for New Testament believers (Hebrews 13:5) in very emphatic terms.

14 Note the allusion to Deuteronomy 6:5. David was telling Solomon that the only way he would be able to render this sort of dedicated service was by learning to love the LORD his God and then yielding his life in willing response.

15 The Books of Chronicles focus in particular upon matters concerning national worship, the Davidic monarchy, the temple and the priesthood. "This historian's purpose is to show that the true glory of the Hebrew nation was found in its

covenant relationship to God, as safeguarded by the prescribed forms of worship in the temple and administered by
the divinely ordained priesthood under the protection of the
divinely authorized dynasty of David" (G. L. Archer, *"A
Survey of Old Testament Introduction",* pg. 412).

[16] Edersheim,V, pg.49, makes the interesting observation
that: "The history of Israel is presented in the Book of Kings
from the prophetic point of view. In other words, it is a history written from the standpoint of 2 Samuel 7:12-16."
Whereas the Book of Chronicles presents the same history
"with special reference to its religious institutions, and to
place it in the context of God's dealings with mankind" (Bro.
Ashton, pg.2).

[17] Thus Wilcock, pg.108, *"With what might be called 'The
Second Assembly of Jerusalem' the Chronicler completes his
story of David".*

6

David's Challenge

LIKE Moses on the plains of Moab,[1] David summoned representatives of the nation to hear his final words of God-given wisdom. Who would have thought, only months before, that the frail bed-ridden king could have summoned up the energy to undertake this huge responsibility? David could not, of course; this was God-given energy, an extension of his natural powers, for God still had work for him to do. Everything had to be "decent and in order" so that Solomon could further God's purpose with His people.[2]

Long before he had petitioned God: *"when I am old and greyheaded, O God, forsake me not; until I have shewed thy strength unto this generation, and thy power to every one that is to come" (Psalm 71:18)*, a prayer that immediately precedes the one *"For (or "of") Solomon"*. Now God answered that prayer and, although David was still feeble and had to sit for much of the Assembly, he was able to speak to the forthcoming generation and to his son and successor. It would have taken a while to issue invitations and make the necessary arrangements for the Assembly that was to be convened. There would have been a lot of people present and, given David's physical condition, there might have been two Assemblies – one of spiritual and the other of secular leaders. The records say that he summoned:[3]

"All the princes of Israel,[4] with the priests and the Levites (1 Chronicles 23:2) ... All the princes of Israel, the princes of the tribes, and the captains of the compa-

nies that ministered to the king by course, and the cap-
tains over the thousands, and captains over the hun-
dreds, and the stewards over all the substance and pos-
session of the king, and of his sons, with the officers,
and with the mighty men, and with all the valiant men,
unto Jerusalem" (1 Chronicles 28:1).

The apparent confusion in the record – which makes it
difficult to be sure about the precise detail of the arrangements – is caused by the addition of lists of the names and
offices of those who were summoned, or who would have
been eligible to attend. *"All"* the people mentioned could
not possibly have been included, for reference is made to
38,000 people altogether. It is likely that representatives
would have been called to the meeting or meetings. It
might appear, at first glance, that the lists of names and
offices are out of place in the record. But, as we know only
too well with the Word of God, when something appears to
be unusual there is usually an important lesson to learn,
and that is the case here.

Temple Worship
No sooner has the Chronicler mentioned that David was
summoning the Levites than he begins to catalogue how
many officials there were in total and how David had
organised them for Temple worship.[5] There were 4 cate-
gories of Levites from which to select representatives –
24,000 who worked in the sanctuary;[6] 6,000 officers and
judges; 4,000 gatekeepers and 4,000 musicians (1
Chronicles 23:3-5).[7] His point in inserting that detail here
should not be missed. Sandwiched in-between the call to
build God's House are details of the people who already
worshipped God in the two Tabernacles that already existed, the old one at Gibeon and the new Tent for the Ark at
Jerusalem.[8]

The inspired historian was making the point that people were, and are, the most important component in the
worship of Almighty God. And they come with various
God-given skills: in David's time, some were sanctuary
workers, some administrators, some doorkeepers, some
musicians, and so on. What God really wants is not an
inanimate building in which to dwell, but a spiritual com-

munity: what the apostle Peter later called *"lively stones
... built up a spiritual house, an holy priesthood, to offer up
spiritual sacrifices, acceptable to God by Jesus Christ"* (1
Peter 2:5). God does not want a church building, but an
ecclesia. David and Solomon would accomplish nothing for
God, nor will we, unless the people whom God has called
are willing to become wholly involved with that calling.

Nor would the Temple that David wanted built be of
any Divine consequence unless it was occupied and attended by people who wholly desired God and gave their lives
as *"a living sacrifice"* (Romans 12:1). This is a New
Testament thought, but the Levites were the very exempli-
fication of that exhortation: they lived for God in every
respect. He was their employer, their Father and their
inheritance. And God had richly endowed them with skills
and abilities, giving us a clear indication that we should
seek to achieve the best we can in our service in ecclesial
life and in serving the brotherhood.[9]

So, it is an important point that the Chronicler makes
in the way that he arranges the narrative. David (and
Solomon with him, in all probability) summoned representatives, who were themselves indicative of all the work he
had already done to prepare God's people for the worship
that would be offered. He was not able to build a House for
God, but there was plenty else for him to do, and he started where it really matters – winning the hearts and minds
of his fellow worshippers.

The King's Message

Now that he had opportunity to talk to Israel, through
their invited representatives, what was it that the aged
and infirm King wanted to say? How did his final exhortation compare with Moses' words of distilled wisdom as he
left Israel to carry on the work which the King so loved?
Some commentators think that David began the National
Convention with a public act of association in which
Solomon was made King with a proper Coronation, the
earlier rush job having served its purpose to head-off
Adonijah's rebellion, but comprising a wholly inadequate
ceremony for the transfer of power that was taking place.
That may be what happened, for the record says, as it

were in one breath, that: *"when David was old and full of days, he made Solomon his son king over Israel. And he gathered together all the princes of Israel, with the priests and the Levites"* (1 Chronicles 23:1,2). But it is more likely that Solomon was anointed and declared king at the end of the gathering.[10] If so, the speech or speeches now spoken by David were the equivalent of Coronation addresses.

Considerable detail is given both of what David said, and how he said it. Remember that he was very infirm by now and that even sitting up in bed had been an effort.[11] Now, the record says, *"David the king stood up upon his feet, and said, Hear me, my brethren, and my people…"* (1 Chronicles 28:2). He summoned up all his strength to pass on to them the commission that first had been given to him, for he wanted all Israel to share what had been his life's desire. It must make us ask if we have such a sense of passing on our part in God's saving work to our children and the young people in our ecclesia; for the House of God is still being built – stone by living stone – and it is still every bit as vital for one generation to pass on to the next their sense of vision and their spiritual priorities.

You can read the inspired summary of the proceedings in 1 Chronicles 28:2-8 and 29:1-9. We have already looked at the intervening verses which summarise the private session David had with Solomon,[12] and now we find that the public encouragement was designed to uphold and encourage the young king in the work he had to do. However able we might be as individuals, and Solomon was exceptionally able, and was destined to become more so with God's help, none of us is sufficient of ourselves. We have got to work together – not only because there is too much for one person to do, but because God's work is given for the salvation of a community, not an individual. Working together with the LORD, we can build one another up and walk together to God's Kingdom. That was why Jesus worked with twelve close companions, not because he needed the help, but because they did.

Personal Example

There is no better exhortation than that of personal example; all parents should remember that, as should all brethren who speak. As someone once said, "when you point the finger at someone, there are three fingers pointing back at you!" An exhortation is not just a Sunday morning or afternoon affair – it is to be a matter of daily practice for each of us. No wonder the apostle said: *"exhort one another daily, while it is called 'Today'; lest any of you be hardened through the deceitfulness of sin"* (Hebrews 3:13). That is what David had tried to do, nearly all his life long, and now he did three more things.

● He shared with the people his vision of the great work that lay ahead – something that was designed to bring about that happy state when God would indeed dwell with mankind.

● He explained what he had done personally to begin the process.

● He invited their involvement.

As David said to Israel, he had longed to build a House for God, so that He could dwell in their midst in a permanent and settled state, never to leave His people. That desire was *"in mine heart"* (28:2), David said. Later he would say that it was *"all my salvation, and all my desire"* (2 Samuel 23:5). But now, he explained, it was Solomon's responsibility to take the work forward. As David had once been chosen by God, so now Solomon was God's choice for the next stage – to sit upon the LORD's throne and to build His House – and the king's address made strong reference back to the Davidic covenant, and its conditional nature.[13] Then, in public, he solemnly charged Solomon to *"keep and seek for all the commandments of the LORD your God: that ye may possess this good land, and leave it for an inheritance for your children after you for ever"* (28:8).

Turning to the congregation, David explained the part they had to play, given that Solomon was only a young man and the work of building God's *"palace"*[14] was a great work. He listed the materials he had already put aside – *"gold ... silver ... brass (or bronze) ... iron ... wood ... onyx stones, and stones to be set, glistering stones, and of divers colours, and all manner of precious stones, and marble*

SOLOMON – WISE AND FOOLISH

stones in abundance" (29:2).[15] These appear to have been riches obtained in part as a result of the various wars David was forced to fight after becoming king in Jerusalem,[16] and the pattern is clear for the future as well (see Haggai 2:6-9). When a king comes to Jerusalem again, the One set by God upon His holy hill of Zion, against whom the nations will rage,[17] will once more appropriate national treasures for the exceedingly magnificent house yet to be built.

Personal Contribution

A building requires building materials of all sorts, then as now. In David's day the materials were as listed, and more. In our day, the *"living stones"* God is fitting together to form His dwelling place will be of diverse nature, including His precious stones and "jewels".[18] And the work we do will be regarded as having different value before God depending upon its lasting worth – *"gold, silver, precious stones"*, or *"wood, hay, stubble; every man's work shall be made manifest: for the day shall declare it"* (1 Corinthians 3;12,13). It matters *what* we do and *why* we do it, for the motive is as vital as the contribution itself.

God wants generous gifts from people with willing and thankful hearts. He loves a cheerful giver. It was so at the time of the Exodus, when Moses asked for materials for the construction of the Tabernacle, and it was like that again now, with King David himself. For although the plunder of the nations around had made a vital contribution towards the building project, that was not enough for David. He wanted to be involved himself and, as he had stated once before, he would not offer to God *"of that which doth cost me nothing"* (2 Samuel 24:24).

So, having listed the commodities resulting from the seven wars he had fought, David now catalogued what he had supplied from his own personal fortune:

> *"I have of mine own proper good, of gold and silver, which I have given to the house of my God, over and above all that I have prepared for the holy house. Even three thousand talents of gold, of the gold of Ophir, and seven thousand talents of refined silver,[19] to overlay the*

walls of the houses withal: the gold for things of gold, and the silver for things of silver, and for all manner of work to be made by the hands of artificers" (1 Chronicles 29:3,4).

He had also procured something else, for which he paid a large sum of money, something vital, without which no house could be built. He had bought the site – that area which is now known as the Temple Mount. First, he purchased enough of the original threshing floor, from Araunah the original Jebusite owner, upon which to build an altar, so the plague could be halted. He paid *"fifty shekels of silver"* for that (2 Samuel 24:24), despite Araunah's generous offer to give it for nothing. But it is clear that, when the immediate danger was past, David thought again about what was involved[20] and negotiated with Araunah to buy a much more extensive parcel of ground in that area. Araunah (also named "Ornan") may have had to accumulate that site from several owners, much as a modern developer would proceed to assemble a development site. For David now paid a very large sum for the whole site – the Chronicler records that *"David gave to Ornan for the place six hundred shekels of gold by weight"* *(1 Chronicles 21:25).*

David's Motivation

So far so good, so far as David was concerned, but the real point of the narrative has still not emerged. We might be prompted, provoked or persuaded to do many things which are right, good and profitable. But God wants something more than just bare works – He wants them offered from a willing heart, for love's sake. Carefully included in this list of things is the record of what motivated David. Notice what the Chronicler observed:

"Solomon my son, whom alone God hath chosen, is yet young and tender..."[21] This was God's work and Solomon could not, and should not, do it alone. There was a God-given opportunity for everyone to get involved in a wonderful collective activity.

"... the work is great: for the palace is not for man, but for the LORD God..." The task was much more important

than anything else they would ever be asked to do: it was the LORD's work, that He might dwell among them. We shall never be asked to do anything more important than the work we are asked to do for the LORD our God; we should always remember that when working out our priorities.

"Now I have prepared with all my might for the house of my God the gold for things to be made of gold, and the silver for things of silver …" David, the King, had made it his first concern. It was a work that had dominated his mind and become his ruling passion. Can we say that? Do we really seek "first" the Kingdom of God and His righteousness? We must.

"Because I have set my affection to the house of my God, I have of mine own proper good … given to the house of my God, over and above all that I have prepared for the holy house." David was doing all this because he loved the LORD, it was a matter of "affection", not duty. He loved God, so he wanted to give something back for all that he had received of God's abundance. It was a *"holy house"* and his holiness, his 'separation to God', meant that he wanted to share in the gracious work that Solomon would be privileged to complete. If we have the same sense of the holiness of the work going on in our day, and want to prepare for the completion of that work by King David's greater Son, we too would be more ready to get involved in the work than is sometimes the case.

David's Challenge

Now, having led by example, and having disclosed his motives and his personal example, David issued the challenge. It was, in fact, as challenging to his son Solomon as to all those who were attending the assembly. Generations later, it echoes down to us. *"Who then is willing"*, David asked, *"to consecrate his service this day unto the LORD?"* (1 Chronicles 29:5). The point was that nothing David had started could come to anything unless it was carried forward by faithful followers. He was dependent upon those whom God had appointed as his successors to fulfil their part of the grand purpose. It has been the same for every generation, and it still is. Should the King delay, the up-

and-coming generation has got to play its part, or the true faith will not be found in the earth.

With this in mind, the Scriptures can be seen to be utterly different from human literature. In a human story, when a new character has been introduced the reader expects the writer's attention to switch to him, not to remain with the old cast. But although Solomon has made his entrance on to the scene – and has already been anointed King in dramatic circumstances – we are continuing to follow David's movements, step by weary step. It is what he says that counts, and the *"young and tender"* lad is silent – listening and learning. His turn will come, after David's death, but for now the older man had much to teach his young successor, placed in such a responsible and demanding situation. And today, there is much for the next generation to absorb, so much to learn.

But the time of waiting for Solomon was rapidly coming to an end. Soon, very soon, he would be by himself and the decisions he took would be wholly his own, right or wrong. Was he, *"willing to consecrate himself today to the LORD"*? Are we?

NOTES

[1] As Bro. Whittaker explains (pgs.288,289), there are strong verbal links between the accounts of Moses handing over to Joshua and King David handing over to Solomon. In both cases, much remained to be done and their predecessors had been unable to finish the work, for it was not their work, but God's. He would oversee its completion.

[2] Bro. Ashton (pg.82) suggests that David memorialised his extension of life, Hezekiah-like, in Psalm 30, which is headed "at the dedication of the house". However William Kay, *"The Psalms with Notes"*, 1871, pg.94, thinks this memorialises David's return to the Palace after Absalom's rebellion; and Bro. Booker, *"Psalms Studies"*, i, pg.173, thinks the heading refers to the setting up in Jerusalem of the Tent in which the Ark was kept, pro tem.

[3] Wilcock, pg.98, notes different wording for the two assemblies: *'gathered together'* (23:2 RV) and *'assembled'* (28:1 RV).

[4] The *"princes of Israel"* might have included all Solomon's remaining brothers, to give them a chance to accept him and pledge their wholehearted support; or it might have been those men listed in 1 Chronicles 27:16-22, who are described as *"the princes of the tribes of Israel"*; or both.

[5] This organisation might have been done earlier, as part of David's on-going preparation for the temple, but the details are recorded here to show that Temple worship was about people, not just about a building. What mattered was the use they were going to make of the magnificent structure that God wanted Solomon to build.

[6] The 24,000 Levites in question were divided into 24 courses which would be responsible for Temple worship all year round. They would all have their duties allocated by lot *"as well the small as the great"* (25:8), which showed that they were all subject to Divine control. They were not free to do as they chose, any more than we are.

[7] These numbers appear to be the result of a Levitical census that had taken place (1 Chronicles 23:3). It also appears that whilst Moses had decreed that the Levitical service was to be from 30 to 50 years of age, David now altered that to 20 to 50 (23:24). Perhaps this was because there was going to be a lot of work building and then organising worship at the new Temple, as well as a wider teaching ministry to ensure that the people came to worship three times a year, as the Law prescribed. His immediate justification, however, was that the heavy physical work of carrying the Tabernacle around would no longer apply, once the Temple had been built (23:26). McConville, pgs.89-96, makes the interesting suggestion that there may have been different age limits for different functions within the priestly orders.

[8] For an illustration of how this might have been configured, see Bro. & Sis. Ritmeyer's *"From Sinai to Jerusalem"* (2000), pg.66.

[9] There are many references in these chapters to God-given skills and abilities (25:7; 26:6,9,30f.; 27:32), the very point that Paul also makes in Romans 12:6-8.

[10] 1 Chronicles 29:22 describes the feast that ended the Assembly then adds: *"They ate and drank with great joy in the presence of the LORD that day. Then they acknowledged*

Solomon son of David as king a second time, anointing him before the LORD to be ruler..." (NIV).

[11] 1 Kings 1:47 "And the king bowed himself upon the bed".

[12] 1 Chronicles 28:9-21 (see pages 39-41).

[13] See page 37.

[14] 1 Chronicles 29:1 *"Solomon my son, whom alone God hath chosen, is yet young and tender, and the work is great: for the palace is not for man, but for the LORD God".* The term *"palace"* is used in Scripture to describe the palaces of eastern monarchs, but only here, and in verse 19, to describe God's dwelling place.

[15] In cataloguing what he had prepared, including the plans for the new Temple, a certain amount of detail is given about the intended construction. We will look at these details when considering the construction of the Temple and its furniture.

[16] Against the Philistines, Moab, Zobah, Edom, Ammon, Syria and Ammon (see 2 Samuel 5-11 and 1 Chronicles 18-20). After the battle against Zobah it is specifically recorded that *"from Tibhath, and from Chun, cities of Hadarezer, brought David very much brass, wherewith Solomon made the brasen sea, and the pillars, and the vessels of brass"* (1 Chronicles 18:8).

[17] *"Ask of me, and I shall give thee the heathen for thine inheritance, and the uttermost parts of the earth for thy possession"* (Psalm 2:8).

[18] Malachi 3:17.

[19] *"Gold, of the gold of Ophir, and seven thousand talents of refined silver"* – notice that only the best is good enough for God.

[20] It seems that God had indicated to David the precise spot where He wanted His House built within Jerusalem. First, Gad had been commanded to require the erection of an altar on the threshing floor in question (1 Chronicles 21:18) on Mount Moriah and, later, David had declared: *"The house of the LORD God is to be here, and also the altar of burnt offering for Israel"* (22:1 NIV).

[21] All these descriptive phrases are taken from 1 Chronicles 29:1-5.

7

Solomon's Coronation

ADDRESSING the assembled congregation, David had begun with a significant form of words. *"Hear me, my brethren, and my people"* (28:2), he had said, making it clear at the outset that they were all in this together, as brethren, and that all needed to work together to fulfil the LORD's commandments.[1] That was a point that was well taken by the assembled company and when David invited their contributions, to add to what he had already assembled, there was a wonderfully encouraging response. *"Who then is willing...?"* he had asked, and the answer was that a lot of people were:

> *"... the chief of the fathers and princes of the tribes of Israel and the captains of thousands and of hundreds, with the rulers of the king's work, offered willingly, and gave for the service of the house of God ... And they with whom precious stones were found gave them to the treasure of the house of the LORD ... Then the people rejoiced, for that they offered willingly, because with perfect heart they offered willingly to the LORD: and David the king also rejoiced with great joy"* (1 Chronicles 29:6-9).

There is a lot of joy to be had from working together and it is indeed the case that *"it is more blessed to give than to receive"*. All that we have comes from God, and belongs to Him; when we contribute we do no more than give back what has been entrusted to our care. It is our duty to do that, as faithful servants, but we are to give for love's sake, not because we feel obliged to respond.[2] There is a real emphasis here upon that point. Building the

56

Temple was going to be a huge project; a very expensive and demanding one. It would take years and much of the productive and economic capacity of the nation; so David spells out, in the clearest possible way, that everything we have in life is given us so that we can use it to glorify God. Look at this progression of thought:

> *"Thine, O LORD is the greatness, and the power, and the glory, and the victory, and the majesty: for all that is in the heaven and in the earth is thine"* (29:11);

> *"Both riches and honour come of thee"* (29:12);

> *"All things come of thee, and of thine own have we given thee"* (29:14);

> *"O LORD our God, all this store that we have prepared to build thee an house for thine holy name cometh of thine hand, and is all thine own"* (29:16);

> *"In the uprightness of mine heart I have willingly offered all these things: and now have I seen with joy thy people, which are present here, to offer willingly unto thee"* (29:17).

Years later, and involved in another attempt to raise a lot of money, this time for the poor saints in Jerusalem, the apostle Paul summed up the Christian challenge in these terms: *"For if there be first a willing mind, it is accepted according to that a man hath, and not according to that he hath not"* (2 Corinthians 8:12). God does not ask us to contribute more than we are able to give; but He does expect us to be willing to do what we can, and, with His help and assistance, many a person has been surprised by what they can accomplish in His service when they put their minds to it.

It was like that in Jerusalem when the people responded to David's challenge. The record in 1 Chronicles makes it clear that the people rejoiced together, because they were fulfilling their heart's desire[3] – they had come to know what they really needed, and to want that. It's a very happy outcome when our wants and our needs are in perfect alignment, for often we want lots of things we don't really need.

Thanks be to God

David's response to this outpouring of communal generosity was typical of the man. He thanked God – doing so in a way which anticipated some of the sentiments later included by the Lord Jesus in the model prayer he taught his disciples.[4] The glory was all God's, as were the things that people were privileged to give in His service:

> *"Thine, O LORD is the greatness, and the power, and the glory, and the victory, and the majesty: for all that is in the heaven and in the earth is thine; thine is the kingdom, O LORD, and thou art exalted as head above all. Both riches and honour come of thee, and thou reignest over all; and in thine hand is power and might; and in thine hand it is to make great, and to give strength unto all. Now therefore, our God, we thank thee, and praise thy glorious name. But who am I, and what is my people, that we should be able to offer so willingly after this sort? For all things come of thee, and of thine own have we given thee..."* (1 Chronicles 29:10-14).

But there was something else as well. David was grateful for the opportunity to have lived with God and to have given Him life-long service. He knew that God wanted a life that was inclined towards Him – worship that came from the heart, not just from the lip. Works, however welcome, were only acceptable provided they were the product of a changed attitude, the fruit of a nature that was being transformed. So, whilst thanking God, David also petitioned Him on Israel's behalf:

> *"... We are strangers before thee, and sojourners, as were all our fathers: our days on the earth are as a shadow, and there is none abiding ... I know also, my God, that thou triest the heart, and hast pleasure in uprightness. As for me, in the uprightness of mine heart I have willingly offered all these things: and now have I seen with joy thy people, which are present here, to offer willingly*

unto thee. O LORD God of Abraham, Isaac, and of Israel, our fathers, keep this for ever in the imagination of the thoughts of the heart of thy people, and prepare their heart unto thee: and give unto Solomon my son a perfect heart, to keep thy commandments, thy testimonies, and thy statutes, and to do all these things, and to build the palace, for the which I have made provision" (29:15-19).

David wanted their hearts and minds – their feelings and their understanding – to be right with God and, most of all, he wanted Solomon's spiritual life to be modelled on his own, for he was pre-eminently the man *"after God's own heart"*.[5] He also wanted this time of dedicated communal commitment to linger in the national consciousness and to be something that changed the course of Israel's life in the land as, once before, the obsession to pursue the ways of sin and violence had been a turning point for the world that then existed.[6]

Getting our hearts right with God is crucially important and is a Bible-long theme. We know that our human condition is deep-rooted in the inclination to follow our own heart's desire and we often refer to passages like Jeremiah 17:9 or Mark 7:21, to show that the problem we experience from within is an inherited inclination towards sin. We are born like that; but we can be reborn into Christ, so that we learn to develop a quite different inclination. There are over 700 references in Scripture to the heart, but not all of them are discouraging: far from it! We are urged to: *"love the LORD thy God with all thine heart"* (Deuteronomy 6:5) and the promise was given that a time was coming when a new covenant relationship would be established between God and man which will fulfil this promise: *"A new heart also will I give you, and a new spirit will I put within you: and I will take away the stony heart out of your flesh, and I will give you an heart of flesh"* (Ezekiel 36:26). That promise is now being fulfilled for those men and women who have made a new relationship with God, through faith in the Lord Jesus Christ.

It was about that new relationship that David was now praying: asking God that the hearts of the nation would be affected for good by what they were now doing together, and hoping, in particular, that Solomon would remain focused on God, and His Law, so that he would always *"incline (his) ear unto wisdom, and apply (his) heart to understanding"* (Proverbs 2:2). If he would do that, it was a recipe for a long and much blessed life, both for the king and for the nation.

Bowing the Knee

It was now that the second anointing[7] and the national coronation of Solomon took place. The earlier occasion, when Solomon had been proclaimed king, had been a hurried affair attended by some people from Jerusalem who spotted what was happening. But now it was necessary to affirm Solomon's kingship with representatives of the entire nation, so that they would all go along with the appointment of Solomon as king. First, they worshipped the LORD and offered sacrifices (29:20,21) and then, on the second day of their assembly, they held a formal Coronation:[8]

> *"They made Solomon the son of David king the second time, and anointed him[9] unto the LORD to be the chief governor,[10] and Zadok to be priest.[11] Then Solomon sat on the throne of the LORD[12] as king instead of David his father, and prospered; and all Israel obeyed him. And all the princes, and the mighty men, and all the sons likewise of king David, submitted themselves unto Solomon the king"* (1 Chronicles 29:22-24).

Where the KJV says that they *"submitted themselves"*, both the KJV and RV margins render the expression *"gave the hand under Solomon,"* or, *"pledged their submission"* (NIV). The literal rendering appears to pick up the way in which a loyal pledge was sworn in times past (Genesis 24:2; 47:29), and would be sworn in the future (2 Chronicles 30:8; Ezekiel 17:18). If done by each of the representatives placing his or her hand under Solomon's thigh, it is worth noting that Solomon's brothers – including Adonijah – would also have pledged their loyal submission. Again this points forward to the time when every knee will bow before the Lord Jesus in submission, which is why we are told that *"he hath on his vesture **and on his**"*

thigh *a name written, KING OF KINGS, AND LORD OF LORDS"* (Revelation 19:16).

It seems possible that Psalm 72 was composed for this very occasion. If so, everyone watching the ceremony would have been looking beyond it to One who one day will sit on David's throne in Jerusalem – 'great David's greater son'. They would have looked forward to the time when an ideal King will reign from Jerusalem over all the earth:

> *"In his days shall the righteous flourish; and abundance of peace so long as the moon endureth. He shall have dominion also from sea to sea, and from the river unto the ends of the earth. They that dwell in the wilderness shall bow before him; and his enemies shall lick the dust. The kings of Tarshish and of the isles shall bring presents: the kings of Sheba and Seba shall offer gifts. Yea, all kings shall fall down before him: all nations shall serve him ... Blessed be the LORD God, the God of Israel, who only doeth wondrous things. And blessed be his glorious name for ever: and let the whole earth be filled with his glory; Amen, and Amen"* (Psalm 72:7-11,18-19).

That King was not being crowned in Jerusalem at this time, although there would be a limited fulfilment of those words in years to come. In anticipation of the Messianic reign of Christ, the record says that:

> *"The LORD magnified Solomon exceedingly in the sight of all Israel, and bestowed upon him such royal majesty as had not been on any king before him in Israel"* (29:25).

Yet, when the Lord Jesus Christ returns, to be acclaimed by those who love him, there will be those who regret his Coming and try to resist his will. It was so even in this phase of the Kingdom of God on earth. Some of those who pledged loyalty – because they had no alternative – were not fully persuaded that this turn of events was wholly to their liking. They were content to bide their time and await a favourable opportunity. Solomon was ruling *"in the midst of (his) enemies"* [13] but, unknown to

them, David had already alerted Solomon of their intentions and had advised him about the appropriate action to
be taken.

NOTES

[1] Selman, pg.248, notes that there is a distinctive emphasis
on the need for obedience to the Divine command in these
chapters.

[2] McConville, pg.91, says that these chapters provide a
reminder that "the function of humanity and creation as a
whole is to worship God. Israel was entrusted for a time with
a duty which lies ultimately upon all".

[3] The very same point – about giving willingly – is made
about the building of the Tabernacle (see Exodus 35:20-29).
There, the people were described as *"willing hearted"* and
"wise hearted".

[4] Bro. Whittaker, pg.371, finds lots of other links between
David's Psalms and the words in the Lord's Prayer.

[5] 1 Samuel 13:14; Acts 13:22.

[6] That was the time when: *"GOD saw that the wickedness of
man was great in the earth, and that every imagination of the
thoughts of his heart was only evil continually"* (Genesis 6:5),
so He sent the flood to take them all away.

[7] Saul and David were both anointed King (1 Samuel 10:1;
16:13) and, although largely unmentioned, there are indications (e.g. 1 Kings 19:16) that this act of sacred association
with God – which linked the King with the Divinely appointed roles of Priest and prophet – was always practised.

[8] Bro. Whittaker, pg.297, thinks that this second coronation
would have taken place at Shechem, but if the Assembly took
place in Jerusalem, it seems more likely that the coronation
would have been there, notwithstanding what happened later
in Israel's history. And there were three thousand animals
sacrificed (1 Chronicles 29:21), which would have necessitated access to an altar – probably the one that had been set up
on the intended site of the new Temple.

⁹ David was himself anointed three times (1 Sam.16:13; 2 Sam. 2:4,5:3).

¹⁰ This appears to mean that Solomon would now be the leader of the joint-rulership, until such time as David died.

¹¹ Notice that Zadok was now formally appointed as High Priest, in association with Solomon. Previously he had been the officiating priest at the Tabernacle in Gibeon.

¹² This kingdom was no ordinary kingdom: it was *"the throne of the LORD"* – the kingdom of God. It is strongly emphasized that Solomon was chosen by God: to sit on His throne, to be God's son and to build the Temple. (See Selman, pg.250.)

¹³ *"The LORD said unto my Lord, Sit thou at my right hand, until I make thine enemies thy footstool. The LORD shall send the rod of thy strength out of Zion: rule thou in the midst of thine enemies. Thy people shall be willing in the day of thy power..."* (Psalm 110:1-3).

8

Unfinished Business

AMONG David's last words to Solomon had been the injunction: *"Arise therefore, and be doing, and the LORD be with thee"* (1 Chronicles 22:16). It was a call to action, for he had left his son some unfinished business; tricky problems to deal with for a young man who had to follow in the footsteps of a much loved and very gifted father who had reigned for the last forty years.

In his private briefing, the concerned father had pinpointed a few problems in the kingdom that needed urgent attention. We have left those details until now, because they lead on to the first executive actions of Solomon's reign, although it is difficult to know how quickly he acted. The indications are that he bided his time with most of the problems but that when he had the opportunity, he acted swiftly and decisively.

Things to Do

David had said that Solomon needed to attend to the following:

- **Joab** – *"Thou knowest also what Joab the son of Zeruiah did to me ... Do therefore according to thy wisdom, and let not his hoar head go down to the grave in peace"* (1 Kings 2:5,6).

- **The sons of Barzillai** – *"Shew kindness unto the sons of Barzillai the Gileadite, and let them be of those that eat at thy table: for so they came to me when I fled because of Absalom thy brother"* (2:7).

- **Shimei** – *"the son of Gera, a Benjamite of Bahurim …
  cursed me with a grievous curse in the day when I went
  to Mahanaim: but he came down to meet me at Jordan,
  and I sware to him by the LORD, saying, I will not put
  thee to death with the sword. Now therefore hold him
  not guiltless: for thou art a wise man, and knowest what
  thou oughtest to do unto him; but his hoar head bring
  thou down to the grave with blood"* (2:8,9).

Notice that David had a lot of confidence in the young
king's ability and perception. Whatever Solomon might
think of his own administrative capabilities, David
thought him well-endowed in that respect. He might
appear to be handing over problems to his son – notably
how to deal with Joab and Shimei – that he had been
unwilling or unable to tackle himself. But there were reasons why he had taken no earlier action, apart from his
personal debility, resulting from his guilty conscience and
the realisation of his sinfulness and unworthiness. And
there were other problems to tackle which Solomon could
see for himself, arising out of Adonijah's failed coup
attempt, including what to do about Adonijah, and
Abiathar the priest, who had supported him.

"A little child"

These were big issues for anyone to tackle. For any new
administration is always studied very closely and their
early decisions and actions are often seen as indicative of
the political direction they will follow and the style they
will adopt. It was especially so for a young man following
the demise of a much-loved father. We cannot be certain of
Solomon's age at his accession. David twice described him
as *"young and tender"* when addressing the Assemblies (1
Chron. 22:5; 29:1) and Solomon makes a similar statement
at Gibeon when, in prayer to God, he says *"I am but a little
child"* (1 Kings 3:7).

In both cases there is a reason why this should be said.
David was highlighting the magnitude of the task that
faced Israel as a whole and the inexperience of the new
king. Who could be worthy of, or capable to accomplish,
such a monumental task, for David wanted the temple to
be the most magnificent dwelling place for God? And

Solomon, faced by the awesome responsibility of ruling for God, on His throne, over His kingdom, was quite properly saying, in so many words, that he was not capable without help from on high. But we should not therefore think that Solomon was in his early teens, or that he would have needed someone to lift him up on to the throne, or to help him down again.

He was already married and had a child, as we learn right at the end of his life. Rehoboam was forty-one years old when he succeeded to the throne after Solomon's forty year reign (2 Chron. 12:13). Solomon was Bathsheba's fourth, or possibly fifth, son and if the tragic circumstances whereby David became her husband can be dated to about 992 B.C., and David's death to 971, then Solomon would have been in his late teens – 16 or 17 at the time he came to the throne.[1] As a working assumption, many commentators have reckoned that he was about 20 years old.

Solomon's Solutions

● **Adonijah**

As it turned out, Adonijah made the first move that prompted Solomon into action. He had been warned by Solomon already, just after the coup attempt, that his conduct was under scrutiny and that he must show himself *"a worthy man"* (1 Kings 1:52) and it would appear that he had later pledged his support to the new king (1 Chronicles 29:24).[2] But now he did something which exposed his discontent and revealed his latent ambition. He approached Bathsheba with a seemingly innocent request: he asked if he could be allowed to marry Abishag, the pretty young lady who had attended David in the few weeks or months before his death. Bathsheba came to Solomon to ask that favour on Adonijah's behalf and Solomon saw through the request at once.[3]

> *"Why dost thou ask Abishag the Shunammite for Adonijah?"*, he remonstrated, *"Ask for him the kingdom also; for he is mine elder brother; even for him, and for Abiathar the priest, and for Joab the son of Zeruiah.[4] Then king Solomon sware by the LORD, saying, God do so to me, and more also, if Adonijah have not spoken*

*this word against his own life. Now therefore, as the
LORD liveth ... Adonijah shall be put to death this day"*
(1 Kings 2:22-24).

Was Solomon being hasty, and was this to be the impul-
sive and headstrong way in which he meant to resolve all
the complex problems that came his way? Or was the
young king being discerning? The Scriptural account
makes it clear that he was showing great insight. How did
he know what his elder brother was planning? First, there
was the implication behind the request; remember how
Absalom had appropriated the Kingdom by taking David's
concubines as his own, as a public display of accession.[5]
Second, although there is no record of the full conversation
between mother and son, as they sat comfortably side-by-
side, it is clear that if he asked her, as he must have done,
Bathsheba could tell him:

(a) that she had been apprehensive about the unusual
    approach made to her by Adonijah,[6] and

(b) that Solomon's elder brother had made it perfectly
    clear when he made the request that he still considered
    himself to be the proper heir to the throne.[7]

So Benaiah[8] was despatched, with no more ado, to execute Adonijah and problem No. 1 was solved – just like
that! It sent the signal that you didn't mess with King
Solomon. Step out of line and you would get swift and
summary judgement against you.

● Abiathar

Having dealt with the chief conspirator, Solomon now
turned his attention to his supporters. Abiathar, the son of
Ahimelech, was the only survivor of the priestly massacre
at Nob.[9] He had been with David all through the wilderness experience; had been loyal through Absalom's rebellion and had served as the king's counsellor. It would
appear that he served as high priest in Jerusalem, ministering before the ark in the Tent of Meeting that David
had pitched, while Zadok, his second-in-command, was left
to minister before the Tabernacle at Gibeon.[10] It is difficult

67

to be certain why Abiathar had abandoned David and gone in support of Adonijah. Perhaps it was just a career move that went wrong – a case of being in the wrong place at the wrong time! Or he may have been picking up signals from David's behaviour that indicated that his days as high priest were numbered, for David had advanced Zadok's career as well, a quite natural development when you consider that there were two centres of worship at this time – Gibeon and Jerusalem. It was, in fact, a pointer for the future.

Unwisely, Abiathar had supported Adonijah and now he paid the price. In dealing with this problem, Solomon's actions were quite different this time, for he made the punishment fit the crime:

> *"Unto Abiathar the priest said the king, Get thee to Anathoth, unto thine own fields; for thou art worthy of death: but I will not at this time put thee to death, because thou barest the ark of the Lord GOD before David my father, and because thou hast been afflicted in all wherein my father was afflicted. So Solomon thrust out Abiathar from being priest unto the LORD; that he might fulfil the word of the LORD, which he spake concerning the house of Eli in Shiloh"* (1 Kings 2:26,27).

God had left a remnant for the house of Eli, and He had not been hasty to fulfil the prophecy about another, more faithful, priestly house.[11] Nor was Solomon hasty now, for although he banished Abiathar and thus separated him from both Tabernacle and Tent, he is still mentioned as a priest along with Zadok in a passage summarising the settled state of Solomon's kingdom.[12] Perhaps this man who had been so faithful and helpful to David came to see the error of his ways and later returned to favour, or perhaps it was that a high priest still retains that title until his death, even if deposed.

● **Joab**

Now Solomon turned his attention to the man who had been David's all-powerful commander-in-chief. There are many reasons why David had not restrained or punished Joab. He was David's nephew, of course,[13] and family ties counted for an awful lot in those days. They had been through a lot together, and David was a very loyal friend. There were times when he had needed the sort of ruthless treatment that Joab meted out, for war was a bloody business. He had acquiesced in some of Joab's most vicious acts of revenge[14] and, once having failed to act, it was more difficult the next time – an important lesson for us.

Then, worst of all, David had compromised himself with Joab in connection with Uriah's death, though there was no question of any blackmail or covert influence over the King, for the whole matter had been made public in the most compromising way. Yet, despite God's declared forgiveness, that whole incident debilitated David and lessened his moral and public authority in a very serious way. Sin has that effect to this very day. So David had advised Solomon that he should take action: *"Let not his hoar head go down to the grave in peace"* (1 Kings 2:6).

Joab was always ahead of the game, and when he saw what was happening to his fellow-conspirators he took avoiding action. He fled to Gibeon – to the Tabernacle – and claimed sanctuary by grasping the horns of the altar of burnt offering. Benaiah, who was again sent to sort the problem out as the King's trouble-shooter, was clearly uncomfortable about this. It seems that his Levitical training got the upper hand and he returned to Jerusalem to report the position: that Joab was not for letting go, but that he preferred to die in the courtyard of the Lord's house, like a sacrifice!

Solomon would have none of that. Joab had never bothered about such niceties before. Abner, for instance, had been brutally murdered in Hebron – a city of refuge, where it was unlawful for the avenger of blood to take vengeance. Now there was no refuge for Joab either and Benaiah returned to deliver summary justice.

"Benaiah the son of Jehoiada went up, and fell upon him, and slew him: and [Joab] was buried in his own house in the wilderness. And the king put Benaiah the son of Jehoiada in his room over the host: and Zadok the priest did the king put in the room of Abiathar" (1 Kings 2:34,35).

Thus Adonijah and Joab died by the orders of Solomon and the sword of Benaiah. Abiathar the priest was banished to the Levitical city of Anathoth. The king appointed Benaiah, the son of Jehoiada, in Joab's place, as his new commander-in-chief over the army; and Zadok became high priest instead of Abiathar. And the young king was not finished yet.

● Shimei

David had also asked Solomon to deal with Shimei and, once again, Solomon produced a quite different regime for him – restraint within Jerusalem, much like 'probation' or 'electronic tagging' in our day. So, it became evident that the young king was very able and imaginative in the way he intended to govern. And there was much more of that to come.

When David was fleeing Jerusalem, to avoid fighting against his much-loved son Absalom, most people were sorry to see him go. There is a touching account of the sad and tearful king leaving the city, crossing the Kidron Brook, then climbing up the Mount of Olives, being encouraged as he did so by his faithful bodyguard and followers. But one man was really glad to see him go – Shimei the Benjamite. He might have thought that the family feud between David and Absalom was the inevitable result of David having stolen the kingship from the tribe of Benjamin, from whence Saul had come. Or he might have wanted to make a protest about David's conduct towards Bathsheba and Uriah.

Whatever his thinking, he expressed his feelings in a very striking way; for, as David left the city, Shimei was to be seen pelting him with stones. And as he threw them at the departing king, he cursed David:

> *"Come out, come out, thou bloody man, and thou man of Belial: the* LORD *hath returned upon thee all the blood of the house of Saul, in whose stead thou hast reigned; and the* LORD *hath delivered the kingdom into the hand of Absalom thy son: and, behold, thou art taken in thy mischief, because thou art a bloody man"* (2 Samuel 16:7,8).

David's soldiers wanted to end the demonstration there and then, but David told them to let Shimei curse on. Perhaps, he said, it was a message from the LORD. It must have been in his mind that the punishment for an act of adultery in the law of God was that *"the adulterer and the adulteress shall surely be put to death"* [15]

Shimei had acted rather differently, however, when David returned from Manahaim the victor over Absalom, albeit the reluctant one. This time he had been one of the first to welcome David home, he and a thousand other Benjamites.[16] The fact that they accompanied Shimei might indicate that he was an important man among the tribe of Benjamin. Certainly it marked him out so far as David was concerned. For, although he accepted Shimei's contrite repentance and swore an oath that he should not die,[17] now he briefed Solomon about him:

"Behold, thou hast with thee Shimei the son of Gera, a Benjamite of Bahurim, which cursed me with a grievous curse in the day when I went to Mahanaim: but he came down to meet me at Jordan, and I sware to him by the LORD, saying, I will not put thee to death with the sword. Now therefore hold him not guiltless: for thou art a wise man, and knowest what thou oughtest to do unto him; but his hoar head bring thou down to the grave with blood" (1 Kings 2:8,9).

Notice, once again, what confidence David had in his son's ability. He recognised that it was not right to let people treat the office of the king of Israel with contempt, whatever his personal feelings might have been. He took no action for his own sake; indeed, he could not have done so once he had sworn not to. But now he felt the need for something to be done, hence his request to Solomon.

So, after David's death, Solomon summoned Shimei and told him that henceforth he must live in Jerusalem and made it perfectly clear that if he ever left the city he would be executed, making him swear an oath of acceptance in the name of the LORD, just as David had done for him years before. Shimei accepted the terms – he had no option – and lived peacefully in Jerusalem for the next three years without causing any trouble. But then he left Jerusalem to visit Gath, to recover some fleeing slaves, and immediately Solomon summoned him again. He explained that as Shimei had broken his oath he had forfeited his right to live, and he had the Benjamite executed.

As Solomon said later: *"Better is it that thou shouldest not vow, than that thou shouldest vow and not pay"* (Ecclesiastes 5:5). The message must have gone through the kingdom loud and clear; Solomon was not a man to be trifled with, for he meant what he said. And the last of David's problem cases had been solved – decisively!

In all these acts Solomon was showing what it will be like when a king reigns in Jerusalem who will execute *"judgement and justice"*. He will not be dependent upon human testimony, or open to special pleading on behalf of the rich and famous, for he will care for the poor and needy and dispense much-needed righteous judgement. As ever, young Solomon was pointing beyond himself. He was an insightful young man, but he was about to become even more able in the service of his God.

● Chimham

That left just one, much easier, remit to fulfil. David had also requested that Solomon should reward the kindness and hospitality shown him by Barzillai at Mahanaim, when the king had been forced to flee from Absalom. At the time David had offered the old man lifelong hospitality in return, but he had declined as he was already of a good age and preferred to die where he had lived. Now, said David: *"shew kindness unto the sons of Barzillai the Gileadite, and let them be of those that eat at thy table: for so they came to me when I fled because of Absalom thy brother"* (1 Kings 2:7).

Nothing is said expressly about Solomon's continuing provision for Chimham, who had returned with David from exile, or about the other sons of Barzillai, but it becomes clear that Solomon never stinted in matters of hospitality. Years later Scripture records that there was a lodging place in Bethlehem known as *"the habitation of Chimham"* (Jeremiah 41:17), from which it is possible to deduce that he was given sufficient funds to settle in that locality and establish his family business there. It is a possibility that this was the very inn which turned Mary and Joseph away when they came seeking refuge, when Mary was heavily pregnant. If so, this is in marked contrast to the hospitality shown to David by Chimham's father, so many generations before.[18]

In these events we see the outworking of truths that would be repeatedly established over the coming years, and that are equally true with regard to our own King, the Lord Jesus Christ:

> *"The wrath of a king is as messengers of death: but a wise man will pacify it. In the light of the king's countenance is life; and his favour is as a cloud of the latter rain"* (Proverbs 16:14,15).

NOTES

[1] Merrill, pg.244, suggests the 992 B.C. date (though he thinks that Solomon was Bathsheba's first surviving child, born the year afterwards), but there can be no certainty about the date he suggests as it is part of his dated reconstruction of David's reign. Theile, *"The Mysterious Numbers of the Hebrew Kings"* (1983) dates Solomon's accession at 970 B.C. (a little later if there was a co-regency with David for a couple of years), but makes no suggestion about Solomon's age. Nolen-Jones, in his quite different chronological scheme, detailed in *"The Chronology of the Old Testament"* (2005), also reckons Solomon to have been about 17 when David died (he thinks in 1015 B.C.).

[2] It is possible, however, that when Solomon said to him *"Go to thine house"* (1 Kings 1:53) he was placing him under house arrest, as later he limited Shimei to the city of Jerusalem.

[3] Farrar, pg.45, observes that the Queen Mother was the real power behind the throne, while the king's wives had much less influence. This, he suggests, is why there is frequent use of the phrase *"...and his mother's name was..."* throughout the Books of Kings and Chronicles.

[4] Notice how Solomon had been considering what to do with

the 3 main conspirators – Adonijah, Abiathar and Joab.

⁵ 2 Samuel 16:21,22. See also 2 Samuel 12:8; 1 Kings 20:7 and 2 Kings 24:15.

⁶ *"She said, Comest thou peaceably? And he said, Peaceably"* (1 Kings 2:13).

⁷ *"He said, Thou knowest that the kingdom was mine, and that all Israel set their faces on me, that I should reign: howbeit the kingdom is turned about, and is become my brother's: for it was his from the LORD"* (2:15). You can almost hear the dissatisfaction in his voice, and his self-delusion was patently evident!

⁸ Benaiah was the son of the high priest Jehoiada, and this Levite/warrior had become the chief of David's bodyguard of Cherethites and Pelethites. Having remained faithful in Adonijah's rebellion, he was now destined to become Solomon's commander-in-chief, the post having been vacated by Joab when he joined forces with Adonijah.

⁹ 1 Samuel 22.

¹⁰ 1 Chronicles 16:39.

¹¹ He was descended from Eli, being the youngest son of Ithamar, and it had long since been forecast that the priesthood was to pass to another line of the family (1 Samuel 2:31-35). *("I will raise me up a faithful priest, that shall do according to that which is in mine heart and in my mind: and I will build him a sure house; and he shall walk before mine anointed for ever.")* Abiathar may have been watching for any indication of that happening. The irony is that it was his own act that now brought it to pass.

¹² 1 Kings 4:4 *"And Benaiah the son of Jehoiada was over the host: and Zadok and Abiathar were the priests"*.

¹³ Joab was the eldest of the 3 sons of Zeruiah, David's sister.

¹⁴ 1 Kings 2:5 is significant, in that David mentions to Solomon two particular crimes – those against Abner and Amasa. It seems that he regretted not having responded to them at the time they occurred.

¹⁵ Leviticus 20:10; Deuteronomy 22:22.

¹⁶ *"Shimei the son of Gera, a Benjamite, which was of*

Bahurim, hasted and came down with the men of Judah to meet king David. And there were a thousand men of Benjamin with him ..." (2 Samuel 19:16,17).

[17] 2 Samuel 19:23.

[18] It could have been that Jesus was born in the stable of that very inn, as some people suggest, but it is much more likely that Mary, being pregnant, and having distant relatives in the village, was given hospitality in a nearby house. See Kenneth E Bailey, "The Manger and the Inn", *Theological Review* (November 1979).

9

"What lack I yet?"

SOLOMON had made an excellent start. He had dealt with problems his father had left in a way that showed everyone that he meant business and that, although he was young, he was capable to rule as king. Both inspired accounts recognise that good start, both when viewed from the standpoint of the prophetic word and that of Temple worship:[1]

- *"The kingdom was established in the hand of Solomon"* (1 Kings 2:46); and

- *"Solomon the son of David was strengthened in his kingdom, and the LORD his God was with him, and magnified him exceedingly"* (2 Chronicles 1:1).

God was with Solomon and He *"established"* the Kingdom in this young man's hand, causing his prestige and influence to increase greatly. Things were going really well and Solomon must have been growing in self-confidence. He had dealt well with one administrative problem after another and now he made a marriage alliance with Pharaoh of Egypt, which also secured his southern border (1 Kings 3:1-3). It would appear that he taught his new bride the ways of the LORD. For nothing is said against her to suggest that she led him astray, indeed the record appears to suggest otherwise:[2]

"Solomon made affinity with Pharaoh king of Egypt, and took Pharaoh's daughter, and brought her into the city of David ... And Solomon loved the LORD, walking

in the statutes of David his father: only he sacrificed and burnt incense in high places" (1 Kings 3:1-3).

Something Missing

But there was something missing, even so, and it is to young Solomon's credit that he knew that to be the case. We all have needs that only God can satisfy, but we do not always recognise them nor do anything to remedy the situation. Those are haunting words in the seventh letter written to the ecclesias in Asia, that:

"Because thou sayest, I am rich, and increased with goods, and have need of nothing; and knowest not that thou art wretched, and miserable, and poor, and blind, and naked: I counsel thee to buy of me gold tried in the fire, that thou mayest be rich ..." (Revelation 3:17,18).[3]

But such can be encouraging words, too, if we acknowledge that we know we need God's help. If we ask Him, He is always ready to come to our aid. It was like that with Solomon. We are left to conjecture precisely why he decided to go to Gibeon, to worship at the Tabernacle and to offer burnt offerings upon that altar, instead of the one that David had established in Jerusalem.[4] As the Kings and Chronicles accounts merge to become close parallel accounts of all that was happening, we get two different perspectives.

It transpires that Solomon was concerned about the fact that the people were still worshipping at "high places", certain geographical locations that had some historical or sacred connection with Israel's history. That practice was understandable in a way, although it had unfortunate Canaanite associations, because the *"place"* where God had said he would place His name[5] – where the Temple was to be built – had not yet become available to the nation. It was going to be a building site for some years and it would be impractical during that time for the tribes to come together to worship there. So Solomon carefully set an example for all the tribes by going to *"the great high place"* (1 Kings 3:4) at Gibeon, where both the Tabernacle and the brazen Altar of Burnt Offering were situated, and he offered a thousand burnt offerings there.

But he did not go alone. Just as David had helpfully conferred with key leaders of the congregation of Israel, so did Solomon (2 Chron. 1:2-6); so they came along too.

It was a clear demonstration to everyone that Gibeon was to become Israel's focal point of worship for the foreseeable future and, if they got into the habit of coming there three times a year, as the Law required, later they would manage the transition to Jerusalem and to the Temple without difficulty. Gibeon is situated about seven miles[6] north-west of Jerusalem and *"the great high place"* in question, where the Tabernacle was then situated, seems to have been one of the two hills which gave the city its name – *"the twin height"*.

> *"The people sacrificed in high places, because there was no house built unto the name of the LORD, until those days. And Solomon … sacrificed and burnt incense in high places. And the king went to Gibeon to sacrifice there; for that was the great high place"* (1 Kings 3:2-4).

There are other suggestions as to why Solomon chose Gibeon. Farrar suggests that Solomon was touching base with the sacred traditions of Israel, going 'back to basics', as it were, to celebrate the secure establishment of his throne.[7] Or he could have wanted to inaugurate his reign as one that would seek to serve God sacrificially. Wordsworth makes the observation that although the Tabernacle was due to be superseded by the Temple, Solomon showed that it was still a place of worship that God had appointed, and so he honoured it accordingly.[8]

"A thousand burnt offerings did Solomon offer upon that altar" [9] (1 Kings 3:4). And that night, in a dream, God appeared to him to pose the vital question – *"Ask what I shall give thee"* (3:5).

"What do YOU want?"

As we have seen, Solomon was a well endowed young man, possessing wisdom and understanding well in advance of what might have been expected from someone his age. Evidently David trusted him to do the right thing with those difficult problems he had passed on to the lad. But how wise was Solomon really? Given the invitation to ask for a gift from God, what would he request? His response confirms our view of his maturity.

First, he responded to the offer itself by reflecting what God had already done for his family – what he had already given the House of David. God had:

- showed David great mercy,[10]

- given him a son to sit on his throne,

- made Solomon, God's servant, king instead of David.[11]

But what a responsibility all this was. Quite clearly the careful teaching of David had left a deep impression. The kingdom would only continue, David had said, *"if"* Solomon remained faithful.[12] So now the young king shared his problem with God. This occasion is full of instruction and challenge for us. Do we impress upon our children and young people how important it is that they should keep the faith and carry the work forward, should the Lord delay his Coming? Do the younger members of the ecclesia appreciate how important their faithful adherence is? Do we all, young and old, share our problems with God and ask for the help that He is able to provide – as Solomon did now?

The King's Need

> *"I am but a little child:*[13] *I know not how to go out or come in. And thy servant is in the midst of thy people which thou hast chosen, a great people, that cannot be numbered nor counted for multitude ... Now, O LORD God, let thy promise unto David my father be established: for thou hast made me king over a people like the dust of the earth in multitude"* (1 Kings 3:7,8; 2 Chronicles 1:9).

Notice how Solomon was aware of the Abrahamic covenant – that Abraham's seed would be multiplied like the *"the dust of the earth: so that if a man can number the dust of the earth, then shall thy seed also be numbered".*[14] He was aware of his own responsibility as a shepherd over God's people – to *"go out"* and *"come in"* before them, as he

79

led them to safe pasture and beside still waters.[15] And he was keenly conscious of the Davidic covenant, founded on God's *"promise unto David my father"*.

The King's Request

> *"Give therefore thy servant an understanding heart to judge thy people, that I may discern between good and bad: for who is able to judge this thy so great a people? ... Give me now wisdom and knowledge, that I may go out and come in before this people: for who can judge this thy people, that is so great?"* (1 Kings 3:9; 2 Chronicles 1:10).

This request, which really pleased God, needs to be fully understood if we are to appreciate what Solomon was really asking for and what God was pleased to give him. Notice the words that qualified Solomon's request. He asked for:

an understanding heart –

• to judge God's people, the nation of Israel, and

• the ability to discern between good and bad;

wisdom and knowledge –

• that he might *"go out and come in"* (be a shepherd to) the nation.

Solomon was not asking for understanding, wisdom and knowledge about everything – every branch of science and all walks of life – or an insight into the way everything works or everybody thinks. He wanted administrative skill and insight, so that he could properly discharge his responsibilities as King of Israel, ruling over God's kingdom. He wanted to know right from wrong for those national issues that would confront him, both when he was deciding policy and administering judgement and justice.

Under the Law, the king had an important role to play in the judicial process. He was the final court of appeal for matters that were referred up from earlier hearings. Deuteronomy made provision for this process when there were questions which were too difficult for the judges in a city to decide. The plaintiff was to come to: *"the priests the Levites, and unto the judge that shall be in those days, and enquire; and they shall shew thee the sentence of judgment: and thou shalt do according to the sentence, which they of that place which the LORD shall choose shall shew thee"* (Deuteronomy 17:9,10). In course of time a central court of appeal was established, consisting of priests, Levites and the heads of fathers' houses (2 Chronicles 19:8); Moses was the first leader of Israel to act in this capacity and afterwards the king assumed the role (see 2 Samuel 15:2).

Case Study

Only one such legal judgement of Solomon is preserved, but it is so striking that people still refer to that incident with respect and admiration to this day. As if to show what gift God had conferred upon Solomon by way of judicial insight, the episode concerns two women who come to seek the king's judgement concerning one child who had died and another who remained alive. One plaintiff argued that it was her child that had survived and that her companion had stolen that child in the night when her own had died. The other said that no such things had happened: the surviving child was hers all along. It was a tricky case to decide for it was one person's word against another's and there were no witnesses and no hospital case notes to consult.

Nowadays a DNA test would have sorted it out scientifically. But Solomon's solution was so breathtakingly striking that, even today, people marvel at the King's daring, psychological insight and his sheer wisdom. His actions resulted in an immediate confession of guilt which concluded the matter absolutely. There were no expensive legal hearings, no legal arguments, no charges, no appeals, and no delay.

"Bring me a sword", the king said, faced with the quandary. *"And they brought a sword before the king ... Divide the living child in two, and give half to the one, and half to the other. Then spake the woman whose the*

living child was unto the king, for her bowels yearned upon her son, and she said, O my lord, give her the living child, and in no wise slay it. But the other said, Let it be neither mine nor thine, but divide it. Then the king answered and said, Give her the living child, and in no wise slay it: she is the mother thereof" (1 Kings 3:24-27).

What a brilliant resolution of a seemingly intractable problem, and so easily done! That was the effect of Solomon's God-given wisdom. Judicial and administrative wisdom was what Solomon had asked for, and what God had willingly conferred. No wonder that *"all Israel heard of the judgment which the king had judged; and they feared the king: for they saw that the wisdom of God was in him, to do judgment"* (3:28).

What a portrayal this was of the King who is Coming; the One who will be imbued with even more insight and understanding. Of him it is said:

"The spirit of the LORD shall rest upon him, the spirit of wisdom and understanding, the spirit of counsel and might, the spirit of knowledge and of the fear of the LORD; and shall make him of quick understanding in the fear of the LORD: and he shall not judge after the sight of his eyes, neither reprove after the hearing of his ears: but with righteousness shall he judge the poor, and reprove with equity for the meek of the earth" (Isaiah 11:2-4).

NOTES

[1] See Note 15 on page 43 about the different perspectives of the Books of Kings and Chronicles.

[2] Jewish tradition maintains that this Egyptian wife, of whom we shall have more to say later, converted to Judaism (so Edersheim,V, pg. 63). Heaton, pg.22, makes the interesting comparison between the request for wisdom made by Solomon and Egyptian scribal tradition, in which the quest for wisdom was much prized. Could his new wife have sug-

gested this to Solomon, for she is mentioned just before the narrative of Solomon's dream at Gibeon?

[3] The title of this chapter *"What lack I yet?"* is the question posed by the rich young ruler, who didn't like the answer Jesus gave him (Matthew 19:20).

[4] See 1 Kings 3:4 and 2 Chronicles 1:1-5 for details of the Tabernacle at Gibeon and, by contrast, 2 Samuel 24:25 and 1 Chronicles 21:26-30 for details of the altar in Jerusalem, perhaps co-located with the Tent that had been pitched for the Ark (2 Chronicles 1:4).

[5] Deuteronomy 12:5.

[6] Ten or eleven kilometres.

[7] Farrar, pg. 58.

[8] Wordsworth, vol iii, pg.11. He further likens Solomon's attitude towards the Tabernacle to that of the apostles in New Testament times, "who were careful to show that in their zeal for the Gospel they did not despise the Law, but honoured it as the minister and servant whom God had appointed to bring His People to Christ".

[9] *"... the brasen altar, that Bezaleel the son of Uri, the son of Hur, had made, he put before the tabernacle of the LORD: and Solomon and the congregation sought unto it"* (2 Chronicles 1:5).

[10] The word translated *"mercy"* is better translated 'covenant love' (see N H Snaith, *"Distinctive Ideas of the Old Testament"*, 1944, pg. 94f.).

[11] 1 Kings 3:6,7; 2 Chronicles 1:8.

[12] See pgs. 36-37 earlier.

[13] Solomon's comment here does not merely reflect his age, but his humility and sense of unworthiness for such a great responsibility.

[14] Genesis 13:16; 28:14.

[15] See Bro. H A Whittaker, *"Enjoying the Bible"*, 1973, pg.78, where he traces these shepherd allusions in Numbers 27:16,17; Joshua 14:11; 1 Samuel 18:13; Acts 1:21 and 9:26.

10

Solomon's many Gifts

ASKED by God at Gibeon to say what he wanted as a gift, Solomon chose wisdom – the ability to govern, administer and judge – so that he could do a worthwhile job when ruling for God over His people. God was pleased with his choice for there were other less valuable things that Solomon might have requested. The Divine response to Solomon's request listed some of them, and contained a surprising tailpiece. God said:

> *"Because thou hast asked this thing, and hast not asked for thyself long life; neither hast asked riches for thyself, nor hast asked the life of thine enemies; but hast asked for thyself understanding to discern judgment; behold, I have done according to thy words: lo, I have given thee a wise and an understanding heart; so that there was none like thee before thee, neither after thee shall any arise like unto thee"* (1 Kings 3:11,12).

Notice the words *"for thyself"*,[1] which occur three times. Solomon could have made the most of God's offer to magnify and glorify himself, and so can we. The truth brings many blessings. It gives us and our families a sound and secure basis for life. Generally we have good relationships, a safe environment for our children and young people, a real and living hope – which shields us from the hopelessness and despair that can prevail for those who have no hope. But if we just appropriate these things "for ourselves", and seek to give nothing back to God, then we are missing the key point. God gives us many blessings – to enable us to "spend and be spent" in His service, and to

His greater glory.

Solomon understood that, wise young man that he already was. He wanted what he really needed, so that he could serve God, and God's people, most effectively. He had an attitude like the one the Lord Jesus urges us to cultivate when he bids us become *"as little children"* (Matthew 18:3). So God was pleased to give him what he had asked for: *"Lo"*, said God, *"I have given thee a wise and an understanding heart; so that there was none like thee before thee, neither after thee shall any arise like unto thee"* (3:12). But what exactly did that gift imply? [2]

"A wise and understanding heart"

Solomon himself makes the point often enough in his later writings that there is nothing more worthwhile in life than the quest for wisdom. He often urges us to choose wisdom rather than anything else – just as he was doing now.

> *"Happy is the man that findeth wisdom, and the man that getteth understanding ... Her ways are ways of pleasantness, and all her paths are peace"* (Proverbs 3:13-17; see also 4:5-7; 16:16).

Within the Book of Proverbs, wisdom can be analysed or grouped into many different facets. Here are a few:

- **Instruction or Training,** which is related to correction and discipline;

- **Understanding or Insight** – this was what Solomon had asked for: he wanted to *"discern between good and bad"* (1 Kings 3:9);

- **Wise dealing;**

- **Shrewdness and discretion;**

- **Knowledge and Learning.**[3]

But "Proverbs" is much more than a catalogue of what wisdom can do for you; it is full of encouragement to seek after and find this attribute, so as to know God and His will. That is the way in which we can turn from evil, so that we can grow in the knowledge of God. Thus, Solomon urges his readers:

> "*Get wisdom, get understanding: forget it not; neither decline from the words of my mouth. Forsake her not, and she shall preserve thee: love her, and she shall keep thee. Wisdom is the principal thing; therefore get wisdom: and with all thy getting get understanding*" (4:5-7).

The quest for wisdom is a profound Old Testament theme, not just in the writings of Solomon. The 'Wisdom' books are grouped together around the common theme of *"the fear of the LORD"*.[4] And the New Testament is no less emphatic about the importance of this life-long quest. The difference is that while Solomon urged his contemporaries to court Wisdom, to love her, and to live happily with her all one's life long (Proverbs, chapters 8 and 9), the New Testament bids us search for Christ, who is the very embodiment of wisdom and knowledge. It was the Lord who said of himself: *"Behold, a greater than Solomon is here"* (Matthew 12:42), and his apostle who said that in him: *"are hid all the treasures of wisdom and knowledge"* (Colossians 2:3).

New Testament Parallels

Understand that parallel and some New Testament passages become much clearer. For example, when James says that we should be like Solomon and seek first for wisdom, his words are a perfect match for something Solomon once said:

> "*If any of you lack wisdom, let him ask of God, that giveth to all men liberally, and upbraideth not; and it shall be given him. But let him ask in faith, nothing wavering*" (James 1:5,6);

> "*If thou criest after knowledge, and liftest up thy voice for understanding; if thou seekest her as silver, and searchest for her as for hid treasures; then shalt thou understand the fear of the LORD, and find the knowledge of God. For the LORD giveth wisdom: out of his mouth cometh knowledge and understanding*" (Proverbs 2:3-6).

If, like Solomon, we want the knowledge of God, His revealed Word will lead us to both knowledge and understanding. We too can be wise. And if we put the search for God and His Kingdom first, just as Solomon received many other gifts from God, we too will be richly blessed. For, Jesus promised:

> *"Seek ye first the kingdom of God, and his righteousness; and all these things shall be added unto you"* (Matthew 6:33).

"All these things..."

It was like that for Solomon too. He asked for discernment and insight, to enable him to rule the Kingdom effectively and God granted that request and then said something else. This was the surprising tailpiece, mentioned earlier. Solomon had chosen wisely and God would now reward him richly for that good choice, with three other things, and a possible fourth:

> *"I have given thee (1) a wise and an understanding heart ... And I have also given thee that which thou hast not asked, both (2) riches (and wealth),[5] and (3) honour: so that there shall not be any among the kings like unto thee all thy days. And if thou wilt walk in my ways, to keep my statutes and my commandments, as thy father David did walk, then I will (4) lengthen thy days"* (1 Kings 3:12-14).

Writing under inspiration in the Book of Proverbs, Solomon would later have a lot to say about (2) riches and wealth and (3) honour, and he was well qualified to comment in the light of his experience. Comparing and contrasting all the things he received from God, Solomon concluded that Wisdom was undoubtedly the best and foremost choice:

> *"Happy is the man that findeth wisdom, and the man that getteth understanding. For the merchandise of it is better than the merchandise of silver, and the gain thereof than fine gold. She is more precious than rubies: and all the things thou canst desire are not to be compared unto her. Length of days is in her right hand; and*

in her left hand riches and honour. Her ways are ways of pleasantness, and all her paths are peace" (Proverbs 3:13-17).

What other gifts?

The record will become explicit about exactly what riches came Solomon's way; what honour was shown him both by his own subjects and by dignitaries from elsewhere; and how long he lived. But to get a flavour of how wide-ranging the gift of wisdom was, the Book of Kings immediately groups together several different aspects of wisdom that made Solomon's talent quite extraordinary. Here's the breakdown:

Happening	References	Category
Solomon's Prayer at Gibeon	1 Kings 3:4-5; 2 Chron.1:7-13	Wisdom
Judgement of the Harlots	1 Kings 3:16-28	Judicial
Solomon's Officials	1 Kings 4:1-19	Administrative
Extent of Solomon's Kingdom	1 Kings 4:20,21	Political
Solomon's Wealth & Power	1 Kings 4:22-28; 2 Chron.1:14-17	Economic
His Wisdom & its Appeal	1 Kings 4:29-34	Proverbial

Notice that whilst the first incident (with the harlots) illustrates Solomon's new-found judicial ability, which made the nation appreciate that he now possessed *"the wisdom of God"* (1 Kings 3:28), there are also indications of his administrative capability (4:1-19); his political astuteness (4:20,21); Israel's economic prosperity and enlarged influence (4:22-28); and his personal insight and understanding which received international acclaim (4:29-34).

As Solomon's wisdom is such a key feature of his reign, and so critical to his personal life, it is worthwhile analysing each of these aspects to better understand what skills he possessed and what they could do for him, if anything, as he made progress towards the life that is to come.

● Judicial wisdom

We have already seen how his new-found perception gave him the ability to discern and decide tricky matters of judgement, and to elicit a confession from the one harlot, much to the benefit of the other and the baby. There must have been many other such judgements over the years to come and it is an intriguing possibility that many of the proverbs Solomon later wrote, under the influence of God's Spirit, started off as conclusions that he reached after a particular court case. If so, the particular happenings might have brought forth a principle of much more general application. Here are a few examples:

"Hatred stirreth up strifes: but love covereth all sins" (Proverbs 10:12);

"A false balance is abomination to the LORD: but a just weight is his delight" (11:1);

"A talebearer revealeth secrets: but he that is of a faithful spirit concealeth the matter" (11:13);

"He that withholdeth corn, the people shall curse him: but blessing shall be upon the head of him that selleth it" (11:26);

"He that tilleth his land shall be satisfied with bread: but he that followeth vain persons is void of understanding" (12:11).

● Administrative wisdom

The Temple could only be built once the materials could be afforded by the nation, for it was to be a major capital investment – at least, that is how we would view it today if such massive public expenditure were to be contemplated. So the nation had to be organised and administered in a way which maximised its economic strength and, to achieve that, Solomon did a very interesting thing. As 1

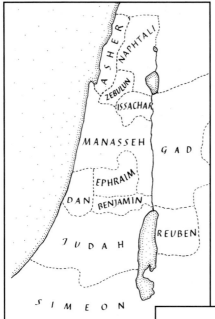

*The Tribal
Boundaries as estab-
lished by Joshua after
the casting of lots.*

*Not all the Tribes
conquered their allo-
cated portions, but
this was how the land
was divided.*

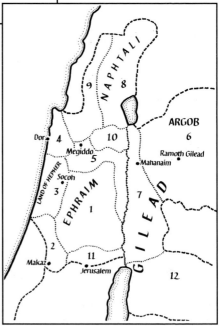

*The Tribal
Boundaries as recast
by Solomon, as part
of the reorganisation
of the Kingdom.*

*These new divisions
did not survive for
long: Israel split
along Tribal lines
during Rehoboam's
reign.*

90

Kings explains in detail,[6] Solomon reorganised the tribal territories and created 12 new economic regions or divisions.[7]

Detailing the civil servants that he appointed – and the quality and organisation of its public servants is always a good indication of a properly run administration – the record indicates that Solomon made wise choices for his key advisers. It is a sign of a developing nation when defined roles begin to emerge, almost like a Cabinet of advisers or counsellors. This is how the Tanakh (a Jewish translation of the Old Testament) lists the key people who worked with Solomon:

"These were his officials:

- *Azariah son of Zadok – the priest;*

- *Elihoreph and Ahijah sons of Shisha – scribes;*

- *Jehoshaphat son of Ahilud – recorder;*

- *Benaiah son of Jehoiada – over the army;*

- *Zadok and Abiathar – priests;*[8]

- *Azariah son of Nathan – in charge of the prefects;*[9]

- *Zabud son of Nathan the priest – companion of the king;*[10]

- *Ahishar – in charge of the palace; and*

- *Adoniram son of Abda – in charge of the forced labour"* (1 Kings 4:2-6).

Note that several of those advisers are described as *"priests"*. The term can have a wider meaning, as "principal officer" or "chief adviser",[11] but it is encouraging to think that Solomon would have included men of God among his advisers. Notice, too, that the young king chose his closest counsellors from his father's close friends, quite possibly children with whom Solomon had grown up.[12] Thus we can see the benefits in life of making good friendships with like-minded people – friendships that will last for life, and which will be the means of furthering the LORD's work.

Solomon did involve members of his family in due course, as the details of his twelve new administrative divisions indicate. Ben-Abinadab (4:11 RV) and Ahimaaz (4:15) were to become Solomon's sons-in-law, so he had at least two daughters. Bear in mind that the twelve principal officers in the provinces, whose main duty was to provide food for the palace,[13] would change over time, so the list of those in office might not be the people who were first appointed. But it may also be the case that, while seeking good husbands for his daughters Taphath and Basemah, Solomon may have pointed them in the direction of people he had come to respect and appreciate. Whichever way it worked out, it is instructive to note that he gave the couples space to develop and mature in their own ways, for neither of them were located in the palace, but in Dor and Naphtali respectively.

For those of us who find change difficult, it is helpful to note that King Solomon, made wise by God, knew that it was time for a change. The old tribal divisions had led to strong vested interests and loyalties to family and locality which threatened the unity and effectiveness of the entire nation. Solomon knew that unless something was done, loyalty to the clan and the family unit would tear the nation apart – and he was quite right, for it did.

Instead, he tried to create new associations, based on geographical areas – Mount Ephraim; Makaz; Sochoh and the land of Hepher; and so on.[14] The king was not seeking to remove the original tribal boundaries, which had a vital part to play especially in matters of land tenure,[15] but he wanted to break the parochial view that was beginning to prevail, in which tribal interests and loyalties had become more important than the national good. The parallel with today's ecclesial scene can readily be drawn – we need to see and respond to the needs of the brotherhood as a whole, not just take a narrow ecclesial view. And our individual lives must not be so dominated by personal or family considerations that we miss the main challenge.[16]

Solomon wanted the district governors to collect taxes and the temple tithe, as well as to supply the court with food for one month each year, and to help both with building projects and the defence of the realm.[17] In that way they would work together, as the LORD's people, everyone contributing. That challenge to our community is undiminished by the passing of time. Engaged upon building a temple in which the LORD dwells by His Spirit, we have to work together in this great endeavour. Personal, family or ecclesial considerations have their proper place, but they must not be allowed to impede the work we have to do if God is to dwell among us.

● Political peace and prosperity

The Kingdom was reorganised for the better under Solomon's gifted administration and as a result of many different activities the nation's wealth increased enormously. The King lived sumptuously, as did the royal court, but so also did the ordinary people of Israel:

> *"Judah and Israel were many, as the sand which is by the sea in multitude, eating and drinking, and making merry. And Solomon reigned over all kingdoms from the river unto the land of the Philistines, and unto the border of Egypt: they brought presents, and served Solomon all the days of his life"* (1 Kings 4:20-21).

God blessed the nation with prosperity and happiness, something which was an aspect of the Abrahamic blessing, as the language makes clear – *"as the sand which is by the sea in multitude"* – but it had an incidental effect. Their prosperity would enable many in the nation to help fund both the construction of the Temple and the necessary sacrifices and offerings. It would allow them to be partners in this remarkable work, if they so chose. To this day, God never asks us to give what He has not first supplied. We only give Him back what He has already given to us.[18] And it was not only Judah and Israel who could participate, for the record includes details of the kingdom's territorial extent – *"from the river (Euphrates) unto the land of the Philistines, and unto the border of Egypt"* – another clear allusion to God's covenant with Abraham.[19] Some of those subject nations paid tribute to Solomon, and others engaged in trade with the entrepreneurial king, so they would indirectly be contributing to the financing of a house which was to be a House of prayer for all nations.

- **Personal and poetic insight**

> *"God gave Solomon wisdom and understanding exceeding much, and largeness of heart, even as the sand that is on the sea shore. And Solomon's wisdom excelled the wisdom of all the children of the east country, and all the wisdom of Egypt.*[20] *For he was wiser than all men ... and his fame was in all nations round about. And he spake three thousand proverbs: and his songs were a thousand and five. And he spake of trees, from the cedar tree that is in Lebanon even unto the hyssop that springeth out of the wall: he spake also of beasts, and of fowl, and of creeping things, and of fishes. And there came of all people to hear the wisdom of Solomon, from all kings of the earth, which had heard of his wisdom"* (1 Kings 4:29-34).

Apart from any other skill or insight he possessed, Solomon was to become a literary man – a poet, singer or composer, and a writer of many proverbs.[21] Not all of these had lasting value for us, or they would have been preserved.[22] Those proverbs and writings that were inspired by God were of an altogether higher value. But the king was evidently a naturalist of considerable repute – trees, shrubs, animals, birds, reptiles, insects, fish: he had studied and apparently written about all these. We know, from Ecclesiastes, that he built parks and gardens in Jerusalem, and pagan rulers had similar enterprises – notably the hanging gardens of Babylon.

Coupled with his administrative and judicial decisions, the combination of all these skills and accomplishments gained Solomon an international reputation. It engendered in Israel something akin to the Renaissance in Europe. One writer observes that "Israel's mental horizons, and in a sense her physical ones as well, were expanding".[23] E. W. Heaton's book has the full title

94

"Solomon's New Men – the emergence of ancient Israel as a national state". He says of Solomon's reign that, *"Israel finally ceased to be anything like a 'tribal' society and emerged as a national state of great complexity and high pretentions, which, for a brief period, ranked as one of the major powers of the Ancient Near East"*.[24]

Inspired by God

As David before him, Solomon was also to be privileged as the means whereby God would convey His inspired wisdom in the Scriptures of truth, which include several of Solomon's writings. And, in his own right, he was challenged to develop his powers of understanding and perception in relation to his spiritual and personal life. So he became wise in a whole range of things and expressed much of his understanding in pithy or epigrammatic sayings, as had wise men before him.

That doesn't mean that he would always *do* what was right, but he would know what ought to be done. His gift from God would mean that he was never to be in doubt about the correct course of action to be taken in any given circumstance. He then had to make the choice himself: to choose to do the right thing. In this, there is a remarkable parallel with the life-long experience of the Lord Jesus, who appears to have had a unique insight, from his earliest years, into the will and purpose of God for him.[25]

Because Solomon was God's appointed king, living a godly life was his first and most important responsibility, so that he could lead the nation by example. Notwithstanding that his gift from God was predominantly to do with government and administration, it would seem to have included discernment in matters that affected his own spirituality. If he went wrong later, it would not be because he was unsure of what to do, but because he wilfully chose to do those things that he knew he should not do.

Model King

God had promised Solomon the wisdom he requested, plus riches, wealth and honour – which he had not asked for, but would get anyway. Riches, wealth and honour are not always an unmixed blessing, for they are very supportive to the natural man and his native affections. They can breed pride, self-sufficiency, avarice and all sorts of other undesirable characteristics. But these further gifts from God served at least two purposes.

- They made Solomon a living example of how God means to reward His faithful servants when they, too, are made kings and priests in His coming Kingdom (not because of his possessions, but because of the way he was gifted by God with abilities and talents far beyond what was normal).

- Because the king was so gifted in material terms, and so able to discern the true benefits of the various gifts he had been given, Solomon was placed in a unique position to advise us about the advantages or disadvantages of the various choices we must make in life. The Book of Ecclesiastes is the King's report to us on that particular aspect of human life.

But there was another aspect to all the blessings that came his way. Solomon had been richly endued by God and would be expected to respond to those blessings – to give back according to the measure that God had given to him. He had things to do for God – a Kingdom to be governed according to God's gracious law and a Temple to build in which God was to be worshipped in the midst of His people. Should he fail, he would be a salutary lesson to believers in all ages.

Meanwhile Solomon's response to God's gracious blessings was as it should have been. Having offered 1000 sacrifices in Gibeon, and having communicated with God: *"Solomon awoke; and, behold, it was a dream. And he came to Jerusalem, and stood before the ark of the covenant of the LORD, and offered up burnt offerings, and offered peace offerings, and made a feast to all his servants"* (1 Kings 3:15). He continued as he had begun – living sacrificially and sharing the blessings he had received with his fellow servants. Together they had a lot of work to do.

NOTES

[1] In the parallel account, Solomon is commended for asking for wisdom and knowledge *"for himself"* so that he could rule over God's people. *"God said to Solomon, Because this was in thine heart, and thou hast not asked riches, wealth, or honour, nor the life of thine enemies, neither yet hast asked long life; but hast asked wisdom and knowledge for thyself, that thou mayest judge my people, over whom I have made thee king: wisdom and knowledge is granted unto thee"* (2 Chronicles 1:11).

[2] Wordsworth, vol.iii, pg.12, has a typically full answer: *"With regard to the true character of Solomon's wisdom, it is not to be limited, with some, to mere practical sagacity, and political prudence, or physical science, such as may be attained by human efforts; nor yet is it to be extended, with others, to the knowledge of supernatural mysteries of faith, which are unfolded by divine Revelation; but it was that wisdom of the heart which loved and embraced whatever truth the human mind, by reason and experience, aided by divine grace, was enabled to discover".*

[3] This analysis is taken from Derek Kidner, *"Proverbs"*, TOTC, 1964, pg.36.

[4] See Job 28:28; Psalms 19:9; 111:10; Proverbs 1:7,29; 15:33; Ecclesiastes 12:13.

[5] 2 Chronicles 1:12.

[6] 1 Kings 4:1-19.

[7] Several writers point out the similarity between the arrangements Solomon introduced and the administrative set-up in Egypt. See Heaton, pgs.47-60, and de Vaux, pgs.127-138.

[8] Azariah is said to be Zadok's *"son"*, but that term really means descendant, for he was Zadok's grandson (1 Chronicles 6:8). Nothing more is heard of Zadok in the Biblical account after his appointment as Solomon's high priest.

[9] Notice that although Abiathar has been sent home and Zadok has been made his replacement, he is still listed as

High Priest. This was a Divine appointment and the title must have lasted for as long as the person lived, whether they were still serving in that capacity or not.

[10] This Nathan may be Nathan the prophet, or it may be that he was one of the sons of Solomon's brother Nathan (who later features in the genealogy of the Lord Jesus: Luke 3:31). The likelihood is that Azariah and Zabud were the prophet's children, as Solomon's nephews would have been too young to hold such offices at the start of his reign.

[11] See Edersheim,vol.v, pg. 67; de Vaux, pg.128. The latter adds this comment about the list as a whole: *"It is noteworthy, too, that some of these high officials, or their fathers, have non-Israelite names, names which have puzzled the copyists or the translators: Adoram has a Phoenician name, like his father Abda. The names of Shisha or Shawsa (1 Ch 18: 16) and his son Elthoreph or Elihaph may be Egyptian or Hurrite. In fact it was to be expected that the young Israelite kingdom should recruit some of its officials from the neighbouring countries, which had an administrative tradition. Even for its organization it had to copy models abroad. Study of some offices suggests the influence of Egyptian institutions, but it does not enable us to decide whether this influence was direct, or whether it came indirectly to Israel from the Canaanite states which Israel displaced. Direct influence seems the more likely."*

[12] De Vaux, pg.128, writes: *"The continuity with the Davidic administration is evident. Solomon employs the same herald as his father, the son of one of his priests, both the sons of his secretary, the son of his army commander and at least two sons of the prophet Nathan, who had been an adviser of David and had favoured the accession of Solomon."*

[13] *"Solomon had twelve officers over all Israel, which provided victuals for the king and his household: each man his month in a year made provision"* (1 Kings 4:7).

[14] Solomon may not, however, have disrupted the arrangements in Judah (his own tribe) although it seems that it was given a governor of its own: *"And there was one officer in the land of Judah"* (1 Kings 4:19 RSV). So, de Vaux, pg 135, although Wiseman, pg.93, thinks that Judah could have been the twelfth province.

[15] See Numbers 36:1-9, where it is commanded that *"Neither shall the inheritance remove from one tribe to another tribe; but every one of the tribes of the children of Israel shall keep himself to his own inheritance"* (verse 9).

[16] This is the main point of the Lord's solemn words: *"If any man come to me, and hate not his father, and mother, and wife, and children, and brethren, and sisters, yea, and his own life also, he cannot be my disciple"* (Luke 14:26). It is a matter of first things, first.

[17] *"Adoniram the son of Abda was over the tribute. And Solomon had twelve officers over all Israel, which provided victuals for the king and his household: each man his month in a year made provision ... And those officers provided victual for king Solomon, and for all that came unto king Solomon's table, every man in his month: they lacked nothing. Barley also and straw for the horses and dromedaries brought they unto the place where the officers were, every man according to his charge"* (1 Kings 4,6-7, 27-28).

[18] Remember David's words in 1 Chronicles 29:14 when he made this very point.

[19] *"In the same day the LORD made a covenant with Abram, saying, Unto thy seed have I given this land, from the river of Egypt unto the great river, the river Euphrates"* (Genesis 15:18).

[20] 1 Kings 4:31 compares Solomon's wisdom favourably with Ethan the Ezrahite, and Heman – these were probably Levites who were in charge of the choir, and who wrote Psalms 89 and 88 respectively. Heman was also *"the king's seer in the words of God, to lift up the horn"* (1 Chronicles 25:5). Chalcol, and Darda, the sons of Mahol are also named, but nothing is really known about them otherwise. All four names appear together, and in this order, in 1 Chronicles 2:6 – as sons (or descendants) of Zerach – in which case they would be great grandsons of Jacob.

[21] The aptly-named Wiseman, pg.86, makes this comment about the genre of wisdom writing then prevalent: *"Solomon, like the academic 'wise men' of contemporary Mesopotamian and Egyptian courts, learned scribal skills and those genres of literature (so-called 'Wisdom Literature') which taught life and nature, ethical and aesthetic values and general behav-*

iour (1 Kings 4:32). These included serious discussions ('The Righteous Sufferer') and didactic works of all kinds. Among these, scribal reference texts listing natural and philosophical subjects can be compared, in literary form, with the biblical books of Job, Psalms, Proverbs, Ecclesiastes and the Song of Solomon".

[22] J. L. Crenshaw, *"Old Testament Wisdom – An Introduction"*, 1998, pgs.40-42, considers several possible reasons why these writings did not survive. Perhaps, he surmises, these lists were noun lists (onomastica) which functioned as a means of ordering the vast store of knowledge achieved by students of nature, for there are strong parallels with writings found on Egypt and Mesopotamia. He concludes, however, that: *"such proverbs and songs may have constituted riddles and fables that became lost over the years. Since animals, trees, and insects are essential to these literary forms, and Israel's sages undoubtedly composed enigmatic sayings, this explanation is more natural than resorting to onomastica, for which no clear evidence exists within biblical wisdom".*

[23] Derek Kidner, *"Wisdom to Live By"*, 1985, pg.14.

[24] Heaton, pg.31.

[25] See Psalm 22:9,10; 40:6-8; Isaiah 50:4,5. These passages appear to indicate that Jesus would have such sensitivity to the mind of God that he would be in tune with his Father's will and purpose. Jesus appears to endorse that in John 5:19-20 and 8:38. The difference between our Lord and Solomon is that he not only knew what God wanted him to do, he always did it!

11

Building God's Temple

WHAT David had longed to do, Solomon was now to achieve. The Covenant that God had made with David contained the promise that a seed from David's loins would build a House for God[1] and whilst this has clear reference to the later work of the Lord Jesus Christ, Solomon's work would foreshadow that and teach some important spiritual lessons in the process. It follows that the extensive details which are recorded about the first Temple have lasting spiritual value.

You might have expected that the narrative account of Solomon's achievements would now concentrate on the Temple building, especially the Chronicles account, where the inspired writer is more concerned with the spiritual aspects of the Kingdom than with the political or secular achievements. It is, therefore, instructive to notice the sequence of recorded events as both accounts guide their readers towards the climax of Solomon's achievements: the construction of a House for God, where He would dwell among His people.

Having reorganised both the civil service and the tribal boundaries, to increase efficiency and to ensure that the nation could afford the capital expenditure they were about to undertake for God, Solomon turned his attention to organising a large workforce which would be well administered. For the project required major civil engineering works, complex building construction, and fine artwork. To do all these properly required the involvement of an international team of labourers and the employment of skilled craftsmen.

101

David's Legacy

The young king was not starting from scratch, of course,
for David had already made elaborate preparations and
had begun to accumulate a lot of the material which would
be needed. In his handover of the Kingdom to Solomon,
David had placed a lot of emphasis upon this task: the one
that he would dearly have loved to undertake. It was a
driving force in his life and God had revealed to his faithful servant just what the Temple was to be like and what
materials were needed.[2] He had, therefore, been able to
give Solomon a full set of plans, which God had revealed to
David:

> *"Take heed now; for the LORD hath chosen thee to build
> an house for the sanctuary: be strong, and do it. Then
> David gave to Solomon his son the pattern of the porch,
> and of the houses thereof, and of the treasuries thereof,
> and of the upper chambers thereof, and of the inner par-
> lours thereof, and of the place of the mercy seat, and the
> pattern of all that he had by the spirit, of the courts of
> the house of the LORD , and of all the chambers round
> about, of the treasuries of the house of God, and of the
> treasuries of the dedicated things ... All this, said
> David, the LORD made me understand in writing by his
> hand upon me, even all the works of this pattern"* (1
> Chronicles 28:10-19).

As these verses indicate, this was much more than a
general indication of what the Temple would be like: it
was a very detailed specification and it enabled David to
plan accordingly. When working out what Solomon's
Temple was like we have three Biblical sources – the
descriptions in the Books of Kings and Chronicles; some
details of what was taken away to Babylon when the
Temple was destroyed;[3] and the specification of what
David accumulated.[4] This is a listing of what he had
already accumulated:

- wrought stones to build the house of God;[5]
- iron in abundance for the nails for the doors of the
  gates, and for the joinings;[6]
- bronze in abundance without weight;

102

- cedar trees in abundance (from the Zidonians and Tyre);
- an hundred thousand talents of gold;
- a thousand thousand talents of silver;[7]
- workmen – hewers and workers of stone and timber, and all manner of cunning men for every manner of work;
- gold for the lampstands and their lamps;
- silver for a lampstand and its lamps;
- gold for each table for the showbread;
- silver for the silver tables;
- pure gold for the forks, the basins, and the cups; for the gold and the silver bowls;
- great quantities of onyx and stones for setting, antimony, coloured stones, all sorts of precious stones, and marble;
- three thousand talents of gold, of the gold of Ophir, and seven thousand talents of refined silver, for overlaying the walls of the house, and even the floor (1 Kings 6:30).

So, even before Solomon begins to marshal his thoughts and work out what needs to be done, we have begun to get a picture of the intended project. David knew that the house had to be such that it would magnify God's name, not just in Israel but in all the earth:

> *"The house that is to be builded for the* LORD *must be exceeding magnifical, of fame and of glory throughout all countries"* (1 Chronicles 22:5).[8]

Solomon's Taskforce

The team Solomon established for the Temple project is carefully detailed in the record. First, mention is made of the King's growing influence and prestige,[9] which resulted in important people coming to visit the Kingdom to take the King's advice. In all probability this was something that occurred throughout Solomon's reign, but it is mentioned up-front to make a particular point. The Temple was not just for Israel – it was to be of significance to people of all nations. Just as God had given the King wisdom which was proving to be an attraction to many of the national leaders around, the wonderful Temple he was to build was meant to be equally influential in teaching those nations some vital truths about the God of Israel.

As if to reinforce that point, when describing the assembly of the taskforce who would be needed for all aspects of the construction – from the hewing and quarrying through to the finest carving and gilding – it is made perfectly clear that Jews and Gentiles would be working together on the project. The forced labour requisitioned from Israel would have been non-Israelite in character, for the law forbade a Hebrew to enslave his brother,[10] though there might have been a hired, or even a volunteer company of Jews working alongside them. And, as a further development towards forming an international team, Solomon now made a formal approach to Hiram, King of Tyre, to get his valuable assistance.

Solomon had explained what he was intending to do early on in his reign, when Hiram sent friendly greetings, just after David's death;[11] but it was a while before Solomon was ready to approach Hiram with a detailed request for practical help. When he did,[12] he made it clear that he needed timber from Lebanon, and assistance with the practicalities of building. Lebanon had an international reputation for quality timber, and Solomon wanted *"cedar trees, fir (or cypress) trees, and algum trees,[14] out of Lebanon"* (2 Chronicles 2:8). He offered to make a substantial labour force available to help the Phoenicians with the felling and transportation, and a contract was agreed whereby Hiram would supply the timber and some skilled assistance and, in return, Solomon would supply agricultural produce for the essentially sea-faring and trading Phoenicians:

> *"Hiram gave Solomon cedar trees and fir trees according to all his desire. And Solomon gave Hiram twenty thousand measures of wheat for food to his household, and twenty measures of pure oil: thus gave Solomon to Hiram year by year. And the LORD gave Solomon wisdom, as he promised him: and there was peace between*

Hiram and Solomon; and they two made a league together" (1 Kings 5:10-12).

This was an annual contract – *"year by year"* – so its terms might have varied from time to time; for the 2 Chronicles record also mentions *"twenty thousand measures of barley, and twenty thousand baths of wine"*, and that account refers to *"twenty thousand baths of oil"* (2 Chronicles 2:10), not *"twenty measures"*, as above. Those differences apart, the general idea is perfectly clear: a trading partnership was established with an annual contract to regulate it, whereby Israel would exchange the God-given fruits of the land for Phoenician timber and the building skill that Hiram's people supplied.[15]

A picture of the task force, and of the underlying arrangements, is thus beginning to become clear: Jew and Gentile working together to fell and transport the timber. Solomon's levy drafted in a huge number of labourers to work a month at a time, with a two months break before they began another stint of felling duties. The well-established forests of Lebanon must have been alive with people from time to time, whenever the weather made felling and logging practical, and whenever the sea was calm enough to let the log rafts[16] be safely floated down from Lebanon to Jaffa, and thence be dragged or carted up to Jerusalem. Teamwork was of the essence, for the record says that:

"Solomon raised a levy out of all Israel; and the levy was 30,000 men. And he sent them to Lebanon, 10,000 a month by courses: a month they were in Lebanon, and two months at home: and Adoniram was over the levy. And Solomon had 70,000 that bare burdens, and 80,000 hewers in the mountains; beside the chief of Solomon's officers which were over the work, 3,300[17] which ruled over the people that wrought in the work" (1 Kings 5:13-16); and

"Solomon numbered all the strangers that were in the land of Israel, after the numbering wherewith David his father had numbered them; and they were found 153,600. And he set 70,000 of them to be bearers of bur-

dens, and 80,000 to be hewers in the mountain, and 3,600 overseers to set the people a work" (2 Chronicles 2:17,18).

Building Programme

As might be expected, the numbers of people press-ganged into service or employed to work on this huge project differed depending upon the inclusion, or otherwise, of the temporary gangs of people brought into service and the variable nature of the work to be done. First, there was timber felling and, separately, quarrying to be done. Then the project widened to include the processes of transporting the various materials, preparing them, clearing the site, laying out the foundations, beginning the building, and so on. Inevitably, the size of the team would vary quite a lot depending upon what was going on, and having regard to the skilled or unskilled nature of the work in question. The Israelites would have had little, if any, experience of major building projects, except perhaps for city walls. But, by working with the skilled Phoenician craftsmen, that would soon have changed.

The quarrying was another big task. The record says that: *"At the king's command, they quarried out great, costly stones in order to lay the foundation of the house with dressed stones. So Solomon's builders and Hiram's builders and the men of Gebal did the hewing and prepared the timber and the stone to build the house"* (1 Kings 5:18). This was high grade stone cut out in large blocks and the skilled craftsmanship needed to quarry and dress it was done with assistance from both Sidon and Byblos – the latter being a port in Lebanon, 25 miles north of Beirut – which was once famed for its temples. Once again, the Israelites had an opportunity to learn new skills from the very best contemporary craftsmen as Jew and Gentile worked side-by-side.

Of course, had God wanted to make this Temple an exclusively Jewish building, with no Gentile involvement at all, He could have arranged matters in that way. He had enabled the builders of the Tabernacle accordingly – when Moses went up the Mount and God sent down the necessary gifts, that He *"might dwell among them"*.[18] But, this time, it was meant to be different, and that must have significance, for God always has a perfect plan of action. Nothing is left to chance and no detail is without its importance. Notice that Solomon did not just ask Hiram for the craftsmen he needed for felling, shaping and quarrying. He also asked him for the loan of one craftsman who would be absolutely vital to the project, a key worker:

"Send me a man skilled to work in gold, silver, bronze, and iron, and in purple, crimson, and blue fabrics, trained also in engraving, to be with the skilled workers who are with me in Judah and Jerusalem, whom David my father provided".[19]

That request acknowledges that David had already started training some workers, perhaps by having them work an apprenticeship in somewhere like Phoenicia. But there was no-one with sufficient skill as yet, and God did not choose to imbue someone, or a group of craftsmen, with the necessary skills. Instead Hiram was given the opportunity to help the God of Israel, and His people, and he was pleased to do so, for he responded thus:

"I have sent a cunning man, endued with understanding, of Huram my father's, the son of a woman of the daughters of Dan, and his father was a man of Tyre, skilful to work in gold, and in silver, in brass, in iron, in stone, and in timber, in purple, in blue, and in fine linen, and in crimson; also to grave any manner of graving, and to find out every device which shall be put to him, with thy cunning men, and with the cunning men of my lord David thy father" (2 Chronicles 2:13,14).

Hiram or Huram?

The Authorised Version calls the master craftsman "Huram" and the King of Tyre *"Hiram"*, but other versions spell the two names differently; as a footnote in the NIV explains,[20] Huram, is merely a variant spelling of Hiram. Despite those spellings, the important point is that King Hiram was now providing a master-craftsman of the same name, a man who is variously described as *"of Huram my father's"* (2 Chronicles 2:13) and *"Huram his father"* (4:16). The designation *"father"* is a way of denoting the respect and esteem in which Huram was held in Tyre, the phrase being rendered *"Huram-Abi"* in some versions. He was not related to the King in any way, and the expression is interestingly paralleled in Genesis, where Joseph says that *"God ... hath made me a father to Pharaoh, and lord of all his house, and a ruler throughout all the land of Egypt"* (45:8).

Hiram-Abi – so named from now on to distinguish him from King Hiram – was of mixed parentage. In 1 Kings 7:14 he is said to be the son of a Tyrian father and a woman of Naphtali. However, in 2 Chronicles 2:12 his mother is said to have been of the tribe of Dan. It appears that she was by birth a Danite, but had married into the tribe of Naphtali; then, when her husband died, she married again, this time to a man of Tyre, to whom she bare Hiram-Abi.[21] It is intriguing to notice how the various details are selectively recorded, perhaps to highlight the parallel in the Chronicles account between Hiram-Abi and Oholiab (who was also of the tribe of Dan), who built the Tabernacle.[22]

It may be of passing interest to note that this master craftsman – Hiram-Abi, called by Masonic ritual "Hiram Abiff" – is supposed by Freemasons to be the first Grand Master of the Masonic movement.[23] This movement, now thought to have originated with the Knights Templar at the time of the Crusades, alleges that Hiram was murdered during the construction of Solomon's Temple and was buried on the Temple Mount in Jerusalem. All that is myth and fable; the interesting fact is that Hiram-Abi was himself part-Jew and part-Gentile. What had been noticed earlier about a combined Jewish and Gentile workforce is now apparent in that this one key workman – provided by a Gentile King – is of joint parentage.[24] The message could not be clearer. Jew and Gentile were at work together to build a House for the LORD. It was to be a House of prayer for all nations.

Time and Place

It was a momentous time in Israel's history when, at last,

Solomon laid the foundations of the Temple. Rather than describing the place in detail, the account in Kings records the precise time when the foundation was laid and, in doing so, gives an important reference point for Biblical chronology.

> *"It came to pass in the four hundred and eightieth year after the children of Israel were come out of the land of Egypt, in the fourth year of Solomon's reign over Israel,*[25] *in the month Zif, which is the second month, that he began to build the house of the LORD"* (2 Kings 6:1).

Biblical chronology is not without its difficulties, and experts hold different views. But it seems likely that Solomon began his reign in 971 B.C.,[26] in which case the Temple would have been started in 966 B.C. – and the Exodus from Egypt would have taken place in 1446 B.C. Helpful as this is in establishing a datum, in the 1 Kings record it is intended to remind us that the times were now changing for the better. It had taken 480 years since the Exodus, but now – when the time was right[27] – a new phase in God's dealings had begun.

The Chronicler concentrates, not on the time, but on the place where the building was to commence. It was, he says, *"in Mount Moriah"* in Jerusalem – the very spot where once Abraham had offered Isaac, before the angel had halted his outstretched hand, poised over the lad. This was the very location where David had later built an altar to halt the outstretched hand of the angel of judgement, poised over Jerusalem.[28]

New Relationship

Both time and place are recorded to help us appreciate the significance of what was happening. The relationship God had with His people was about to take on a more permanent appearance. The tented dwelling-place, which had represented His presence since the time of the Exodus, was about to be replaced by another structure – this time with foundations, walls and a roof – a permanent presence in the midst of the nation. Of course, the structure itself was not going to make any difference to the relationship

SOLOMON – WISE AND FOOLISH

God had with them, any more than a nice ecclesial hall makes our worship more acceptable to God. But the change had something important to tell them, and us.

God wants to dwell in the midst of His people. He wants to inhabit our lives and always be at the centre of our affections – to dwell in our lives and in our hearts, not in our ecclesial halls. Nice surroundings may make it easier for us, because we may find them more conducive to quiet contemplation, or diligent study; but facilities are really just accessories to the main pursuit.

In Israel, the Temple was to be a powerful visual aid of God's abiding presence and a permanent declaration of His continual interest in the welfare and worship of His people. It was never intended to be a shrine, or a place of magical or mystical significance.[29] At the very least, by its splendid presence in their midst, it would show the people that God was in their midst and that He was to be worshipped in the way He had appointed. And because it was the finest structure in all Israel – an exceedingly splendid construction – it would teach them, as it still teaches us, that God deserves the very best we have to give.

Awed by the beauty of this jewel in Jerusalem's crown, the worshipper who drew near to God was meant to see something of the beauty of the God he or she worshipped and respond accordingly. No wonder the sons of Korah would declare: *"We have thought of thy lovingkindness, O God, in the midst of thy temple. According to thy name, O God, so is thy praise unto the ends of the earth"* (Psalm 48:9,10). And we, who now live "at the ends of the earth", by comparison, must now prolong that note of grateful praise.

NOTES

[1] See 2 Samuel 7:12,13.

[2] There are strong parallels with Moses who was allowed to view the Promised Land even though he was not allowed to enter it.

[3] The deportation of material from the Temple is described in

110

Jeremiah 52:17-23.

4 David's preparation is described in 1 Chronicles 22:1-5,14-19; 28:11-19 and 29:1-9.

5 Bro. Whittaker, pg.292, quotes a geologist who says that the limestone of Jerusalem is very durable yet easily worked. It is a very finely grained white marble which has the property of being relatively soft when first cut, but on exposure takes on a tough outer skin.

6 Iron is not specifically mentioned elsewhere in the construction of the Temple. It was probably used for cramps, to join pieces of stone together, for hinges for the doors, and for nails or fastenings. Note the way in which various metals combine – bronze, silver and gold – to give the same sense of increasing value as progress is made towards the Most Holy Place, just as in the Tabernacle.

7 Curiously, in the details of construction little is said about the use of silver, except in 1 Chronicles 29:4: *"and seven thousand talents of refined silver, to overlay the walls of the houses withal"*. Either the stone walls were lined with silver before they were boarded with cedar, although none of that silver could then be seen, or the silver was on the outside. Given the pattern of the Tabernacle, where much of the work was hidden by other layers, the former would seem the more likely. As silver seems to be related to redemption in Scripture, it would seem that we should appreciate that nothing would have been possible without the redeeming work of God in Christ.

8 David was not saying that Solomon had to build a magnificent Temple, but that it should be one that caused God's name to be magnified. For the Hebrew word means just that: *"(gādal)* grow up, become great or important, promote, make powerful, praise, (magnify), do great things" (TWOT, No 315).

9 1 Kings 4:20-21 and 2 Chronicles 1:14-17. In both records this data precedes the record of the Temple building process.

10 Leviticus 25:39,40. And, when describing Solomon's later building projects – his store cities and suchlike – we are expressly told that he drafted those: *"that were left of the Amorites, Hittites, Perizzites, Hivites, and Jebusites, which were not of the children of Israel ... but of the children of*

SOLOMON – WISE AND FOOLISH

Israel did Solomon make no bondmen: but they were men of war, and his servants, and his princes, and his captains, and rulers of his chariots, and his horsemen" (1 Kings 9:19-22). Although they were not made slaves, the native Israelites were made to work hard (note their complaint to Jeroboam in 1 Kings 12:4).

[11] *"Hiram king of Tyre sent his servants unto Solomon; for he had heard that they had anointed him king in the room of his father: for Hiram was ever a lover of David"* (1 Kings 5:1).

[12] 1 Kings 5:2-6.

[13] About 2100 B.C. Gudea, ruler of Lagash in southern Mesopotamia had acquired cedar from the region, and in 1100 B.C. the Egyptian Wen-Amon came to Lebanon in search of cedar for building a ceremonial barge in Egypt – J. B. Pritchard (Ed.), *"The Ancient Near East"*, Vol.1, pg.16.

[14] In 1 Kings 10:11, mention is made of *"almug trees"*. There is some doubt about the precise timber being sought, including whether it is one and the same species. The *"almug"* felled in Lebanon is now thought to be the Grecian juniper *(Junipera excelsa)*, whilst the *"almug"* is thought to be an imported timber, Indian red sandalwood *(Pterocarpus santalinus)*. See E. N. Hepper, *"Encyclopaedia of Bible Plants"*, 1992, pg.158.

[15] Josephus mentions that copies of the letters between Hiram and Solomon, which set out the terms of this contract, were still in existence in the time of Menander (c.300 B.C.). *Antiquities,*viii.5.3.

[16] 1 Kings 5:9; 2 Chronicles 2:16.

[17] In all, Solomon had 550 higher ranked overseers, 250 of whom were Israelites, the rest Canaanites (see 1 Kings 9:23 and 2 Chronicles 8:10). The total number of overseers is therefore the same in both accounts – 3850; it is just that the people who are included in the counts are different in the two records.

[18] Psalm 68:18, with an evident backward glance at Exodus 31:1-6, and the enabling of Bezaleel and Aholiab.

[19] 2 Chronicles 2:7.

[20] Footnote to 2 Chronicles 2:3. It appears that "Hiram" was

the form of the original Hebrew text, and that "Huram" was an alteration in the margin of the Massoretic text.

²¹ Fausset, in his *"Bible Dictionary"*, and Blunt, *"Undesigned Co-incidences"*, suggests that she would have lived in the colony of Dan that was situated near Phoenicia, right on Israel's northern border.

²² ABD, article *"Hiram"*, makes that connection and adds that *"in the Chronicler's account Huram arrives at the very beginning of the building of the temple and is responsible for extensive craftwork corresponding to the timing and range of work carried out by Oholiab on the Tabernacle".*

²³ See any of the recent books describing Masonic ritual, such as *"Freemasonry – a Religion?"* by John Lawrence, or *"The Hiram Key"* by Knight and Lomas. Freemasonry ritual is a travesty of Scriptural teaching and no true believer should have any part in the practices and rituals involved.

²⁴ Timothy was also chosen by Paul despite, or because of, his mixed parentage, at a time when the gospel was being preached to both Jew and Gentile.

²⁵ Wordsworth, iii,20, sees this as a type of Christ who: *"did not supersede the Tabernacle of the Levitical Law till his crucifixion and ascension in the fourth year after his baptism".*

²⁶ See E. R. Thiele, *"The Mysterious Numbers of the Hebrew Kings"*, for a widely accepted chronological system from the division of the Hebrew kingdom onwards.

²⁷ Note the parallel with Luke 3:1,2, when external events are used to pinpoint the coming of the Word of God to John, the King's herald.

²⁸ 2 Chronicles 3:1 – *"Solomon began to build the house of the LORD at Jerusalem in mount Moriah, where the Lord appeared unto David his father, in the place that David had prepared in the threshingfloor of Ornan the Jebusite".*

²⁹ This was exactly what it became, however, in Israel's later days – a place in which to localise God, or so they thought; and a place of supposed magical power, the mere mention of which was thought to be enough to confer a blessing (see Jeremiah 7:4).

12

Temple Truths

David gave to Solomon his son the pattern of the porch and the pattern of all that he had by the spirit, of the courts of the house of the Lord, and of all the chambers round about, of the treasuries of the house of God, and of the treasuries of the dedicated things ... All this, said David, the Lord made me understand in writing by his hand upon me, even all the works of this pattern (1 Chronicles 28:11-12,19).

PROPHET and seer that he was, David had been shown what God required, just as Moses had been instructed, centuries before, to *"make them after their pattern, which was shewed thee in the mount" (Exodus 25:40).* Commenting on that experience, and its significance, the writer to the Hebrews observed that the Levitical priests then in office: *"serve unto the example and shadow of heavenly things, as Moses was admonished of God when he was about to make the tabernacle: for, 'See', saith he, 'that thou make all things according to the pattern shewed to thee in the mount' "* (Hebrews 8:5). His point was that Moses was shown *"heavenly things";* the Tabernacle revealed Divine truths, or heavenly realities, to the discerning eye, and that turns out to be true of the Temple as well.[1]

Heavenly Realities

What further heavenly realities did the Temple declare – with its *"porch, and ... houses ... and ... treasuries, and ... upper chambers, and ... inner parlours, and ... the place of the mercy seat"?* Notice that David had more than a mere

114

glimpse of what God wanted; he was given a detailed spec-ification – courts, chambers, treasuries, lampstands, tables and suchlike.[2] There was significance in the detailed design as well as in the general layout. The design followed the general arrangement of the Tabernacle, which had a Courtyard, with an altar and laver; a Holy Place with a lampstand, table and incense altar; a Most Holy Place in which the Ark of the Covenant rested.

Then as now, there was only one way to worship God: only one acceptable way of approach. The Temple taught that as clearly as the Tabernacle had done, and the New Testament reiterates that fundamental truth.[3] That *"Way"* demands both sacrifice and washing – altar and laver – before the worshipper can draw near to God. The ultimate sacrifice was to be that of the Lord Jesus Christ, the God-given preliminary to the believer's own sacrificial service. And the washing would eventually be that of Christian baptism, accompanied by the daily cleansing that comes from the believer's contemplation of God's Word.[4] But the Temple, although modelled upon its predecessor, taught some other lessons as well.

Permanent dwelling place

The Temple was to be a permanent structure, not a move-able one, and this was a crucial difference. David had wanted to build the Temple to ensure that God would set-tle down among His people, so that He would never leave them. The king said to Nathan the prophet, *"See now, I dwell in an house of cedar, but the ark of God dwelleth within curtains"*, and God had responded that –

- He never asked Israel to build him a house of cedar;

- He had always been with them, even so, to rescue them from their enemies; but, God acknowledged, there was a long-standing promise[5] whereby He would *"appoint a place for my people Israel, and will plant them, that they may dwell in a place of their own, and move no more"* (2 Samuel 7:10), and now He amplified that promise to David. It was to be Solomon who would

115

"build an house for my name", for he was the promised man of peace, who was given rest from his enemies.

Whereas the Tabernacle was planted on bare earth, so that the bare-footed priests would never forget the desert encampment, the Temple was floored with cedar boards overlaid with gold (1 Kings 6:15,30). The curtained walls of the Tabernacle, visible through the timber frames, were replaced by stone walls overlaid with cedar boards, again overlaid with gold and richly decorated. So everything about the structure indicated that God was indicating to His people that symbolically He had come to dwell in their midst, and that He was staying.

Piece by Piece

The masonry for this permanent structure was being hewn off-site, so accurately and precisely that when it was transported to Mount Moriah it could be pieced together without further cutting or sawing (1 Kings 6:7). Some of the original Phoenician markings have been found: directions that were given at the quarry to ensure that a particular stone went to its intended destination.[6] The stonework was of the best quality available, as we would expect,[7] but none of that was evident from within, for it was all concealed by the lining of ornamented cedar boards.

Consider what an impression the building of the Temple would have given to an observer. No hammer, axe or iron tool was heard as the stones were being slotted into their intended places. Order, design, preparation and planning would have been the overall effect, and it should still be like that as God's purpose proceeds. Step-by-step God is preparing us for the work that lies ahead; we are like stones being shaped for that living Temple experience and our worship should be of that character. As one writer expressed it: *"let not the axes of schism and the hammer of violent contention be heard in the Sanctuary of God"*.[8]

Bigger and better

The next obvious difference about the Temple was that it was much bigger than the Tabernacle, which measured 30 cubits long x 10 broad x 10 high.[9] The Temple measured 60

cubits long x 20 broad x 30 cubits[10] high, plus a porch of 10
cubits long and 20 cubits broad, which was not a feature of
the original Tabernacle. During Bible times two different
cubits were in use,[11] so we are told (in 2 Chronicles 3:3)
that the unit of measurement was *"in cubits of the old
standard"* (RSV). Overall the Temple would thus have
measured 26.67m x 8.89m x 13.33m high;[12] it was not all
that big a building, even though it was twice the size of
the Tabernacle. Quantity has never mattered to Almighty
God, who invariably works through a remnant; what matters to Him is quality, and that is something we must
never forget in our preaching and our worship.

The measurements given are internal, not external, as
the records give no express details about the thickness of
the walls, although we are told that they became thinner
as they ascended, to support the chambers that abutted
the main structure. No doubt the Temple was glorious to
look at, with its white marble shining in the mid-day sun.
Josephus has a famous description of Herod's Temple as
follows:

*"Now the outward face of the temple in its front wanted
nothing that was likely to surprise either men's minds or
their eyes, for it was covered all over with the plates of gold
of great weight, and, at the first rising of the sun, reflected
back a very fiery splendor, and made those who forced
themselves to look upon it to turn their eyes away, just as
they would have done at the sun's own rays. But this temple appeared to strangers, when they were at a distance,
like a mountain covered with snow; for, as to those parts of
it that were not gilt, they were exceeding white."* [13]

By contrast, the description in the Books of Kings and
Chronicles concentrates on what was within, not on what
was outside. In just the same way that the beauties of the
Tabernacle were covered by animal skins, so the wonders
of the truth are progressively revealed to us as we draw
nearer to God, though Christ, in our understanding and in
our affection for things divine. As the apostle Paul said,
outward things perish in time; what matters is the life
within.

We are not even really sure about the appearance of the
Temple despite all the information we are given. Bro. and

Sis. Ritmeyer have written a lot about the Temple in its various phases.[14] Bro. Leen Ritmeyer's drawing of what Solomon's Temple might have looked like shows a ramp up to the Most Holy Place (which he believes to have been situated exactly where the Dome of the Rock is now erected),

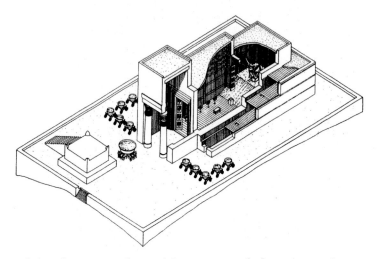

and in that way the cubic nature of that space is preserved.

Other illustrators suggest that there was a chamber or chambers above the Holy Place, as there was in Herod's Temple,[15] and these *"upper chambers"* are referred to in 1 Chronicles 28:11 and 2 Chronicles 3:9. Such a space is

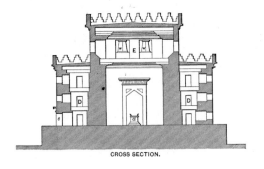

CROSS SECTION.

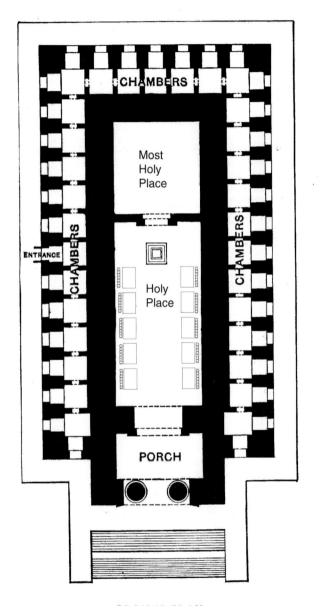

GROUND PLAN.

marked as "E" in this illustration, and reference will be made to that in a later chapter.[16]

The Way In

There is some detail given about the front of the Temple, by which the priests would have access into the Holy

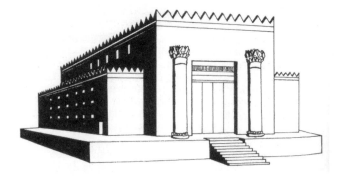

Place. An addition to the Tabernacle, at least when it was in the wilderness,[17] is the Porch or Portico which was fronted by two massive pillars of bronze.

The height of that porch is uncertain, as are some other architectural details, which is why conjectural illustrations vary quite considerably. It is sometimes assumed that as the 1 Kings 6:3 record says nothing about the height of the Porch at the front of the Temple, it was of the same height as the structure it abutted – 30 cubits, or even lower. But the parallel record says something quite different:

> *"These are the things wherein Solomon was instructed for the building of the house of God. The length by cubits after the first measure was threescore cubits, and the breadth twenty cubits. And the porch that was in the front of the house, the length of it was according to the breadth of the house, twenty cubits, and the height was an hundred and twenty"* (2 Chronicles 3:3,4).

120 cubits is about 180 feet tall (54.8 meters) – a skyscraper for those times, but not without some precedent in the ancient world. It is generally accepted, however, that

the text has got corrupted at this point,[18] and it is even possible that a marginal note has crept in to confuse mat-

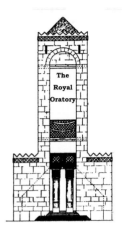

The Royal Oratory

This is Shaw Caldecott's suggestion, in *"Solomon's Temple: Its History and its Structure"*, for a tower at the front entrance. He thinks this could have been the King's vantage point (The Royal Oratory), which would have given him a view of the Outer Courtyard, but not of the Holy Place.

ters. That is why other modern versions – like the NIV – have chosen to render the text differently.[19] But this possible confusion explains why you sometimes see illustrations of the Temple with a tower at the eastern end.

The existence of a porch, of whatever design, emphasizes the fact that there is only one way into a right relationship with God. We have to approach God in the way that he specifies. Everything about the Temple points to this, as we have seen, and everything points forward towards the One who later called himself: *"the door of the sheep"* and *"the way, the truth, and the life: no man cometh unto the Father, but by me"* (John 10:7; 14:6). So, as you paused at the Porch and saw the great doors leading into the Temple, you were bound to recall that you had no right of approach into the presence of God, except by invitation and on God's terms.

Living with God

If the porch was a departure from the original model, there was one other difference which had a major impact on the appearance of the structure. Abutting the main structure – resting on it, not jutting into it – were three stories of side chambers, comprising rooms for priests and

121

temple storage space, measuring 5 cubits wide on the ground floor and increasing in size by one cubit per storey, as the Temple wall reduced in thickness. The details are in 1 Kings 6:5-10. Those chambers were entered by means of a door on the right side of the House, and by spiral staircases, and there would appear to have been a way onto the roof. As mentioned earlier, there may have been other rooms, too, that existed over the Holy and Most Holy Places.

These were rooms where the priests would live, perhaps when their allotted time had come and they were invited to worship at the Sanctuary. Leaving their Levitical city, the Temple would offer some of them temporary accommodation; they would come to live with God for a term. Nothing could be more forceful in reminding us that God wants us to live all our days with Him in mind. He wants to live and dwell in us, and we in Him. So the Temple is not just a place of worship; it is also an abiding place. And in the age to come, the saints will worship and dwell with God. As Jesus said, and he must have had the Temple structure in mind:

> "In my Father's house (the Temple) are many mansions (abiding places): if it were not so, I would have told you. I go to prepare a place for you. And if I go and prepare a place for you, I will come again, and receive you unto myself; that where I am, there ye may be also. And whither I go ye know, and the way ye know … I am the way, the truth, and the life: no man cometh unto the Father, but by me" (John 14:2-6).

By the grace of God we can now live, as baptised believers, *"in Christ"* and he can live in us, so that we can be: *"strengthened with might by his Spirit in the inner man; that Christ may dwell in your hearts by faith"* (Ephesians 3:16,17).

Solomon's Reminder

The detailed specification of God's House is being given in the Kings record and more information is about to come about the interior construction and furnishing, when the account includes a message from God to the King:

"He built chambers against all the house, five cubits high: and they rested on the house with timber of cedar. And the word of the LORD came to Solomon, saying, Concerning this house which thou art in building, if thou wilt walk in my statutes, and execute my judgments, and keep all my commandments to walk in them; then will I perform my word with thee, which I spake unto David thy father: and I will dwell among the children of Israel, and will not forsake my people Israel. So Solomon built the house, and finished it" (6:10-14).

It is so easy for us to get caught up in what we are doing and to be utterly absorbed in the sheer mechanics of it. The work itself might be of vital importance – ecclesial arrangements, maintaining the ecclesial hall, caring for the sick or old, preaching, studying the Word of God – but we must never lose sight of what it is all about. God does not want mere outward observance or lip service. He is interested in the life within, in the reasons why we serve Him, wanting it to be for love's sake, wishing for our obedience from the heart.

So, God sent a message to Solomon, in the middle of this most demanding and fascinating building project, to say that He really cared – and cares – most of all about faithful obedience. He would come and live with His people if they really loved and obeyed Him, not because they were building Him a nice house! That ancient message has a searching modern challenge.

NOTES

[1] There are several books which examine the spiritual lessons taught by the Tabernacle, notably the *"Tabernacle Study Guide"*, 1989, by Bro. Michael Ashton; *"The Tabernacle in the Wilderness"*, by Bro. Keith Cook; *"The Tabernacle of Israel"*, 1987, by James Strong and *"The Tabernacle"*, by H. W. Soltau. There are far fewer books of this sort about the Temple.

[2]See the detailed specification of items listed in the last chap-

ter (pgs.102-103).

[3] See, for example, Ephesians 4:4,5: *"One hope of your calling; one Lord, one faith, one baptism"*.

[4] *"After that the kindness and love of God our Saviour toward man appeared, not by works of righteousness which we have done, but according to his mercy he saved us, by the washing* [laver, Revised Version] *of regeneration, and renewing of the Holy (Spirit); which he shed on us abundantly through Jesus Christ our Saviour" (Titus 3:4-6).*

[5] The promise of a *"place"* that God would choose is hinted at in Genesis 22:3,4,9 and clearly promised in Exodus 15:17; 23:20; 32:34; Leviticus 4:33; 6:25, etc.

[6] See SBD, pg.677.

[7] Further detail about the stonework is given in 1 Kings 7:9,10, in connection with the details of the house later built for Pharaoh's daughter and the great court.

[8] Quoted by Wordsworth, Vol iii, pg.21.

[9] These dimensions resulted in a volume of 2000 cubic cubits for the Holy Place and 1000 cubic cubits for the Most Holy Place – usually taken to broadly equate to the time which is to pass before Jesus returns to the earth, and then the period of the Kingdom (see Exodus 26:15-25).

[10] *"The house which king Solomon built for the LORD, the length thereof was threescore cubits, and the breadth thereof twenty cubits, and the height thereof thirty cubits. And the porch before the temple of the house, twenty cubits was the length thereof, according to the breadth of the house; and ten cubits was the breadth thereof before the house"* (1 Kings 6:2,3). It may be, however, that the internal dimensions were only 20 cubits, and that there was a second storey, accessible from the surrounding chambers. That was certainly the case for the Most Holy Place which, like the Tabernacle, was a perfect cube – this time 20 x 20 x 20 cubits (1 Kings 6:20). If that was so, the Temple would be exactly twice the size of the Tabernacle.

[11] The cubit is about 18 inches (46 cm) in length. See *"The New Bible Dictionary", IVP,* (Weights and Measures) for a helpful description of the various cubit measures thought to

exist – standard Hebrew (17.5 inches); common Egyptian (17.6); royal (20.4), etc.

[12] If you are more comfortable with imperial measurements, the internal dimensions would have approximated to the porch (30 x 15 feet); the holy place (30 x 90 ft.); the most holy place (30 x 30 ft.) – widths first. The height of the rooms would have been 45 ft., the most holy place being 30 ft. (to form a perfect cube).

[13] Josephus, F., & Whiston, W. (1996). *"The works of Josephus : Complete and unabridged"* (*Wars* 5.222-223).

[14] See the Bibliography for details of two of their recent works.

[15] This is detailed in The Mishnah, as follows: *"And in the upper room were openings into the house of the holy of holies, through which they would lower down craftsmen in boxes [closed on three sides] so that they should not feast their eyes on the house of the Holy of Holies" (Middot 4.5).* See also Bro. Ritmeyer *"The Quest"*, pgs.398,399.

[16] See Chapter 19.

[17] It is conjectured that a porch was added when the Tabernacle entered the land and it became more static than hitherto (see, for example, Shaw Caldecott, *"The Tabernacle"*, 1906).

[18] For a well-balanced commentary on this verse, see Keil & Delitzsch, *"Chronicles"*, pg.316, or Selman, pg.307.

[19] *"The portico at the front of the temple was twenty cubits long across the width of the building and twenty cubits high"* (NIV). The LXX offers a variant reading, *"And the portico in front of the house, its length in front of the breadth of the house was twenty cubits, and its height [twenty cubits]."*

13
Temple Worship

WHAT would it be like to enter into the Temple that Solomon was building when, as a priest, you had access into the Holy Place? What thoughts would be provoked and what associations with ancient times, as you went about your priestly duties, trimming the lamps, replacing the shewbread, or burning incense on the altar?

Inside Out

The narrative in the Book of Kings begins by describing the outward appearance of the House (1 Kings 6:2-10) but it then details the interior at much greater length (6:15-36). Chronicles takes the same approach. It gives some overall dimensions (2 Chronicles 3:3,4a) before adding: *"and he overlaid it within with pure gold"* (verse 4b).

What the Temple was like within really mattered and the details given serve two lasting purposes.

- They were an insight for worshippers who would become familiar with the exterior of the complex, but who were never allowed inside, and

- They help us, years after the Temple has been entirely destroyed, to appreciate what it was like and what spiritual lessons it was meant to teach.

So what was it like inside? No stonework was visible at all. The walls, floors and ceiling would have been panelled in cedar, overlaid with gold leaf. There may have been windows at a higher level – like clerestory windows that you sometimes see nowadays; there is some doubt about that, but it's possible. If so, the Holy Place would have been even lighter than the light from the ten lampstands would make it, and there would have been some ventilation:

> *"He built the walls of the house within with boards of cedar, both the floor of the house, and the walls of the ceiling: and he covered them on the inside with wood, and covered the floor of the house with planks of fir. And he built twenty cubits on the sides of the house, both the floor and the walls with boards of cedar: he even built them for it within, even for the oracle, even for the most holy place ... And the cedar of the house within was carved with knops*[1] *and open flowers: all was cedar; there was no stone seen"* (1 Kings 6:15-18).

Priestly Progress

Any priest walking into this new environment, especially one who had recently been ministering in the Tabernacle at Gibeon, would have noticed a lot of differences. For a start it was new where the Tabernacle was now old (nearly 500 years old).[2] Presumably the Tabernacle fittings had been regularly maintained, or replaced as necessary, over the years but now it had become old and, like a worn out garment, was *"ready to vanish away"* (Hebrews 8:13). That quotation refers to the removal of the old covenant and its replacement by the new and better covenant, sealed in the blood of Christ. But a similar contrast must have been evident in Solomon's day – the old was being replaced by the new.

● Altar and Lavers

Key things remained the same. The inner courtyard,[3] where the priests would offer the sacrifices, was still dominated by a brazen Altar[4] and a Laver, even though the one that Solomon had built was much larger and more imposing:

> *"He made a molten sea, ten cubits from the one brim to the other:*[5] *it was round all about, and his height was five cubits: and a line of thirty cubits did compass it round about ... It stood upon twelve oxen, three looking*

127

*toward the north, and three looking toward the west,
and three looking toward the south, and three looking
toward the east: and the sea was set above upon them,
and all their hinder parts were inward ... it was an
hand breadth thick, and the brim thereof was wrought
like the brim of a cup, with flowers of lilies: it contained
two thousand baths"* (1 Kings 7:23-26).

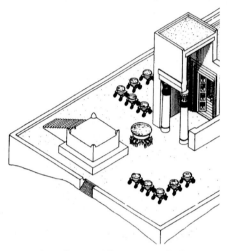

The spiritual significance of these items could easily
form a separate study, and this one is focused upon
Solomon and his part in God's purpose. But even a quick
glance at what this implies suggests that sacrifice and
washing is imperative if we would be made clean before
God. And the large sea pointed forward to a time when
people from the four corners of the earth would be sanctified, all because of the service rendered on their behalf.
For the Ox typifies service, and the twelve oxen signified
that the work of serving God had to begin with Israel and
that it would be continued by the disciples, who must discharge the 'great commission' to the nations of the world.[6]
But there was something else as well, that could have
stopped a new priest in his tracks:

*"He made also ten lavers, and put five on the right
hand, and five on the left, to wash in them: such things
as they offered for the burnt offering they washed in*

them; but the sea was for the priests to wash in" (2 Chronicles 4:6).

There were another ten, portable, lavers around the courtyard. These, much smaller, ones were erected on heavily decorated bases which could be wheeled around. They were closely associated with the brazen altar, being used for the washing of the sacrifices and the decorative motifs and, because they featured cherubim, lions, oxen and palm trees, they were inextricably linked with the Temple itself. The message was inescapable: these outward things of sacrifice and washing were fundamental for anyone who sought access into the presence of God. That truth remains despite the passage of time.

● **Porch and Pillars**

Approaching the Temple his eye would next be drawn to the magnificent porch adorned with the two great bronze pillars, named Jachin and Boaz.[7] They were 18 cubits high (8.1 metres or 26.5 feet tall) and 1.9m in diameter (6.2 feet across), so they were big. We know they were hollow, and that they were richly ornamented, for the capitals were embellished with chain work, rows of pomegranates and lily work.[8] All these features had spiritual significance; they encouraged a worshipper to look upwards – towards heaven, the source of fruitfulness and purity, and to remember 'the ties that bind'. It was unusual to have pillars which were expressly named, but these two were, and their names meant:[9]

- *Jachin* – He shall establish;
- *Boaz* – Strength.

Perhaps the names were engraved upon the pillars, but certainly they were meant to signify something to the enquiring mind. It could be that the worshipper was to enter the Holy Place with the thought in mind that *"God will Establish Israel and in Him alone is our Strength"*. One attractive suggestion, based on allusions in the Psalms, is that these were keywords to two dynastic oracles, such as *"Yahweh will establish thy throne forever and in the strength of Yahweh shall the king rejoice".*[10] But there was something else as well.

The nation of Israel had been led in the Wilderness by a pillar of cloud by day and a pillar of fire by night (Exodus 13:21); they had been the indication that God was with them to strengthen and establish them as a nation, day and night. That same Divine protection had brought them to the Promised Land and to the place that God had chosen, where His presence would again dwell among them. In that way, the Temple becomes a collection of spiritual memorabilia, designed to reinforce the lessons of their past history and to help the priests relive some of those events, so that they would be strongly impressed upon their minds. As the great cedar doors[11] swung open to allow access to the Holy Place, there was another such experience awaiting the priestly worshipper.

● Holy Place

A great deal is told us about the interior of this working area for the priests and for them alone. No layperson was allowed inside. On the occasion that Uzziah, the king of Israel, thought to enter to burn incense on the altar, the outcome was disastrous for him (2 Chronicles 26:16-21). To enter you had to be ordained as a priest, consecrated to that office, and attired in linen garments. Only then could you draw near to God. You did not come in your own merits, but because of a status that had been conferred by God. But what exactly did you see as you entered into this area of the Temple?

The inside of the Temple is described in considerable detail, much more so than the outside. Here's just a sample:

> *"He built the walls of the house within with boards of cedar, both the floor of the house, and the walls of the ceiling: and he covered them on the inside with wood, and covered the floor of the house with planks of fir ... And the cedar of the house within was carved with*

130

*Palm trees, flowers, buds, cherubim, a place of fellow-
ship with God, lampstands like almond trees, an abundance of food to eat – what does this place remind you of?*

knops and open flowers: all was cedar; there was no stone seen ...And the whole house he overlaid with gold, until he had finished all the house: also the whole altar that was by the oracle he overlaid with gold" (1 Kings 6:15-22).[12]

Inside it would have been light enough to see those intricate carvings on the walls, for there were windows high up, and the light from the lampstands would have reflected against the gold-plated walls and ceilings.[13] It was like a garden, for the ornamentation consisted of knops (ornamental buds), flowers in bloom, and precious stones. There were also palm trees there (7:29) and depictions of the cherubim; not only on the walls, but also on the Vail[14] that hung before the olive-wood doors that led into the Most Holy Place (2 Chronicles 3:14), and on the doors themselves (1 Kings 6:32,35).

Gazing around the interior, there was something else that reinforced the idea of a garden scene. There were ten golden lampstands, burning olive oil and illuminating the scene.[15] Modelled on almond trees, like the one Bezaleel had sculpted for the Tabernacle, with knops and flowers and branches,[16] they would have reminded a perceptive onlooker of the bush that Moses had seen: the one which burned but was not consumed. But the whole scene was reminiscent of something else.

Barefoot, the priest had walked back into a scene reminiscent of the Garden of Eden. He was among the trees of the garden and its verdant fruitfulness. He walked in the light and everywhere around him there were glimpses of angelic beings, among the trees of the garden (Genesis 3:8). These carved cherubim were not there to exclude worshippers; they were keeping the way open into the Divine presence (3:24).

It was impossible not to remember how it had all gone wrong and how God had arranged a way back for fallen mankind. And now the priest was standing in a similar environment – a little bit of heaven on earth, if you like to think of it like that – with something else to ponder. *"Take and eat",* had been the opportunity in Eden; for God had provided an abundance of food on every tree of the garden, save for the one that was forbidden them. It was the same again, here in the Holy Place. Where there had been twelve loaves provided each week in the Tabernacle, on the Table of Shewbread, now there were ten such tables,[17] each with twelve loaves upon them – 120 loaves in all. Once again the Almighty was providing in abundance for His people, and all of it was on offer, if they would but come and eat of that which He provided.[18]

There was light from God to illuminate the priest's way and bread that God had provided in abundance to sustain him. How could he express his appreciation for all that God had given him? The Altar of Incense gave that opportunity, situated as it was next to the Vail which covered the Door that led into the Most Holy Place. Incense symbolises prayer, and thus when the priest had the allotted task of offering such incense, he would represent the entire nation in giving thanks and praise to the Almighty.

Spiritual Education

From this we can see that the Temple was a place that had been divinely designed to educate and stimulate the priesthood. It would give them a sense of the presence of God as never before and they would see themselves as part of that process of recovery that was bringing mankind back to true and lasting fellowship with God.

This process of national education will be reinstated when the future Temple is constructed in Jerusalem and representatives of the nation come to learn once again about Divine things. They will be looking back in time so they can understand the way in which the sacrifice of the Lord Jesus Christ was a vital part in God's purpose, and why they need to identify with him.

The priests in Solomon's temple were looking forward; for them the things that had been made pointed to something new and better that was coming – something that would last forever. They might, for the moment, be walking on golden floors, a type of that eternal life that is to come, but that gold would wear off in time, or be removed. What God was offering – symbolised by the perfect cube of the Most Holy Place – was something they could not then enter. It would require a greater High Priest than Zadok to make such access possible for them, and for us too.[19]

All these things are written for our learning, of course, even though we cannot tread the boards and enter that Holy Place, which has long since perished. These descriptions enable us to imagine what it must have been like so that we share something of their experience, and marvel as they must have done at such a profound and searching reconstruction of things gone by. But we have a huge advantage too, in that we can see where all this was leading. There would come a time when the Son of God would fulfil all these types and shadows.

● He would be the One who offered the perfect sacrifice to take away sin and by his shed blood it would be possible for us to be washed and made clean;

● He would open the Door into a new life for us – now God will establish (Jachin) salvation for us and will strengthen (Boaz) us in our walk before Him;

● He would bring us into that state of enlightenment and fellowship that was long-ago lost in Eden, for Christ can be for us *the light of the world"* and we can 'eat and live' of that which he provides: the bread of life.

● Through him, we too can offer up the incense of prayer to the Father and, marvel of marvels, he can give us access into the Divine presence and confer upon us eternal life. The Vail has been torn apart and a new and living way has been opened up.

So the Temple still has something to say to us about our spiritual worship. It encourages us to live like priests and to draw near to God, through Christ.

"Having therefore, brethren, boldness to enter into the holiest by the blood of Jesus, by a new and living way, which he hath consecrated for us, through the veil, that is to say, his flesh; and having an high priest over the house of God; let us draw near with a true heart in full

assurance of faith, having our hearts sprinkled from an evil conscience, and our bodies washed with pure water" (Hebrews 10:19-22).

NOTES

[1] *"ornamental buds"* (NKJV); *"gourds"* (NIV, RSV, NJB).

[2] *"It came to pass in the four hundred and eightieth year after the children of Israel were come out of the land of Egypt, in the fourth year of Solomon's reign over Israel, in the month Zif, which is the second month, that he began to build the house of the LORD" (1 Kings 6:1).* It may be that this detail is included specifically to make the comparison between the old and the new.

[3] There was an outer courtyard too, in which those people would assemble who had come to worship (1 Kings 6:36; 7:12).

[4] The only reference to the altar, and that just one verse, is 2 Chronicles 4:1: *"Moreover he made an altar of brass, twenty cubits the length thereof, and twenty cubits the breadth thereof, and ten cubits the height thereof".* Presumably so little is said because what needs to be said has been said already in connection with the Tabernacle (Exodus 27:1-8; 38:1-7).

[5] The brazen sea was 5 metres in diameter and 2.5 metres high, so it was a big vessel. Presumably it had spigots, or taps, set around the rim, so that water could be drawn off. Perhaps the water came out of the mouths of the twelve oxen, similar to the way that gargoyles sometimes act as drainage outlets on some older public buildings, although that seems unlikely in view of the fact that king Ahaz later removed the basin from the base (2 Kings 16:17).

[6] Mark 16:15,16.

[7] See 1 Kings 7:15-17,20-21; 2 Chronicles 3:15-17; Jeremiah 52:20,21. In the 2 Chronicles account, the length of the pillars is combined. When account is taken of the added height of the capitals (half a cubit each) the different length in the two accounts is reconciled.

[8] The chain work might have been wound around to make the pillars look as though they were trees; the pomegranates would symbolise the fruitfulness of the promised seed (as pomegranates are full of seeds); the lily would be a symbol of holiness and purity. There is a suggestion (largely based on the LXX translation) that the lilies were not visible from outside, but only from within the porch. If so the pomegranates might have symbolised outward fruitfulness in the LORD's service; the lilies would have spoken of the inner purity we all must strive to cultivate. Note that the motif of the lily matches the Brazen Sea, *"the brim thereof was wrought like the brim of a cup, with flowers of lilies"* (1 Kings 7:26). Again, the link is made between the courtyard and the House itself.

[9] There is some dispute about the meaning of these names, as you might expect. Farrar, pg.85, says they cannot mean *"He will establish"* and *"In strength"*. But the *"Enhanced Briggs Driver Brown"* lexicon confirms the usual meaning of Jachin and says that, whilst the meaning of Boaz is obscure, it can mean *"strength"*.

[10] This was suggested by R. B. Y. Scott in the *"Journal of Biblical Literature"* (1939) pg.143ff.

[11] The doors are described, somewhat ambiguously, in 1 Kings 6:34. Farrar, pg.87, surmises that they may have been two-leaved doors made into four squares (like a stable-door), so that only a quarter of the entirety needed to be opened to allow access. Alternatively, they could have been folding doors (concertina-like).

[12] Further descriptions of the interior are given at 1 Kings 6:23-36; 7:48-51 and 2 Chronicles 3:5-13.

[13] Kitchen, pg.125, gives examples of Egyptian major buildings which also used "sheet gold and electrum (gold/silver alloy) on temple walls, columns, obelisks, doorways, etc., and silver on floors." Slots have been discovered for fitting metal sheathing to columns and suchlike and parallels exist in Assyria and Babylon as well.

[14] Remarkably, 2 Chronicles 3:14 is the only reference to the Vail that hung in the Temple, which, at a much later date and in a different Temple, featured so dramatically at the time of the Lord's death.

[15] Ten lampstands this time, not one (1 Kings 7:48,49; 2 Chronicles 4:7,19). It seems that the original one (at Gibeon until the Tabernacle was subsumed into the Temple) was not used in Solomon's Temple. It perhaps ended up in one of the side-chambers as a reminder of years gone by.

[16] Exodus 25:31-36.

[17] Ten Tables of Shewbread (1 Kings 7:48; 1 Chronicles 28:16; 2 Chronicles 4:8,19).

[18] Isaiah 55:1,2.

[19] Details of the Most Holy Place are considered when reviewing the procession of the Ark from the Tent in which it had been located to the Temple itself.

14

The Ark enters the Temple

AFTER seven years of hard and meticulous work the Temple was complete and would soon be ready to become the focal point of all Israel's worship. In recent years there had been at least two such places, for the Tabernacle was still at Gibeon, with its own appointed priesthood there, and David had pitched a Tent for the Ark in Jerusalem – the so-called *"Tabernacle of David"* – where separate services were conducted. There was a different order of priests officiating there, as David had ordained:

> *"He left there before the ark of the covenant of the LORD* [in Jerusalem] *Asaph and his brethren, to minister before the ark continually, as every day's work required: and Obededom with their brethren ... and Zadok the priest, and his brethren the priests, before the tabernacle of the LORD in the high place that was at Gibeon, to offer burnt offerings unto the LORD upon the altar of the burnt offering continually morning and evening, and to do according to all that is written in the law of the LORD, which he commanded Israel" (1 Chronicles 16:37-40).*

Tabernacle of David

It is uncertain exactly where in Jerusalem David pitched the tent – or *"tabernacle"* – which sheltered the Ark of the Covenant. If it was near his palace it would have been within the original City of David[1] and, at least for security purposes, that seems the most likely site. If that was so, there was a third place where worship was offered, for when the angel indicated the site upon which the Temple was to be built – then the threshing floor of Araunah the Jebusite – David built an altar there, and sacrifices were offered in that place:

> *"When David saw that the LORD had answered him in the threshingfloor of Ornan the Jebusite, then he sacrificed there. For the tabernacle of the LORD, which Moses made in the wilderness, and the altar of the burnt offering, were at that season in the high place at Gibeon. But David could not go before it to enquire of God: for he was afraid because of the sword of the angel of the LORD. Then David said, This is the house of the LORD God, and this is the altar of the burnt offering for Israel"* (1 Chronicles 21:28–22:1).

It seems unlikely that David would have pitched the Tent containing the Ark of the Covenant near that altar, for at least three reasons.

- When the Ark was moved into Jerusalem its eventual site had not been designated – that came after the plague – and there is no record of the Ark having been moved within Jerusalem until Solomon moved it.

- Even when the site was known, the threshing floor was outside the city walls and was therefore vulnerable to attack and loss.[2]

- Once David knew that the Temple was to be built on that site, he would hardly have been inclined to pitch the tent in the middle of what was to become a major building site.

Instead, it appears that the worship offered to God in the Tabernacle of David, nearby the Ark, comprised the singing of hymns, the offering of prayers, and perhaps the offering of incense. Sacrifices could have been offered a little distance away, at Araunah's former threshing floor, but it would be difficult to envisage this happening during Solomon's time. If so, the distinction points forward in an interesting way to a time when sacrifice and offering would no longer be required, because of a sacrifice that was offered, once for all, at a site outside the city walls.

It would appear to be equally significant that there is a first century reference to David's Tabernacle in a context which concerns a total change of the way in which God was to be worshipped. Gentiles had been baptised into the saving name of the Lord Jesus and this caused consternation among the Jewish community of believers. So a conference was called at Jerusalem to consider the matter and various arguments were advanced. Matters came to a Spirit-guided conclusion when James, the brother of Jesus who was now a very well-respected elder in the Jerusalem ecclesia, rose to his feet.

Quoting from the prophet Amos, James referred to the promised time when, God said, *"After this I will return, and will build again the tabernacle of David, which is fallen down; and I will build again the ruins thereof, and I will set it up: That the residue of men might seek after the Lord, and all the Gentiles, upon whom my name is called, saith the Lord, who doeth all these things"* (Acts 15:16,17).

James was pointing out that, in the days of David, a movement away from an all-Jewish Tabernacle had taken place and, as a result, a different way of worship had been instituted. If necessary, he could have gone on to explain that the Temple Solomon built clearly demonstrated the intended bringing together of Jew and Gentile. For, as we have seen, it was a joint project and was intended to be a house of prayer for all nations. But he did not need that further argument; his first – about the change brought about by the Tabernacle of David – was considered entirely convincing!

Among the Treasures ...

Now, years after David had pitched his tent for the Ark, Solomon was to bring everything together again in one united place of worship. The construction work having been completed, the various items of sacred furniture were positioned in their allocated places, and the various items that David had prepared were integrated with those that had been fashioned more recently:

140

"Solomon made all the vessels that pertained unto the house of the LORD: the altar of gold, and the table of gold, whereupon the shewbread was,[3] and the candlesticks of pure gold, five on the right side, and five on the left, before the oracle, with the flowers, and the lamps, and the tongs of gold, and the bowls, and the snuffers, and the basons, and the spoons, and the censers of pure gold; and the hinges of gold, both for the doors of the inner house, the most holy place, and for the doors of the house, to wit, of the temple. So was ended all the work that king Solomon made for the house of the LORD. And Solomon brought in the things which David his father had dedicated; even the silver, and the gold, and the vessels, did he put among the treasures of the house of the LORD" (1 Kings 7:48-51).

There were storage chambers abutting the Temple structure, as well as some living accommodation (1 Kings 6:5,6), and into these chambers went the Temple treasure. The Ark was to be moved from its Tent into the Temple, which had now been built on the threshing floor of Araunah, and both David's Tent and the Tabernacle at Gibeon were to be dismantled. Some of the furniture from the original Tabernacle – the lampstand or the table of shewbread – could have been integrated with that commissioned by Solomon; it may have been melted down or, more likely, have been stored in the Temple chambers, at least for the time being.[4] As we have seen, the Tabernacle itself was worn out; it had decayed and waxed old, and was *"ready to vanish away"*, just as the Law given to Moses was destined to wear itself out in due course, when something better had come. We are told expressly that:

"they brought up the ark of the LORD, and the tabernacle of the congregation, and all the holy vessels that were in the tabernacle, even those did the priests and the Levites bring up" (1 Kings 8:4).

The record does not say what happened to the Tabernacle, or its furnishings, but it seems that they were absorbed, one way or another, into the Temple. One writer, with an eye on the typology of all this, says:

141

SOLOMON – WISE AND FOOLISH

"The Ark was not taken by Solomon to the Tabernacle at Gibeon, but he brought up the 'Tabernacle of meeting' to Jerusalem; and the Tabernacle was absorbed into the Temple. In like manner the Gospel (which was the essence of the Levitical Law itself), was not infused into the Law (as the Judaisers desired that it should be), nor was the Gospel set up as co-ordinate with the Law of Moses, but the Levitical Law was absorbed by Jesus Christ, the Divine Solomon, and by his Apostles, into the Temple of the Christian Church." [5]

The Return of the Ark

When the time came for the Ark to be moved, in the seventh month of the 11th year of his reign, at the Feast of Tabernacles,[6] Solomon assembled all the leaders of the nation, elders, tribal heads and, no doubt, his court officials. They were to accompany the Ark of the Covenant as it was moved from the Tabernacle of David into the Most Holy Place in the Temple. It was only a short journey, probably only a few hundred yards from within the City of David – what had been Jebusite Jerusalem – to the newly extended part of the city, due north, although they may have taken a more circuitous route in order to give the people of the city more participation:

"Solomon assembled the elders of Israel, and all the heads of the tribes, the chief of the fathers of the children of Israel, unto Jerusalem, to bring up the ark of the covenant of the LORD out of the city of David, which is Zion. Wherefore all the men of Israel assembled themselves unto the king in the feast which was in the seventh month. And all the elders of Israel came; and the Levites took up the ark. And they brought up the ark, and the tabernacle of the congregation, and all the holy vessels that were in the tabernacle, these did the priests and the Levites bring up" (2 Chronicles 5:2-5).

It may only have been a short journey, but it was a very important symbolic move. The Ark of the Covenant symbolised God's footstool – His resting place in the midst of His people. From above the mercy seat God had communicated with Moses and now, if the change of residence was

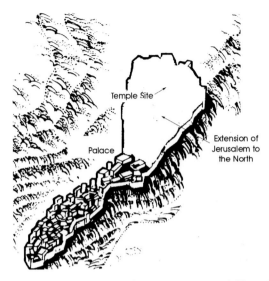

Temple Site

Palace

Extension of
Jerusalem to
the North

acceptable to God, God would continue to fellowship with His people in a new situation – one of permanence and stability. That was what Solomon hoped would happen, if everything was acceptable to God.

We can be confident that the ark was transported precisely in accordance with the law given to Moses – covered, borne upon the shoulders of the Kohlathite family of the Levitical priests, accompanied by sacrifices, prayers and praises.[7] Just as David had performed a priestly function when the Ark was being brought to Jerusalem, wearing a linen ephod and making sacrifices, now it was Solomon who performed that function, demonstrating his role as a King-priest, no doubt after the order of Melchizedek.[8]

Israel had learned that lesson well, when Uzzah had been smitten by God during David's reign, for, at that time they had wrongly imitated Philistine ways of transport and failed to show proper respect for God's gracious commandments. This time everything went well and, at last, the ark was brought into its ordained place in the Most Holy Place:

> *"The priests brought in the ark of the covenant of the LORD unto his place, into the oracle of the house, to the*

most holy place, even under the wings of the cherubims"
(1 Kings 8:6).

The Most Holy Place

We have deferred our consideration of this crucial part of
the temple complex until now. Our imaginary priest, pro-
cessing into the Temple could go no further than the Holy
Place, for it was only the High Priest who could enter
within the Veil, then only once a year – on the Day of
Atonement – and only then by virtue of the shed blood of
the atoning sacrifice (Hebrews 9:7). But when he entered
on that annual occasion, what might he have seen?

The room itself was a perfect cube – twenty cubits by
twenty cubits by twenty cubits (1 Kings 6:20).[9] The very
shape was representative; for when the eternal life of the
saints is depicted in the Apocalypse, it is seen as the New
Jerusalem whose dimensions are as follows: *"The city lieth
foursquare, and the length is as large as the breadth: and
he measured the city with the reed, twelve thousand fur-
longs. The length and the breadth and the height of it are
equal"* (Revelation 21:16).[10]

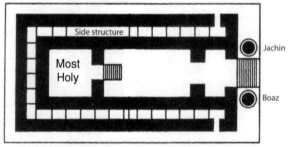

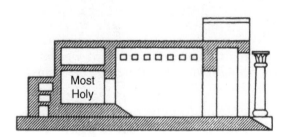

Lined with cedar boards, like the Holy Place, it too was richly ornamented with knops, flowers in blossom and palm trees; and both gold and precious stone adorned it.[11] Once again the motifs were Edenic; but now they were pointing forward to that time when Paradise will be restored and the people of God will dwell with Him for evermore. So because this enclosure was meant to represent God's very dwelling place, where He was figuratively enthroned above the mercy seat, cherubim were depicted everywhere. They were on the embroidered Veil, the olive-wood folding Doors, on the Walls, and free-standing – right in the centre of the space. For, under God's direction, Solomon had made two large cherubim out of olive wood, covered with gold (1 Kings 6:23-28). They were so large that their wings touched in the middle and reached to the outer walls. It was full of depictions of heavenly beings reflecting the Divine glory.

Now, underneath the outstretched wings of the large cherubim, came the cherubim that were one with the mercy seat – they nestled underneath, sheltered and protected by the large cherubim already there (1 Chronicles 28:18). With the cherubim foursquare, God was demonstrating that His providential care would overshadow everything that had to do with the quest for holiness, including the work to be done by His Son – whose coming and accomplishments were typified by the Ark of the Covenant. Father and Son were to work together to bring holiness.

Bear in mind that the ark would have gone in poles first – on an East/West axis – and, because of the length of the poles and the presence of the large cherubim, there would have been no room to turn it through 90 degrees, as is sometimes suggested.[12] Thus the cherubim – large and small – would have been at right angles to one another. The two faces of the cherubim on the Ark looked inward, towards the blood-sprinkled mercy seat;[13] the two faces of the free-standing cherubim looked "inward"– toward the house – (2 Chronicles 3:13), toward the priests and the worshippers.[14]

The Ark of the Covenant

There are a few things to note about the Ark:

- Whilst the Lampstand, the Altar of Incense and the Table of Shewbread that were in the Tabernacle might not have made it into the Temple, for reasons already considered, the Ark remained unchanged. God never changes and this was the figurative symbol of His dwelling place. In fact the entire temple was built to house the Ark (2 Samuel 7:1,2), so this item of Divine furniture has pride of place. It was the first item to have been made – in the Wilderness – but now it was the last item to be put in place; just as the Lord Jesus Christ, whom it typifies, was *the first and the last* in the purpose of God.[15]

- There was no table or stand for the Ark. It rested on the ground, in all probability on the rocky outcrop that had once been part of the threshing floor. There is a strong likelihood that it now rested on the very spot where once Abraham showed himself willing to sacrifice Isaac (2 Chronicles 3:1; Genesis 22:2) and it may well be that the very spot it rested can still be seen on the Rock-hewn floor of the Dome of the Rock.[16] This also meant that when the High Priest entered on the Day of Atonement, he would need to bend low, or even to kneel as he ministered at the Ark which would have been most appropriate in view of what it represented.

- At least he would not have been in danger of tripping up over the poles which were threaded through the four rings by which it had been carried in the past. According to the Talmud, these were 10 cubits long,[17] but now the Ark had reached its resting place, the poles were to be pulled out. The Law as given in Exodus precluded that happening, as the Ark was then to be kept in a state of permanent readiness for departure, as Israel moved forward towards the Land (Exodus 25:15), but now they could be removed, or extended if they were not entirely taken out.[18]

- Comforting as that was, as a visual sign that God's presence was settled among His people, it did not mean that He would never leave them. Solomon knew only too clearly that obedience was a prerequisite to Divine favour and that the nation had to be responsive if they were to continue as a blessed people who had God close to them. There was something in the language of the Divine specification for the free-standing cherubim which contained a warning that God could move away from His people as easily as He had drawn near, if things went wrong between them. David had been told to provide:

"Gold for the pattern of the chariot of the cherubims, that spread out their wings, and covered the ark of the covenant of the LORD. All this, said David, the LORD made me understand in writing by his hand upon me, even all the works of this pattern" (1 Chronicles 28:18,19).

That very terminology showed that if God chose to move His presence away from the midst of Israel, He would do so without their assistance. That was the very movement that Ezekiel later saw, when he saw the heavenly counterparts of those temple cherubim – the angelic chariot of God – departing from the Temple.[19] But, although the language warned that God could "move out" of the Temple as easily as He had "moved in", it was Solomon's fervent hope, and prayer, that this symbol of God's dwelling in the midst of His people would remain a perpetual reality.

● The last item of information given about the Ark is that it now only contained the two tablets of stone upon which the Law of God had been written in the Mount (1 Kings 8:9). The pot of manna had served its purpose, as had Aaron's rod that budded. God's people were now settled in a land which would yield its fruits to them; and the priesthood was securely held by Aaron's descendants, as we have seen. Only the Book of the Law (Deuteronomy) would have been there alongside the Ark, for safe keeping, as a constant reminder that the people were to live by faith if they were to please God.[20]

Final Flourish

It was nearly finished. The work that had taken seven years and huge expenditure was almost complete and the worship of God could commence in earnest. The priests who had borne the Ark began to withdraw from the Most Holy Place, coming through the Holy Place, and returning to the Inner Courtyard, through the Temple porch and past the two great pillars. There the entire company of priests had assembled, for the process of serving according to an allotted schedule had not yet begun (2 Chronicles 5:11), and the Levites, too, including the choirs and the musicians.

One hundred and twenty trumpets sounded; there was a clashing of cymbals and the raising of voices in tuneful accord. They *"praised the LORD, saying, For he is good; for his mercy endureth for ever"* (5:13). What an occasion that was to keep in the corporate memory of the nation; the people were in perfect accord praising God and offering Him thanksgiving.

But was all this pleasing to God? Would He signify to

Israel that He accepted their work and that He would be close to them forever? Solomon looked for such an indication and was not disappointed. That occasion of sublime harmony in the House of God presents a challenge to all succeeding ages, our own included. There is still only one way of rendering acceptable worship to God, the way He has appointed. The goodness and mercy of God in calling us to be the people among whom He now seeks to dwell should bring from us the same united expression of praise. Before Jesus entered into the heavenly counterpart of the Most Holy Place – into heaven itself – it was the earnest prayer of our great High Priest that:

> *"They all may be one; as thou, Father, art in me, and I in thee, that they also may be one in us: that the world may believe that thou hast sent me. And the glory which thou gavest me I have given them; that they may be one, even as we are one: I in them, and thou in me, that they may be made perfect in one; and that the world may know that thou hast sent me, and hast loved them, as thou hast loved me"* (John 17:21-23).

We should think of those Priests and Levites, with the King, the elders and the fathers of the tribes in Israel, all with one united desire, with their voices raised in communal praise. And we should then ponder our own desire to be fully united with all our brothers and sisters, in praise of Almighty God. It is a challenge that stands the test of time. For if we do not want to be with them now, why should God want us to be with them throughout the ages of eternity?

"He is good; for his mercy endureth for ever", sang the choir lustily, with the orchestral accompaniment, and God signified His approval by demonstrating His presence.

> *"It came even to pass, as the trumpeters and singers were as one, to make one sound to be heard in praising and thanking the LORD ... that then the house was filled with a cloud, even the house of the LORD; so that the priests could not stand to minister by reason of the cloud: for the glory of the LORD had filled the house of God"* (2 Chronicles 5:13-14).

SOLOMON – WISE AND FOOLISH

It is a sobering thought that God, who is now waiting to signify His presence on earth once again, by sending His Son to sit on David's throne, might now be waiting for us to offer a united expression of our ardent desire for that Coming, and for His glory to be manifest before the nations. Remember that when Israel were at one with one another, and with God, then God came near to them.

NOTES

[1] Shaw Caldecott (*"The Tabernacle"*, 1906, pg. 64) suggests that a site was prepared for the tent housing the ark adjoining the king's house at the northernmost part of the old city ("just below the south wall of the Haram area"). Bro. Leen Ritmeyer has illustrated one possibility, as mentioned earlier (page 54, footnote 8), and his sketch is based in part upon the work of the archaeologist Eilat Mazar, who in recent years is thought to have uncovered the ruins of King David's Palace near the massive Stepped Stone Structure. See BAR January/February 1997 and January/February 2006.

[2] It seems likely that Levitical guards would have been posted by David to guard the altar and the enclosure it made sacred. (See 1 Chronicles 26:12-19, for details of those who would later man the temple gates at the cardinal points; this arrangement could have been brought forward to meet the exceptional circumstances that now arose.)

[3] Note that whilst there were, in fact, ten tables of shewbread (2 Chronicles 4:8,19), they are regarded as one table, at which God provided heavenly fare – bread from heaven.

[4] The details, in 1 Kings 7:48-50 and 2 Chronicles 4:7-8,19-22, seem to imply that none of the earlier items (like the lampstand, altar of incense, table of shewbread, censers, etc., were used in the temple. It was to be a complete break with the past. An alternative explanation (offered by Shaw Caldecott, op cit., pg.100) is that Solomon ended the worship being offered at Gibeon after God appeared to him there, in a dream (1 Kings 3). Having offered 1000 burnt offerings there, he suggests that *"the Tabernacle was taken down and carried to Jerusalem, where its golden furniture furnished models for*

similar articles to be constructed by Hiram. Having served this purpose, the gold of which they were made was doubtless melted down and formed a part of a new service".

[5] So, Wordsworth, vol iii, pg.230. See also 2 Chronicles 24:6, where King Josiah refers to the Temple as *"the Tent of the Testimony"*, clearly seeing the Temple as having absorbed and replaced the Tabernacle.

[6] The feast of the seventh month (1 Kings 8:2) was the Feast of Tabernacles, representative of God dwelling with His people, and them living in fellowship with Him.

[7] Some difficulty exists between the records when designating those who carried the Ark, for they are variously described as *"priests"* and *"Levites"* (1 Kings 8:3; 2 Chron. 5:4-7). All Priests were, of course, Levites; though not all Levites were Priests. It may be that the Levites brought the Ark to the Temple and the Priests carried it inside, to the Most Holy Place. If so, this act would have united them in a corporate act of worship.

[8] See Bro. Whittaker, pg.188, with regard to King David as a priest after this divinely ordained order of priesthood.

[9] 390 cubits is 8.89m or 30ft. It is worth noting that the floor plan of the Most Holy Place accorded precisely with that of the brazen altar (which was also 20 x 20 cubits: 2 Chron. 4:1).

[10] There are other links as well, for the streets of the city were paved with pure gold (like the Most Holy Place); and the city was illuminated by the glory of God, just as the Shekinah glory of God was to fill the oracle. See Revelation chapters 21 and 22.

[11] The Most Holy Place is also called *"the inner house"* (1 Kings 6:27); *"the holiest of all"* (Hebrews 9:3); and *"the oracle"* (1 Kings 6:16,19,20-23).

[12] The illustration is adapted from The NIV Study Bible. Some earlier editions had the Ark the other way around, with the cherubim pressed right against the back wall, out of the way.

[13] Exodus 25:20; 37:9.

[14] The NIV translation says: *"The wings of these cherubim extended twenty cubits. They stood on their feet, facing the*

main hall".

¹⁵ Here's Wordsworth again, vol iii, pg.30, with a typical comment: *"The rest of the Tabernacle passed away. There were more cherubims, more golden candlesticks, and there was greater splendour in the Table of Shewbread in the Temple of Sion, than there had been in the Tabernacle of Sinai. But the Ark remained the same. The Ark was God's Throne. His Presence was there enshrined on the Mercy Seat, which was sprinkled with blood on the Day of Atonement".*

¹⁶ See pages 117,118 and the Bibliography, for the conclusions offered by Bro. & Sis. Ritmeyer.

¹⁷ 10 cubits equates to 5.25 m (17.2 ft). The Talmudic reference (Yoma 54a) is given in Bro. & Sis. Ritmeyer's book, *"From Sinai to Jerusalem"* (2000), pg.13.

¹⁸ *"They drew out the staves, that the ends of the staves were seen out in the holy place before the oracle, and they were not seen without: and there they are unto this day"* (1 Kings 8:8, and 2 Chron. 5:9). It seems that the ends of the poles could be seen from the Holy Place, pressing up against the Vail; that would have given an assurance that the Ark was there, even though neither it nor the poles were in fact visible.

¹⁹ See Bro. John Allfree, *"Ezekiel"*, 1999, pgs.20-32,119-122.

²⁰ Deuteronomy 31:26.

15
Man of Prayer

THE Ark of the Covenant had been installed in the Temple and that had resulted in a sublime display of unity on the part of the Priests and Levites. The people were one – with one another, and with God — who had signified His presence when *"the house was filled with a cloud, even the house of the LORD; so that the priests could not stand to minister by reason of the cloud: for the glory of the LORD had filled the house of God"* (2 Chronicles 5:13,14).

Divine Confirmation

Solomon took the cloud as a sign – like the pillar of cloud in the wilderness. It was, for him, the Divine confirmation he had been awaiting.[1] Now he knew the House could be dedicated as a place where God would be worshipped. The seventh month was when the feast of Tabernacles was enjoyed,[2] the best attended of all Israel's feasts, held after the harvest had been gathered. The proceedings associated with the dedication give us a real insight into Solomon's spiritual life at this time.

It was the twelfth year of his reign. The Temple was finished in the eighth month of his eleventh year (1 Kings 6:38); but this dedication had been deferred for nearly a year. It is not obvious why Solomon should have waited so long, given his commitment to this project and his undoubted desire to get the Temple operational. Perhaps the extra time was needed to finish all the external work that needed to be done – courtyards, landscaping and suchlike. Or the king may have wanted to give the nation plenty of time to prepare for the occasion, for it was an immensely significant moment in their spiritual history, more significant by far than even a king's coronation. Or Solomon may have been given Divine guidance that told him to wait.

God was coming to tabernacle among His people and the Feast of Tabernacles might have been the divinely fitting time for this point to be made.[3] It could be that in the Divine calendar there was a particular fitness about this moment. It has been suggested that it could be the start of the Jubilee Year, for example, but that began and ended on the Day of Atonement (Leviticus 25:9). It is more likely that a Sabbatical Year *ended* on the Day of Atonement in Solomon's twelfth year, just a few days before this Dedication.[4] For this signified rest and, after the hard physical labour of the building work, everyone involved would have had respite for nearly a year and, whether they kept the Sabbatical Year or not, that rest would have signified an important spiritual principle. They were to rest from their labours (Hebrews 4:9-11) and were to put their trust entirely in God, who would care for them and bring about their salvation.

Solomon the Servant
It was not the king who took centre stage at this Dedication but the LORD, and the king was merely the *"servant"* of the LORD:

> *"Yet have thou respect unto the prayer of thy servant, and to his supplication, O LORD my God, to hearken unto the cry and to the prayer, which **thy servant** prayeth before thee to day"* (1 Kings 8:28).

That expression is used 15 times in the 1 Kings account of these events. Twice Solomon refers to Moses as God's servant (perhaps because he saw himself as following in Moses' footsteps); four times he refers to David his father as God's servant; six times he makes mention of himself in that capacity; and three times of Israel likewise.[5] Evidently this servile attitude of mind was pleasing to God.

154

Solomon wanted to be seen and heard, not only by God but also by all the people of Israel; for his prayer was meant at once to be a petition to God, and an instruction to the nation. So he had constructed a bronze or copper platform, which was positioned in front of the altar (1 Kings 8:22), in the Temple courtyard, and he began his prayer standing on that:

"Solomon had made a brasen scaffold of five cubits long, and five cubits broad, and three cubits high, and had set it in the midst of the court: and upon it he stood, and kneeled down upon his knees before all the congregation of Israel, and spread forth his hands toward heaven" (2 Chronicles 6:13).[6]

First he stood and then he knelt, which is probably the first record of that posture being adopted in prayer. As one writer has commented: "A king upon his knees in public, leading the nation in humble supplication to God! A rare spectacle!"[7] It was thus expressive of his earnestness in prayer and of his willingness to submit himself entirely to God, as he humbled himself before Him.

Model Prayer

It is helpful to note how Solomon went about addressing the God of the Universe, in this fine example of intercessory prayer, which is recorded for us at some length, in both 1 Kings 8 and 2 Chronicles 6.[8] Primarily, Solomon focuses upon God's presence and purpose. He had just finished building the Temple, and could easily have allowed external things to dominate his thinking – as we can in our own prayers, sometimes being more conscious of what is going on around us, than about the One to whom we are speaking.

In his prayer, Solomon made immediate contact with God, who had just signified His presence by sending the cloud and driving everyone out – a clear statement that it was His House, not theirs! Starting from that experience, Solomon remembered that the Tabernacle in the wilderness had been built without windows and had been covered with several layers of cloth and animal skins, to block out all light from inside; for God was, and is, our only source of true enlightenment.[9] Then he referred to the fact that the Temple was now finished, as a place which He could inhabit – in the midst of His people, for ever. No sooner were the words uttered, than Solomon knew that the God of glory could not be so contained. Turning to the entire congregation, he blessed them and said:

> *"Blessed be the* LORD *God of Israel, who hath with his hands fulfilled that which he spake with his mouth to my father David, saying, Since the day that I brought forth my people out of the land of Egypt I chose no city among all the tribes of Israel to build an house in, that my name might be there; neither chose I any man to be a ruler over my people Israel: but I have chosen Jerusalem, that my name might be there; and have chosen David to be over my people Israel"* (2 Chronicles 6:4-6).

Bring the two accounts of the prayer together and you will notice that Solomon thought through God's purpose since the Exodus: His choice of David, and David's willing response,[10] which led on to the commission given to Solomon to build the Temple for God. God had made a covenant with His people, and that covenant – expressed by the tablets of stone within the ark – was now physically at the centre of Israel's national life. This, Solomon recalled before God, had happened because of God's gracious promises – made to the fathers and re-iterated to David. Now Solomon pleaded the promises, asking that God would continue to do what He had said:

> *"O* LORD *God of Israel, there is no God like thee in the heaven, nor in the earth;* **which keepest covenant, and shewest mercy unto thy servants, that walk before thee with all their hearts:** *thou which hast kept with thy servant David my father that which thou hast promised him; and spakest with thy mouth, and hast fulfilled it with thine hand, as it is this day. Now therefore, O* LORD *God of Israel, keep with thy servant David my father that which thou hast promised him, saying, There shall not fail thee a man in my sight to sit upon the throne of Israel; yet so that thy children take*

heed to their way to walk in my law, as thou hast walked before me. Now then, O LORD God of Israel, let thy word be verified, which thou hast spoken unto thy servant David" (6:14-17).

As the words picked out in bold type indicate, Solomon knew this was a two-sided relationship. God had been utterly faithful to His Word – He had spoken with His mouth and fulfilled it with His hand (1 Kings 8:24). Now Solomon hoped that God's people would be responsive, that they would fulfil their part of the covenant deal – just as we must be if we are to see God's purpose come to its inevitable and gracious conclusion. [11]

House of Prayer

As Isaiah would later remind Israel, at a time when the Temple was under threat by a foreign invader, God was not limited by the Temple – it was not a box in which to shut Him away! The God of the Universe fills time and space, but He also wants to dwell with us – in the middle of our community life and, every day, in every aspect of our personal lives, if we will let Him.[12] Solomon knew that, and was keen to explain to Israel that the Temple was really just a focal point, to help God's people centre their minds upon the unseen God who dwells in *"highest heaven"*. So, as Isaiah would later reiterate, Solomon asked the vital question, and supplied the answer:

"But will God in very deed dwell with men on the earth? Behold, heaven and the heaven of heavens cannot contain thee; how much less this house which I have built! Have respect therefore to the prayer of thy servant, and to his supplication, O LORD my God, to hearken unto the cry and the prayer which thy servant prayeth before thee: that thine eyes may be open upon this house day and night, upon the place whereof thou hast said that thou wouldest put thy name there; to hearken unto the prayer which thy servant prayeth toward this place. Hearken therefore unto the supplications of thy servant, and of thy people Israel, which they shall make toward this place: hear thou from thy dwelling place, even from heaven; and when thou hearest, forgive" (6:18-21).

In our terms, Solomon envisaged the Temple as essentially a point of contact with God – rather like a switchboard in a modern office. He asked for God's assurance that acceptable prayers directed towards that "place" would be redirected to God's actual presence, in heaven.[13] He wanted to make sure that, wherever God was, He would hear and respond to His people's needs, and he went on to specify what he anticipated some of those needs would be.

Solomon wanted an assurance that God would *"hear"* and *"forgive"* His people when they came to Him in contrite prayer.[14] What needs did he anticipate? Evidently Solomon knew his Scriptures well; for the problems he foresaw were those that Moses had already predicted, so he built on that foundation:

Expected Problems		2 Chronicles 6 *Verses:*	Pentateuch
1	Oath at the Altar	22,23	Exodus 22:6-12; Leviticus 5:21-24
2	Defeat	33,34	Lev. 26:17; Deut. 28:25
3	Drought	35,36	Lev. 26:19; Deut. 11:17; 28:23
4	Famine and Pestilence	28-31	Lev. 26:19-26; Deut. 28:22-23, 38
5	The Stranger	32,33	e.g. Exodus 12:48,49; Numbers 15:14–16, Deut. 28:10
6	In Battle	34,35	
7	In Captivity and Exile	36-39	Leviticus 26:33,44; Deut. 28:45ff., 64ff., 30:1-5

Petitions 2-7 refer mainly to Leviticus 26 and Deuteronomy 28, where Moses had recorded a prophetic portrait of Israel's future.

Petition 6 contains the only reference to offensive action, as opposed to defensive behaviour. Here Solomon asks God to uphold Israel's cause.

Whatever might come, Solomon was saying, he hoped that God would be gracious to His people – that He would hear their prayers,[15] be merciful, and help them. And his prayer was not only that God would hear and help His people Israel, but that He would do the same for others as well, all – from anywhere and everywhere – who came to Him in faith.[16]

> *"Moreover concerning the stranger, which is not of thy people Israel, but is come from a far country for thy great name's sake, and thy mighty hand, and thy stretched out arm; if they come and pray in this house; then hear thou from the heavens, even from thy dwelling place, and do according to all that the stranger calleth to thee for; that all people of the earth may know thy name, and fear thee, as doth thy people Israel, and may know that this house which I have built is called by thy name"* (2 Chronicles 6:32,33).

Gentiles had helped build the Temple, and it is clear that Solomon understood that they, too, were to be allowed the privilege of worshipping the God of Israel, if they so desired. His prayer was a remarkable preface to the process of magnifying God in other nations also; a work in which he was to play a vital role.

Solomon's Insight

Something else is clear, too, from this remarkable prayer. Solomon had a keen insight into the human condition – the nature of all people, Jew or Gentile. For, intermingled with the seven petitions, listed above, is his analysis of what was likely to be the main problem for those who would worship God in the years ahead. Notice these asides in the prayer:

> *"What prayer or what supplication soever shall be made of any man ... when every one shall know his own sore and his own grief ... the plague of his own heart ... then hear thou from heaven thy dwelling place, and forgive, and render unto every man according unto all his ways, whose heart thou knowest; (for thou only knowest the hearts of the children of men:)"* (2 Chronicles 6:29,30 and 1 Kings 8:38, conflated).

If only Solomon could have foreseen his own situation some years on! The *"plague of his own heart"* was going to need some attention, and he was going to be completely reliant upon God's forgiveness, covenant love and compassionate help, if he was ever to find the way back to God's favour. But, for the moment, all was well. Solomon, the man of prayer, was totally in tune with God. One writer says of this prayer of dedication:

"It seems like presumption and impertinence to refer in laudatory terms to what for comprehensiveness, sublimeness, humility, faith, and earnestness has no parallel in the Old Testament, and can only be compared with the prayer which our Lord taught His disciples. Like the latter, it consists of an introduction (1 Kings 8:23-30), of seven petitions (the covenant-number, verses 31-53), and of a eulogetic close (2 Chronicles 6:40-42). The Introduction sounds like an Old Testament version of the words 'Our Father' (verses 23-26), 'which art in heaven' (verses 27-30)." [17]

Another writer comments that the prayer neither shows great variety of thought nor expression, in that it is quite repetitive in part, but that it concentrates upon one great theme and it is that concentration which is arresting. It concentrates Solomon's longing that future generations should find God and His blessing and thus challenges us to consider whether or not our prayers are sufficiently focused upon what we really want God to accomplish in our lives. And it also reveals Solomon's appreciation of what the Temple was really all about – it was a focal point for the spiritual aspirations of God's people. When they looked or prayed towards God's Temple, they were really looking towards Him.[18]

So, with Solomon, it is a case of 'So far, so good'. There were years of faithful service ahead before things would begin to go wrong. He was doing well and was walking with God.

NOTES

[1] Similar confirmation was given by God that the Tabernacle was acceptable to Him, being built according to His specification, and under His direction. See Exodus 40:35.

[2] 1 Kings 8:2; Leviticus 23:34 ("Ethanim" is the same month as "Tisri"). Phoenician names for the months are used in these chapters, perhaps because of the nationality of the key builders and workers. It's yet another reminder of the major Gentile involvement in the project.

[3] See John 1:14 (RV) and Rev. 21:3, for the spiritual import of what was being typified.

[4] Bro. W. H. Carter, *"Times and Seasons"* (1961), pg.30, suggests that the completion of Solomon's Temple coincided with a Sabbatical year cycle that had begun at Creation. According to his calculations, the Year of Jubilee fell in the 4th year of Solomon's reign, when the foundation of the Temple was laid (Table 27). That would have indicated to the spiritually-minded that freedom from sin would come about for all those whose lives were founded upon God.

[5] The sequences are (Moses) 1 Kings 8:53,56; (David) 8:24-26,66; (Solomon) 8:28,30,36,52,59; (Israel) 8:23,32,36.

[6] This scaffold, in the middle of the Temple court, was the same size as the altar of burnt offering (5 cubits x 5 cubits x 3 cubits), so it appears that Solomon was presenting himself to God as though he wished to be a *"living sacrifice"*.

[7] Fereday, pg.75.

[8] Analysing the structure of 2 Chronicles, McConville, pg. 129, says that this prayer of Solomon's *"is perhaps the central prayer in the two books, following as it does the most significant single event in them [the ark having come to its final resting place], and containing, moreover, the essence of [Chronicles'] theology of salvation".*

[9] There were also clear statements to that effect, e.g. Exodus 19:9; Leviticus 16:2.

[10] Several times Solomon refers to the fact that the desire to build God a Temple was *"in the heart of David"*, an indication that Solomon knew that desire matters every bit as much as

realisation. It is not just doing God's will that counts, but wanting to do it!

[11] Our Hymn, *"Shall we behold the promised land?"*, poses precisely that challenge to 21st century followers of God.

[12] *"Thus saith the LORD, The heaven is my throne, and the earth is my footstool: where is the house that ye build unto me? and where is the place of my rest? For all those things hath mine hand made, and all those things have been, saith the LORD: but to this man will I look, even to him that is poor and of a contrite spirit, and trembleth at my word"* (Isaiah 66:1,2); *"Thus saith the high and lofty One that inhabiteth eternity, whose name is Holy; I dwell in the high and holy place, with him also that is of a contrite and humble spirit, to revive the spirit of the humble, and to revive the heart of the contrite ones"* (Isaiah 57:51).

[13] See 1 Kings 8:39,43,45,49.

[14] Solomon wanted both forgiveness and restitution by Divine action: *"Hear thou in heaven, and forgive the sin of thy servants, and of thy people Israel, that thou teach them the good way wherein they should walk"* (1 Kings 8:36). This was the very help he would need himself a little later in his walk with God.

[15] For God to *"hear"* is a key theme (see 2 Chronicles 6:19,20,21,23,25,27,30,33,35,39,40).

[16] Selman, *"2 Chronicles"*, pg. 329, observes that "the idea that other nations will 'fear', i.e. worship, Yahweh (v.33) is typical of Chronicles".

[17] Edersheim, vol v, pg. 92.

[18] McConville, pg.130.

16

The Temple: Open for Worship

THE dedication of the Temple was a remarkable spiritual experience, both for the king and for the nation. The prayer Solomon offered was a remarkable testimony to his spirituality, and the whole sequence of events was such that, years later, a Psalmist would memorialise the coming of the ark to the Temple as the end of a spiritual journey.

> *"Now, my God, let, I beseech thee, thine eyes be open, and let thine ears be attent unto the prayer that is made in this place"*, Solomon prayed – then he added: *"Now therefore **arise, O LORD God, into thy resting place,** thou, and the ark of thy strength: let thy priests, O LORD God, be clothed with salvation, and let thy saints rejoice in goodness. O LORD God, turn not away the face of thine anointed: remember the mercies of David thy servant"* (2 Chronicles 6:40-42).

God at Rest

The words shown in bold type constituted the cry which had sent the ark of God's covenant forward into battle in times of war.[1] Now, with Israel at peace, Solomon was using them to signify his understanding that God had, at last, found the rest He so long intended – now He was settled in the midst of His people. For the ark was only meant to travel until God's *"resting place"* [2] had been found. Later the Psalmist would celebrate the end of a process which had begun with David's desire to rescue the ark from

Kirjath Jearim, to bring it to Jerusalem. When it reached there it was at journey's end; so, in Psalm 132, he recalls the very words of Solomon:

> *"Arise, O LORD, into thy rest; thou, and the ark of thy strength. Let thy priests be clothed with righteousness; and let thy saints shout for joy".* Then the Psalmist adds his own conviction that, *"the LORD hath chosen Zion; he hath desired it for his habitation. This is my rest for ever: here will I dwell; for I have desired it"* (Psalm 132:8,9,13,14).[3]

The quest for rest had been a crucial factor in God's choice of Solomon, rather than David, to build the Temple, for he had been told:

> *"Behold, a son shall be born to thee, who shall be a man of rest; and I will give him rest from all his enemies round about: for his name shall be Solomon, and I will give peace and quietness unto Israel in his days"* (1 Chronicles 22:9).[4]

But how did Solomon know that God was indeed pleased with the present events? How could he be sure? Look at the sequence of events, including the prayer of dedication:

EVENT	1 Kings	2 Chronicles
The Temple is completed	7:51	5:1
The ark is carried in	8:1-9	5:2-10
Musical praise to God, in harmony		5:11-13a
Cloud/Glory fill the House	8:10-11	5:13b-14
King blesses the congregation (1st)	8:14	6:3
Solomon's opening Words	8:15-21	6:4-11
Prayer of Dedication	8:22-53	6:12-42
King blesses the congregation (2nd)	8:54-56	
Solomon's closing Words	8:57-61	
Burnt Offering & Sacrifices prepared		Implied
Fire from heaven consumes them		7:1a
Glory of God fills the House		7:1b-2
People worship & gave thanks		7:3
Sacrifices made – and shared	8:62-64	7:4-7
Feast (of Tabernacles) kept	8:65-66	7:8-10

Moses and Solomon

As you might expect from an occasion as solemn and important as this, there was a measure of repetition to add emphasis to what was happening. The cloud, which signified to onlookers that God was in their midst – as it had done most dramatically in the wilderness – filled the Temple almost as soon as the ark had been moved in. This was a clear association with God's acceptance of the Tabernacle, signifying in the clearest possible terms that God was now willing to accept the Temple as His new place of worship:

● **Tabernacle:**

> *"Then a cloud covered the tent of the congregation, and the glory of the LORD filled the tabernacle. And Moses was not able to enter into the tent of the congregation, because the cloud abode thereon, and the glory of the LORD filled the tabernacle"* (Exodus 40:34,35).

● **Temple:**

> *"And it came to pass, when the priests were come out of the holy place, that the cloud filled the house of the LORD, so that the priests could not stand to minister because of the cloud: for the glory of the LORD had filled the house of the LORD"* (1 Kings 8:10,11).

There is a carefully designed parallel between the acts of Moses and those now performed by Solomon, as if he took what happened with the Tabernacle as his model for the Temple ceremony. And God responded again, to signify His pleasure, as He had done before:

● Moses had blessed the people when the Tabernacle structure was completed; so did Solomon (Exodus 39:43/1 Kings 8:14);

● When Moses and Aaron entered the Tabernacle for the first time, they came out and blessed the people again (Leviticus 9:23a/1 Kings 8:54-56);

165

- The glory of the LORD appeared to the people (Leviticus 9:23b/2 Chronicles 7:1b-2);

- Fire from heaven consumed the offerings (Leviticus 9:24/2 Chronicles 7:1a);

- The people worshipped (Leviticus 9:24/2 Chronicles 7:3).

Solomon was quite aware of these parallels, for his second blessing of the people expressly makes the link with his spiritual predecessor:

> He stood, and blessed all the congregation of Israel with a loud voice, saying, "Blessed be the LORD, that hath given rest unto his people Israel, according to all that he promised: there hath not failed one word of all his good promise, which he promised by the hand of Moses his servant. The LORD our God be with us, as he was with our fathers: let him not leave us, nor forsake us: that he may incline our hearts unto him, to walk in all his ways, and to keep his commandments, and his statutes, and his judgments, which he commanded our fathers" (1 Kings 8:55-58).

Even the language he uses is reminiscent of Moses' appeal to Israel, in Deuteronomy – that the people should incline their hearts to God in faithful obedience. But there was one important difference, and that was a deliberate one. Whilst Moses and Aaron had worked together (as prophet and priest), now there is no mention of the High Priest throughout these ceremonials. It is Solomon, type of the great King/Priest to come, who holds centre stage. He utters the blessings, he addresses the people, he makes the intercessory prayer of dedication, he offers the sacrifices. Of course, he would have been assisted by the Priests and Levites; but they get little mention in the record. For example:

> "And the king, and all Israel with him, offered sacrifice before the LORD. And Solomon offered a sacrifice of peace offerings, which he offered unto the LORD, two and twenty thousand oxen, and an hundred and twenty

thousand sheep. So the king and all the children of Israel dedicated the house of the LORD. The same day did the king hallow the middle of the court that was before the house of the LORD: for there he offered burnt offerings ... And at that time Solomon held a feast, and all Israel with him, a great congregation ... On the eighth day he sent the people away: and they blessed the king, and went unto their tents joyful and glad of heart" (1 Kings 8:62-66).

Solomon was a representative man, representative of the One who was to come – Solomon's greater Son – and of the faithful in all ages, who would be allowed the privilege of directly worshipping God, and living a sacrificial life. But, as he now made clear, such a privilege would only continue if those called to worship God responded to his final exhortation:

"Let your heart therefore be perfect with the LORD our God, to walk in his statutes, and to keep his commandments, as at this day" (1 Kings 8:61).

God would do His part in inclining their hearts towards Him (8:58), but they must be responsive to those evident expressions of God's love and gracious favour – made even more expressive towards us, since Solomon's day, in the gift of His Son. All this was left on the record to counsel and challenge Solomon later in his life. And it challenges us still.

Feasting with God

Eager though Solomon was, and all Israel were, to show their appreciation of all that God had done, and the mercy He had shown,[5] we should not think of the sacrifices then offered as a mere "Thank you" to God – an abundance of slaughter and self-denial. A lot of animals were slaughtered – 22,000 oxen and 120,000 sheep – as burnt offerings and peace offerings, together with meal offerings.[6] There were so many that Solomon had to sanctify the middle of the courtyard, for the altar of burnt offering would never have coped with the volume of animals now being offered.[7]

The record does not distinguish between the number of

burnt and peace offerings,[8] though in practical terms there was an important distinction. Voluntary burnt offerings were a way for the worshipper to say to God that he or she wanted to live in total dedication to God, so everything was consumed upon the altar, except for the animal's skin.[9] But a peace offering was an expression of thanksgiving which led to a meal of fellowship, the worshipper being allowed to eat the remainder, once the fat had been burnt on the altar and the priests had been given the breast and thigh.[10]

The Feast of Tabernacles, which immediately followed this act of dedication,[11] required the offering of 13 bullocks, 2 rams and 14 lambs – as burnt offerings – for the first seven days of the eight day feast, as well as meal offerings and sin offerings.[12] But these offerings preceded those of the second week. For, first, Israel enjoyed seven days of festive dedication, then followed the eight days of the prescribed Feast:

1 Kings 8:65,66	2 Chronicles 7:8-10
"At that time Solomon held a feast, and all Israel with him, a great congregation, from the entering in of Hamath unto the river of Egypt, before the LORD our God, **seven days and seven days,** even fourteen days.	"Solomon kept the feast seven days, and all Israel with him, a very great congregation, from the entering in of Hamath unto the river of Egypt. And in the eighth day they made a solemn assembly: **for they kept the dedication of the altar seven days, and the feast seven days.**
On **the eighth day** he sent the people away: and they blessed the king, and went unto their tents joyful and glad of heart for all the goodness that the LORD had done for David his servant, and for Israel his people."	And on **the three and twentieth day** of the seventh month[13] he sent the people away into their tents, glad and merry in heart for the goodness that the LORD had shewed unto David, and to Solomon, and to Israel his people."

These 15 days, including the 8th day, which was to be a special Sabbath, are a clear pointer to us that we must first dedicate our lives to God, and thus yield our bodies as a Temple in which God comes to dwell – or tabernacle – and then we too can rejoice in the knowledge that God has once again drawn near to His people. First, there was the sharing together of a meal of fellowship – signified by the peace offerings, of the first week – then, there was the dwelling with God, representative both of God's abiding with us now, and of the coming age when *"the tabernacle of God is with men, and he will dwell with them, and they shall be his people, and God himself shall be with them, and be their God"* (Revelation 21:3).

Joyful and Glad

God had shown Himself to be pleased with the worship that had been offered and Israel had rejoiced together in His presence and in fellowship with one another, just as we should. They had gone home rejoicing – *"joyful and glad of heart"* – and, year by year, would return to Jerusalem to keep the feasts, and to worship at the Temple. The building work was finished, but the approach to its courtyards would have shown them that construction work was still going on around about it.

For the completion of the Temple, on the huge platform Solomon had constructed for the purpose – since enlarged by Herod, and now known as the Temple Mount – was just the start of the Temple complex. Over the next 13 years Solomon added other components to his grand design – various porches, the ivory throne, the House of the Forest of Lebanon, and two Palaces.

It follows that we should think of the Temple complex as a two-stage development which took 20 years to complete. We have been considering the events that took place at the end of the first stage – 7 years into the project. But would God be equally pleased with the finished product? Or would the king who had shown himself to be so spiritual and well-attuned to God now stray from that position? What would the next thirteen years bring, as Solomon passed the half-way point of his forty-year long reign?

NOTES

[1] Numbers 10:35.

[2] *"The ark of the covenant of the LORD went before them in the three days' journey, to search out a resting place for them"* (Numbers 10:33).

[3] For a helpful note on the interpretation of Psalm 132, see George Booker, *"Psalm Studies"*, ii, pg. 785.

[4] See also 1 Chronicles 22:18; 23:25 and 28:2, where the Temple is called *"an house of rest for the ark of the covenant of the lord, and for the footstool of our god"*.

[5] Significantly, both at the beginning and end of the Dedication process, Israel rejoiced in the merciful kindness of God towards them, as though they saw the Temple as an architectural expression of the sure mercies of David being vouchsafed to them. See 2 Chronicles 5:13 (at the beginning of the celebration) and 7:3 (at the end).

[6] 1 Kings 8:63-64; 2 Chronicles 7:5-7. This number of animals could only have been sacrificed in 7 days if there were several teams of Levites working together – hence the need for the court to be sanctified. But the sacrifices could have been spread over the entire 14 days, including the following week's Feast of Tabernacles.

[7] Notice that it is Solomon that sanctifies the Court, not the High Priest, which is again expressive of his representative role.

[8] The animals could have been bullocks, male goats or rams for a burnt offering; male or female from the flock or herd for a peace offering.

[9] Burnt Offering: Leviticus 1:1-13; 6:8-11; 7:8-9.

[10] Peace Offering: Leviticus 3:1-17; 7:11-21,29-34; 10:14-15.

[11] See page 142, earlier.

[12] Numbers 29:12-38.

[13] The Feast of Tabernacles was scheduled to run from the 15th day of the 7th month (Tisri) until the 23rd day (eight days later).

17
Remaining Faithful

SOLOMON had been earnestly employed for many years in building the temple. We saw earlier that he commenced the building in 971 B.C. – in the 4th year of his reign (1 Kings 6:37) – and that the building work took seven years, for it was 964 B.C., in his 11th year, when the building was completed. It could have been regarded as a big drain on the nation's finances, because a civil engineering project of that size would have consumed a lot of energy and revenue, even though it might have generated some wealth, through employment, for both skilled craftsmen and unskilled labourers. Or it could have been viewed as a major expression of Israel's appreciation for their calling by God to be His people – it all depended on your point of view!

It is right that the building of the Temple should have been a substantial cost to the nation, for true and faithful service given to God should cost the worshipper, as David had observed at the outset.[1] For building – or becoming – a dwelling place for the Almighty takes time: it requires years of patient endeavour before our minds and hearts become attuned to the things of God.[2] And that is a price we should willingly pay, by careful reading and thoughtful meditation and prayer over many years, if we are to learn the full import of what God has done, and continues to do for us, both as a community and as individuals.

Faithful Service
All this time Solomon was properly focused upon his calling and his commitment as the one whom God had chosen

171

to build the House at Jerusalem. It must have taken a great deal of his energy and a lot of dedication to the task in question to produce God the dwelling He had requested – the place of his footstool.[3] But what an outcome! When it was finished it was a visual representation of God's gracious presence in the midst of His redeemed people; a blessing that Israel would never ignore, surely, and something that would speak volumes to the nations around should they come to see this new marvel in their midst.

Solomon spent seven years building the Temple and now he began a lot of other building work in Jerusalem:

"But Solomon was building his own house thirteen years, and he finished all his house. He built also the house of the forest of Lebanon ... And he made a porch of pillars ... Then he made a porch for the throne where he might judge, even the porch of judgment ... And his house where he dwelt had another court within the porch, which was of the like work. Solomon made also an house for Pharaoh's daughter, whom he had taken to wife, like unto this porch ... And the great court round about was with three rows of hewed stones, and a row of cedar beams, both for the inner court of the house of the LORD, *and for the porch of the house"* (1 Kings 7:1-12).

Much of this building work was taking place in and around the Temple site,[4] although nobody can know exactly where it was or what it looked like, for the whole area was destroyed by the Babylonians, built upon by the returning exiles and was then totally restructured by Herod, when he rebuilt the Second Temple. It might have looked something like the drawings opposite, but they can only be indicative.[5]

Next Thirteen Years

Notice that it took Solomon a further thirteen years to build these royal palaces for himself and for his Egyptian queen.[6] We need not assume that he did nothing else at all during that time; he also had to administer the affairs of the Kingdom and see to all the necessary day-to-day matters. But it seems reasonably clear, from the sparse chronological data in the Kings and Chronicles record,

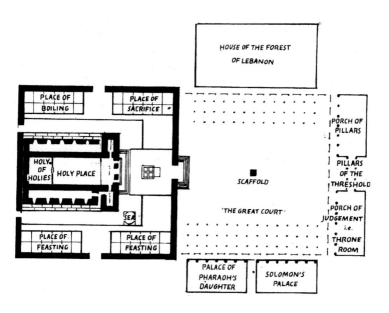

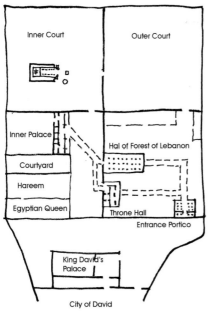

Two possible layouts for the configuration of the Temple and the Palace, to the north of the City of David.

The first is based on *"Solomon's Temple"* by Shaw Caldecott; the second on *"The Reliability of the Old Testament"* by Kenneth Kitchen.

Details of both books are given in the Bibliography

173

that Solomon was spiritually-minded at this time and was not busying himself with marriage alliances, complicated trade arrangements (beyond that with Hiram which had to do with the building work), or the luxuries of life at Court. All that came later.

Because we know how things worked out later, it is easy to find fault with Solomon when no fault is implied in the Scriptural account – just as we find it easy to make unjust judgements about people we know, by assuming the worst instead of the best! For example, no criticism would appear to be implied in the juxtaposition of the two building projects comprising the Temple and the Palace – when we are told that one took seven years, the other thirteen. Viewed impassively, the writer may be commending Solomon for the fact that he made every effort to get the Temple finished as soon as possible, but took longer with his own Palace, because there was less national importance with that. He would not appear to be inferring that the King sought to make his Palace even more splendid, so that he took nearly twice as long to build it.

But is it safe to assume that Solomon gave the Temple absolute priority and did not start his Palace until the Temple was complete? Of course, he already had David's palace – within the old city – which Hiram had helped the King build. He was not homeless. And the chronological sequence appears to highlight Solomon's dedication to the Temple, and to indicate that for the King, as it should be for us, he quite rightly put "first things first". For this is the recorded sequence:

> *"In the fourth year was the foundation of the house of the* LORD *laid, in the month Zif: and in the eleventh year, in the month Bul, which is the eighth month, was the house finished throughout all the parts thereof, and according to all the fashion of it. So was he seven years in building it. But Solomon was building his own house thirteen years, and he finished all his house"* (1 Kings 6:37-7:1) ... *And it came to pass at the end of twenty years, when Solomon had built the two houses, the house of the* LORD, *and the king's house* (9:10) ... *the* LORD *appeared to Solomon the second time, as he had*

appeared unto him at Gibeon. And the LORD said unto
him, I have heard thy prayer and thy supplication, that
thou hast made before me: I have hallowed this house,
which thou hast built, to put my name there for ever;
and mine eyes and mine heart shall be there perpetually" (9:1-3).

Sequence of Events

Notice a detail about God's expression of approval towards
Solomon in this early part of the King's reign. If he had
begun to reign when he was about 20 years old (although
he may have been a little younger),[7] it is easy to compute
his age at the different stages of construction. And as we
know that he reigned 40 years in all,[8] plotting Solomon's
developing spiritual state is quite easy:

Year	B.C.	Percentage of His reign	Event
3?	972	7.5%	*God's **first** appearance to Solomon at Gibeon* (1 Kings 3:1-15; 2 Chron. 1:2-13)
4	971	10	Temple begun
11	964	27.5	Temple finished God's approval signified by fire (2 Chron. 7:1-3)
11	964	27.5	Palace begun
24	952	60	Palace finished *God's **second** appearance to Solomon in Jerusalem* (1 Kings 9:1-9; 2 Chron. 7:11-22).
40	932	100	The end of Solomon's reign

This second appearance to Solomon is really very
important as an indication that things were still going
well, over halfway through Solomon's reign:

175

SOLOMON – WISE AND FOOLISH

"It came to pass, when Solomon had finished the build-
ing of the house of the LORD, and the king's house, and
all Solomon's desire which he was pleased to do, that
the LORD appeared to Solomon the second time, as he
had appeared unto him at Gibeon" (1 Kings 9:1,2).

God had given an earlier indication to Solomon, at the
dedication of the Temple, that all was well, but this
appearance shows that Solomon's good start was maintained well into his reign. From his accession to his 24th
year—from when he was about 20 years old to when he
was 40 – things were going well with Solomon spiritually.
During this period he was:

- *overseeing these major building works in Jerusalem,*
- *administering the Kingdom, including its judiciary,*
- *arranging the necessary finances and the labour force*
  needed to keep the projects on schedule and the adminis-
  tration solvent,
- *maintaining some foreign alliances, notably those with*
  Egypt and Phoenicia, and
- *composing and recording some Divinely-inspired*
  Proverbs and other expressions of the Wisdom God had
  given him and which was now disseminated in the
  nation and elsewhere.

The last activity requires a little more consideration at
this stage, for it was a key part of God's plan to reach out
to the nations around when the *"house of prayer for all*
nations" had been built in Jerusalem. The Temple was
never meant to be exclusively for Israel. Gentiles had been
involved in its construction, both bond and free, and when
it was finished it was like a magnet in the midst of the
nations, for it attracted interest and many visits, not just
for its architectural splendour. It was, remember, a visual
aid to teach people about God, that:

- He is there, to be approached;
- There is a Way into His presence; and that
- He is a God of Glory,

- Who demands Sacrifice and Cleansing, without and within, in all those who seek to come to Him.

People came to look and to learn those lessons, because they had heard about both the House and the King. Solomon was an integral part of the package. For, the Scripture records: *"There came of all people to hear the wisdom of Solomon, from all kings of the earth, which had heard of his wisdom"* (1 Kings 4:34).

Temple and Palace

Everything was going well, and God was well pleased with his beloved son,[9] Solomon. How do we know? Because of the two Divine 'seals of approval' that were given in respect of Solomon's work at this time. The first was in the 11th year of Solomon's reign (when he might have been about 30 or 31), when the Temple was completed; the second was in the 24th year, when the Palace and Temple were finished.

Before we look at what God did and said on those two occasions, it may be helpful to note the reason why there was a second seal of approval after the Palace was finished, for that might seem an entirely secular construction, not meriting God's endorsement, far less a second appearance to Solomon. The city of David had occupied only a small portion of what we now think of as the old city of Jerusalem. As any good Bible Dictionary will show, it existed mainly to the south of the later settlement. When David purchased the land-holding belonging to

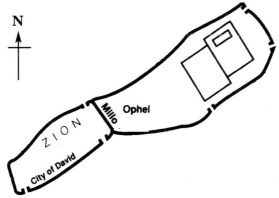

SOLOMON – WISE AND FOOLISH

Araunah the Jebusite, at the angel's direction, he was buy-
ing land outside the boundaries of the then walled city of
Jerusalem, to the north of the existing settlement.

Solomon was instrumental later in extending the whole
city northward to include the Temple site, around which
area he also extended the walls of the city, to ensure
Jerusalem's security. But this would have been easier said
than done on an undulating site. There was a huge job to
be done to level out the foundations for the Temple, by
constructing a vast platform, which exists to this day –
now known as the Temple Mount. Then he probably had to
bridge the gap between the old city and the new Temple
site, by terracing, or filling the intervening area with earth
or hardcore, so that it could become an integral part of the
city. Precisely how this was done is still a matter for
debate amongst archaeologists,[10] largely because there
have been so many other subsequent changes in the vicini-
ty, some of them aimed at destroying the city's defences or
demolishing its public buildings, and because access is cur-
rently prohibited to key areas, like the Temple Mount.
Reviewing the position over several years, the record says
that:

> "David dwelt in the castle; therefore they called it the
> city of David. And he built the city round about, even
> from Millo[11] round about: and Joab repaired the rest of
> the city (1 Chron. 11:7,8) ... This is the reason of the levy
> which king Solomon raised; for to build the house of the
> LORD, and his own house, and Millo, and the wall of
> Jerusalem (1 Kings 9:15) ... Solomon built Millo, and
> repaired the breaches of the city of David his father"
> (11:27).

On the platform of the Temple Mount, Solomon had
already erected the Temple when he proceeded to enlarge
and develop that complex. As the record in Kings indicates, two palaces were constructed,[12] apparently near to
the Temple, interlinked to the complex by a porch of pillars, the House of the Forest of Lebanon – which appears
to have housed armour and weapons, to be used mainly for
ceremonial purposes, and a porch above a throne, where

178

Solomon could sit to issue judicial decisions.

The result was a spiritual and administrative centre, where the work of both King and priests could be viewed and appreciated. The vital issue that now faced the King was: 'How would he fare, when the works were finished and the challenge lay before him of living as a faithful follower of God?' That is precisely the challenge that now confronts each of us. When we have responded to God's gracious call, will we *"continue in the faith grounded and settled, and be not moved away from the hope of the gospel, which ye have heard"* (Colossians 1:23)?

NOTES

[1] David made the comment about sacrifice having to be costly when he bought the Temple site from Araunah (2 Samuel 24:24). At the time Araunah, who had two sons himself, would have given anything to stop the oncoming plague, but David knew that a price had to be paid if God was to dwell among mankind. That principle of costly expenditure is strongly emphasised in preparation for and the execution of the temple project. In the 1960s an American Society of Architects tried to calculate what the Temple had cost to build, including labour and materials, and suggested a total, in today's values, of more than \$87,000,000,000 (more than £40,000,000,000). Much of that expenditure came from the conquest and subjection of the nations that had made war with Israel, and lost. This accords with Haggai 2:7-9 with regard to the future Temple that is to be built.

[2] See page 43, footnote 10, and the comments of Bro. Roberts about the need for patience as the spiritual mind develops.

[3] The Ark of the Covenant is called the *"footstool"* of the LORD in 1 Chronicles 28:2; Psalms 99:5; 132:7 and Lamentations 2:1.

[4] André Lemaire, *"Ancient Israel"* (Ed. Hershel Shanks, 1998) thinks that the recently excavated site of David's palace might, in fact, be Solomon's.

[5] What we can be sure of is that there was a complex of build-

ings, religious and administrative, which were part of a new development to the north of the original City of David, the Jebusite citadel that he had captured and then redeveloped.

[6] *"Solomon made affinity with Pharaoh king of Egypt, and took Pharaoh's daughter, and brought her into the city of David, until he had made an end of building his own house, and the house of the LORD, and the wall of Jerusalem round about"* (1 Kings 3:1).

[7] Solomon's age when he began to reign was considered earlier, at pages 65-66 .

[8] 1 Kings 11:42

[9] Jedidiah, the name that God conferred upon Solomon, means *"beloved of the LORD",* and God promised David that Solomon, as the primary fulfilment of the Davidic covenant, would be His son (2 Samuel 7:12).

[10] See, for example, the debate in *"Biblical Archaeology Review",* July/August 1998, pages 24-44.

[11] The word *"Millo"* is thought to refer to the stone terraces that existed from Jebusite times onwards, or to a citadel that was further fortified by David and others, or to the process of infilling structures – perhaps with hardcore – to level areas off. See *"Jerusalem"* , by Herschel Shanks, pages 25-33.

[12] One was for Solomon, the other for Pharaoh's daughter (1 Kings 7:8).

18

God Warns Solomon

GOD does not appear to people today in the way in which He revealed Himself to Solomon. Twenty years before,[1] at Gibeon – where the Tabernacle was then sited – God had appeared in a dream. Now in Jerusalem – at the new complex – God showed Himself again to His chosen king. In between, there had been visible evidence of God's approval of the Temple when a cloud had filled it,[2] just as it had the Tabernacle in the days of Moses. And God had answered by fire, when the sacrifices were consumed.

God's Answer

All that happened thirteen years before, when Solomon had uttered that remarkable prayer of dedication in which he had asked God to grant certain favours.[3] Then he had listed 7 main circumstances in which God's assistance might be required by Israel, and by individuals –

For an Oath at the Altar
In Defeat
In Drought
In Famine and Pestilence
For the Stranger
In Battle
In Captivity and Exile

Solomon had asked that in every such case of need, and in others that he instanced, God would graciously hear the

181

petition, and give the requested help.

> *"Have respect therefore to the prayer of thy servant, and to his supplication, O LORD my God, to hearken unto the cry and the prayer which thy servant prayeth before thee: that thine eyes may be open upon this house day and night, upon the place whereof thou hast said that thou wouldest put thy name there; to hearken unto the prayer which thy servant prayeth toward this place. Hearken therefore unto the supplications of thy servant, and of thy people Israel, which they shall make toward this place: hear thou from thy dwelling place, even from heaven; and when thou hearest, forgive"* (2 Chronicles 6:19-21).

When Solomon had finished, and the fire had fallen from heaven, to consume the burnt offering and the sacrifices, the House was filled with the glory of the LORD and all the congregation bowed themselves *"with their faces to the ground upon the pavement, and worshipped, and praised the LORD, saying, For he is good; for his mercy endureth for ever"* (2 Chronicles 7:1-3). No doubt Solomon took that as Divine acceptance of the petitions he had made on Israel's behalf. But, so far as we can tell, there was then no verbal response, either by vision, prophet or seer.

It was 13 years before God made such a response, and that a detailed one. Like Gibeon, it was a night-time vision, perhaps a dream. Read the requests Solomon had made,[4] and the Divine response now received,[5] and you will see that:

- God had indeed heard Solomon's prayer, petition by petition, and had remembered everything for which Solomon had asked; nothing had been forgotten;
- He now responded in the affirmative;
- God reinforced Solomon's requests, by repeating them, so that the petitioner could recall precisely what he had wanted earlier in his reign.[6] Perhaps this is an indication that God knew that Solomon's wants were in the process of changing, and not for the better;

182

- In responding positively to the prayer, God was empha-
  sising the key things Solomon had to do;[7]
- In keeping the king waiting, God was also teaching him
  about patient endurance, the same lesson we have to
  learn.[8]

Solomon's Petition	God's Delayed Response
O LORD God of Israel, keep with thy servant David my father that which thou hast promised him, saying, There shall not fail thee a man in my sight to sit upon the throne of Israel; yet so that thy children take heed to their way to walk in my law, as thou hast walked before me. Now then, O LORD God of Israel, let thy word be verified, which thou hast spoken unto thy servant David (2 Chron. 6:16-17)	*As for thee, if thou wilt walk before me, as David thy father walked, and do according to all that I have commanded thee, and shalt observe my statutes and my judgments; then will I stablish the throne of thy kingdom, according as I have covenanted with David thy father, saying, There shall not fail thee a man to be ruler in Israel. But if ye turn away, and forsake my statutes and my commandments, which I have set before you, and shall go and serve other gods, and worship them; then will I pluck them up by the roots out of my land which I have given them* (2 Chron. 7:17-20).
When the heaven is shut up, and there is no rain, because they have sinned against thee; yet if they pray toward this place, and confess thy name, and turn from their sin, when thou dost afflict them; then hear thou from heaven, and forgive the sin of thy servants, and of thy people Israel, when thou hast taught them the good way, wherein they should walk; and send rain upon thy land, which thou hast given unto thy people for an inheritance (6:26-27).	*If I shut up heaven that there be no rain, or if I command the locusts to devour the land, or if I send pestilence among my people; if my people, which are called by my name, shall humble themselves, and pray, and seek my face, and turn from their wicked ways; then will I hear from heaven, and will forgive their sin, and will heal their land. Now mine eyes shall be open, and mine ears attent unto the prayer that is made in this place. For now have I chosen and sanctified this house, that my name may be there for ever: and mine eyes and mine heart shall be there perpetually* (7:13-15).

SOLOMON – WISE AND FOOLISH

God's Solemn Warning

Solomon pleaded the promises God had made – the *"sure mercies of David"* – and God duly reminded him that *"if"* he wanted to be part of that blessed outcome, when a King sits forever upon David's throne, reigning once more from Jerusalem, *"then"* he must be faithful and obedient. If not, he could miss out, despite having sat on that very throne in his mortal life. Notice the careful parallel. In his petition, Solomon acknowledged that before the worshipper could reasonably expect God to respond to his or her request there would have to be a spiritual response. They would have to *"pray toward this place, and confess thy name, and turn from their sin, when thou dost afflict them"*, before they could expect deliverance.

God's response to Solomon was that he, too, must *"walk before me, as David thy father walked"* – that means "by faith" – *"and do according to all that I have commanded thee, and shalt observe my statutes and my judgments; then"*, said God, *"will I stablish the throne of thy kingdom, according as I have covenanted with David thy father" (2 Chronicles 7:17)*. And God added a very specific warning, something that was clearly tailored for Solomon, anticipating the key problem he was about to face. Perhaps this problem was beginning to get a grip on Solomon's life, or God could see that the circumstances were such that it was only a matter of time before it struck. And it concerned the very first of God's Ten Commandments:

> *"If ye turn away, and forsake my statutes and my commandments, which I have set before you, and shall go and serve other gods, and worship them; then will I pluck them up by the roots out of my land which I have given them; and this house, which I have sanctified for my name, will I cast out of my sight, and will make it to be a proverb and a byword among all nations. And this house, which is high, shall be an astonishment to every one that passeth by it; so that he shall say, Why hath the LORD done thus unto this land, and unto this house? And it shall be answered, Because they forsook the LORD God of their fathers, which brought them forth out of the land of Egypt, and laid hold on other gods, and wor-*

184

shipped them, and served them: therefore hath he brought all this evil upon them" (7:19-22)".[9]

Everything that Solomon had worked for in building the House of the LORD, so that God would settle in the midst of His people, in Jerusalem, would be lost if they abandoned their foundation of implicit faith in the living God. He must ensure they did not. Spiritual leadership was of the essence and David was their exemplar. First and foremost they must be true to God and worship Him above all else. God would consider it utterly abominable if they abandoned Him, after all He had done for them. If Solomon wanted to have the blessings promised to his father, he must live the life of faith, like him. If he saw himself as a latter-day Moses[10] – building a Temple to replace the Tabernacle – he must never forget from whence Moses had brought Israel. Out of Egypt!

Latter-Day Moses

There are some indications that God gave Solomon the opportunity and ability to fulfil a role similar to that which Moses had undertaken for Israel at an earlier stage of their worship. Then Moses had both received and interpreted the law for a people who were on the verge of entering their inheritance, an interpretation we know as "Deuteronomy". In that series of final addresses Moses had shown Israel how to live by faith, within the framework of law. And he had spelled out the consequences if they failed to live up to their calling – in chapters 27-32.

Now Solomon did much the same thing, for a people who were entering the second stage of their national relationship, what might be described as their "settled state". They were in the land; God had given them rest from all their enemies; there was a Temple, and a restructured priesthood. They were ready to become God's ambassadors in the midst of the earth. Years before, Moses had anticipated this happening, when he said:

"Behold, I have taught you statutes and judgments, even as the LORD my God commanded me, that ye should do so in the land whither ye go to possess it. Keep therefore and do them; for this is your wisdom and your under-

standing in the sight of the nations, which shall hear all these statutes, and say, Surely this great nation is a wise and understanding people. For what nation is there so great, who hath God so nigh unto them, as the LORD our God is in all things that we call upon him for? And what nation is there so great, that hath statutes and judgments so righteous as all this law, which I set before you this day? Only take heed to thyself, and keep thy soul diligently, lest thou forget the things which thine eyes have seen, and lest they depart from thy heart all the days of thy life: but teach them thy sons, and thy sons' sons" (Deuteronomy 4:5-9).

Now they *were* in the midst of other nations, with God's House in their capital city, and His law governing the nation, administered by His anointed King. People from the nations around were going to be attracted to this marvel of the ancient world; they would come to Jerusalem to learn about the LORD, and to worship Him themselves. But that would only happen, as God intended that it should, if the people obeyed Moses' command to *"take heed to thyself, and keep thy soul diligently, lest thou forget the things which thine eyes have seen"*. So, like a father to his children, Solomon set about interpreting the provisions of the Law of God in everyday terms. He might have called the publication "Laws for Life", or suchlike. We call it the *"Book of Proverbs"*, or at least that part of it written by Solomon,[11] under Divine inspiration.

Laws for Life

Solomon picks up the injunctions given by God through Moses and interprets them, like worked examples.[12] Notice the parallels between Deuteronomy 4:5-8 (cited above) and Proverbs 1:2-7; and between Deuteronomy 6:6-12 (the injunction to put the law in the heart) and Proverbs 6:20-23. Both Moses and Solomon had the same burning desire to see the law written in the heart of the believer – to encourage their people to love God and to serve Him wholeheartedly; because they *wanted* to. Things are exactly the same for us today, except that now we are further urged to respond in that way because of all that God has done for us, including through Christ, His Son.

186

Moses warned against the perils of prosperity, at a time when riches were evidently a burden that had to be carried through the wilderness (see Deuteronomy 8:17) and Solomon amplified and developed that warning, at a time of unequalled prosperity for God's settled people. Like a latter-day Moses, he warned against the dangers of material excess:

"My son, if thou wilt receive my words, and hide my commandments with thee; so that thou incline thine ear unto wisdom, and apply thine heart to understanding; Yea, if thou criest after knowledge, and liftest up thy voice for understanding; if thou seekest her as silver, and searchest for her as for hid treasures; then shalt thou understand the fear of the LORD, and find the knowledge of God. For the LORD giveth wisdom: out of his mouth cometh knowledge and understanding" (Proverbs 2:1-6);

"Treasures of wickedness profit nothing: but righteousness delivereth from death ... The blessing of the LORD, it maketh rich, and he addeth no sorrow with it" (10:2,22);

"Riches profit not in the day of wrath: but righteousness delivereth from death ... He that trusteth in his riches shall fall; but the righteous shall flourish as a branch" (11:4,28);

"There is that maketh himself rich, yet hath nothing: there is that maketh himself poor, yet hath great riches" (13:7).

Of course, the real challenge was: would Solomon take his own advice? Could he on the one hand urge Israel to beware the perils of materialism, and then remain entirely unaffected by his own vast riches?

Material Provisions

The record progresses, in both Kings and Chronicles, to deal with the financing of the building work that had been taking place. It would be wrong, of course, to think that this account was simply chronological, so that there were no financial problems whilst the building was taking place, only when it was finished! Building the Temple necessitated a huge capital expenditure for the nation and Solomon had to manage the national finances accordingly. He needed money so that his work for God could proceed and had several ways of raising the income and capital. They included:

- **Forced labour** – both Jeroboam, the son of Nebat, and Adoram are said to have been employed by Solomon to supervise the *"burden of the house of Joseph"*[13] and *"the tribute"*,[14] respectively;

- **Taxation**;

- **International loans or financial arrangements** – at least this is what Solomon's deal with King Hiram seems to be about;[15]

- **International treaties** to secure peace with the nations around;

- **Trading enterprises** including **International trade** with Hiram.

As a consequence, in this well-managed and entrepreneurial nation, the balance of payments position was remarkably good. *"The king made silver and gold at Jerusalem as plenteous as stones, and cedar trees made he as the sycomore trees that are in the vale for abundance"* (2 Chronicles 1:15). Any Chancellor would be pleased with that fiscal statement. But how would all that affluence affect Solomon? Would he remain true to his calling? Would he be wise or foolish with regard to his spirituality?

Things would get out of control, but not before Solomon had the opportunity to show just what potential he, and Israel, had been given by God to witness for Him to the people that lived round about. He had been given so much, and had become so able in so many ways, so that he could use those talents and possessions to glorify God. The parallel is inescapable so far as we are concerned, richly endowed as we are so many centuries later.

NOTES

[1] See Chapter 9.

[2] See pg. 153.

[3] Some commentators prefer to think that God's response to Solomon's prayer was instantaneous, not delayed as suggested. For example, Lumby, pg.99, asks: *"Was the answer of God delayed through the 13 years that elapsed between the finishing of the Temple and the finishing of the king's house? We can hardly accept the latter supposition as possible. It appears far more likely that the dedication was delayed"*. Others think that the Chronicler has merely included God's response as a tailpiece to the account of Solomon's building work in Jerusalem, though it actually happened when the dedication took place in the king's 7th year. On balance, the idea that it was a delayed response seems to do most justice to the inspired text.

[4] Solomon's petitions are detailed in 1 Kings 8:12-61 and 2 Chronicles 6:1-42.

[5] God's response is in 1 Kings 9:1-9 and 2 Chronicles 7:12-22.

[6] This point is important whether there was a 13 year time lapse or not (see note 3 above). Do we always *want* the things for which we pray, or do we ask for them because we think they are the things for which we ought to ask, especially in public? If that was what Solomon had done (though there is no indication of that), God would have been calling Solomon's bluff!

[7] God also showed Solomon how to keep focused upon the promises, by making the declaration about His own desires: *"I have heard thy prayer and thy supplication, that thou hast made before me: I have hallowed this house, which thou hast built, to put my name there for ever; and mine eyes and mine heart shall be there perpetually"* (1 Kings 9:3). That is exactly how it must be with us, if we are to develop the Divine likeness, always living with Jerusalem in mind.

[8] Someone once wisely said that God gives three answers to prayer – "Yes, No and Wait".

[9] See also 1 Kings 9:3-9, with another express warning about idolatry and the warning that the Temple and the Land could

be lost in that case. God would either bless them or curse them, with strong reference back to Deuteronomy chapter 28.

[10] See pg. 165.

[11] Proverbs 1:1–22:16 and 25:1–29:27 (which were circulated later, in the time of Hezekiah).

[12] See Bro. David Radford's article, *"Proverbs in All Ages"* (published in *"The Bible Student"*, Vol. 4, No. 1, pg.15).

[13] 1 Kings 11:28.

[14] 1 Kings 12:18.

[15] 1 Kings 9:10-14 and 2 Chronicles 8:1-2.

19

Solomon's Witness and Worship

THE prophet Ezekiel would later write about Jerusalem in these terms: *"I have set it in the midst of the nations and countries that are round about her..."* Sadly, he would then proceed to remind the people of what the nations around had seen – a city filled with people who had wickedly rebelled against God's laws, more than the nations around. So, Ezekiel said, God had no option but to remove them far away and give the land some rest from their iniquities.

In Solomon's days such a fate was the last thing on anybody's mind. These were boom years. Unparalleled prosperity was being enjoyed and Jerusalem was a showpiece for the nations around, just as it was meant to be. Moses had said that when the people settled in the Promised Land, *"the nations ... shall hear all these statutes, and say, Surely this great nation is a wise and understanding people. For what nation is there so great, who hath God so nigh unto them, as the LORD our God is in all things that we call upon him for?"* (Deuteronomy 4:6-7).

Solomon and Hiram

That process, of attracting and instructing other nations, had begun when Solomon started the Temple project. As we have seen,[1] Jew and Gentile worked together to build God's House at Jerusalem. Hiram, King of Tyre, played a major role himself. Not only was he supportive of the project – willing to help in every way, in pursuance of the

191

commercial agreement he and Solomon had made – he was enthusiastic about its success. Remember his original response to the suggestion that he should become involved: *"When Hiram heard the words of Solomon ... he rejoiced greatly, and said, Blessed be the LORD this day, which hath given unto David a wise son over this great people"* (1 Kings 5:7).

So far as we can tell, the commercial arrangement, whereby Israel paid Tyre for the manpower and raw materials, seems to have continued throughout the duration of the work, though the quantities of food supplied by Solomon may have varied, dependent upon the profiling of the work over the extensive building period.[2] At the end of the work there is a curious detail recorded about a gift of cities in Northern Galilee. It reads as if Solomon had initiated the idea at the end of the 20 years, perhaps as a "Thank you" to Hiram now that the work had been completed so successfully, but it may be that this had been an understanding from the beginning, as Phoenicia might have wanted some territory where they could grow crops and thus have a more balanced economy. They could have been Solomon's collateral against the substantial loans he obtained from Hiram[3] and they might have been redeemed in course of time, which is why Solomon eventually regained and rebuilt them.[4] This is what the record says:

● **1 Kings 9:10-14**

"It came to pass at the end of twenty years, when Solomon had built the two houses, the house of the LORD, and the king's house (now Hiram the king of Tyre had furnished Solomon with cedar trees and fir trees, and with gold, according to all his desire), that then (1) king Solomon gave Hiram twenty cities in the land of Galilee. And (2) Hiram came out from Tyre to see the cities which Solomon had given him; and they pleased him not. And he said, (3) What cities are these which thou hast given me, my brother? And (4) he called them the land of Cabul unto this day. And (5) Hiram sent to the king sixscore talents of gold. It came to pass at the end of twenty years, wherein Solomon had built the

house of the LORD, and his own house ..."

● **2 Chronicles 8:1-2**

"... that (6) the cities which Huram had restored to Solomon, (7) Solomon built them, and caused the children of Israel to dwell there."

The numbering suggests the most likely sequence of events, whereby:

(1) Solomon passed the cities over;

(2) Hiram surveyed the cities (probably we would have called them "villages");

(3) entered into correspondence with Solomon about them;

(4) expressed some dissatisfaction with the gift;[5]

(5) even so, Hiram advanced Solomon some gold;

(6) then restored the settlements to Solomon, at some later time, who

(7) improved them and settled (or re-settled) Israelites in them.

Kenneth Kitchen has a slightly different view of what happened, whilst explaining that this sort of exchange between rulers was not that unusual in ancient times. He thinks that Hiram wanted an ongoing supply of grain, oil and wine, such as he had been paid by Solomon during the Temple building work, and that David's conquests had given Israel control of the coastland that had previously been Philistine territory. Hiram wanted the coastland; Solomon offered him the slopelands not the coastal plain; and they came to an agreement whereby Hiram got the villages on the coastal plain and Solomon was given some villages which had previously been part of Hiram's occupation, and which was part of Asher's allocated territory.[6]

Brothers Together

By describing the settlements as *"Border Towns"*, next to Phoenicia, the record seems to clear Solomon of any criticism that he was parting with a portion of God's Promised Land, but there is another reason why the transaction appears to have been acceptable. Hiram is described as Solomon's brother – *"What cities are these which thou hast given me, my brother?"* (1 Kings 9:13) – and this term appears to signify more than a commercial partner. It seems to imply a covenant relationship,[7] and this could explain Solomon's willingness to enter into such a transaction, quite apart from any temporary shortage of funds that might have existed.

Solomon and Hiram were partners. That partnership included commercial and trading ventures. It had begun when Hiram made craftsmen and materials available, first for David and then for the Temple project. It had involved the advance of capital funds for Solomon's building projects; if the transfer of villages was to sort out unpaid debts, then Hiram had made a substantial advance of funds. It continued when he supplied servants and sailors to man Solomon's navy, which sailed out of Elath; their expertise was undoubtedly invaluable and no doubt there was a sharing out of the commercial profits in due course. For the venture gave the Phoenicians ready access to the Red Sea, Persian Gulf and Indian Ocean, rather than their usual Mediterranean and Atlantic trading areas.[8]

> *"King Solomon also built ships at Ezion Geber, which is near Elath in Edom, on the shore of the Red Sea. And Hiram sent his men – sailors who knew the sea – to serve in the fleet with Solomon's men. They sailed to Ophir and brought back 420 talents of gold, which they delivered to King Solomon. When the queen of Sheba heard about the fame of Solomon ..."* (1 Kings 9:26 – 10:1 NIV).

Notice, in passing, that the trading undertaken by Solomon's men was the direct means of publicising his Kingdom and his Kingly splendour. Just as we should be telling people about the glories of the King we love, they went out trading and, as a result, people were attracted into Jerusalem and to Solomon. This would hardly have happened if the presence of Hiram's men had meant that commerce was the sole consideration. They do not seem to have had any dampening effect on what might be considered the "missionary" aspect of those visits – to tell the nations about the glory of Jerusalem. The reason is quite simple. Hiram had embraced the faith – he too worshipped Israel's God.

The Covering Cherub

We have already noted Hiram's cooperation in all sorts of ways, including his willingness to engage in a risky maritime trading project with untried and inexperienced landlubbers. But Ezekiel puts the matter beyond doubt. Writing about the then King of Tyre, he laments the fact that Phoenicia no longer had a covenant relationship with Israel's God. In his terms, once they were sheltered under God's wings; now they had been cast out from under cherubic protection, and disaster would surely overtake them:

> *"The Lord Yahweh says this: You used to be a model of perfection, full of wisdom, perfect in beauty; you were in Eden, in the garden of God.*[9] *All kinds of gem formed your mantle: sard, topaz, diamond, chrysolite, onyx, jasper, sapphire, garnet, emerald,*[10] *and your ear–pendants and spangles were made of gold; all was ready on the day you were created.*[11] *I made you a living creature with outstretched wings, as guardian,*[12] *you were on the holy mountain of God; you walked amid red hot coals.*[13] *Your behaviour was exemplary from the day you were created until guilt first appeared in you, because your busy trading has filled you with violence and sin. I have thrown you down from the mountain of God and destroyed you, guardian winged creature,*[14] *amid the coals"* (Ezekiel 28:12-16, NJB).

There had been a time, said Ezekiel, when the King of Tyre had been in covenant relationship with God when he was allowed access to the Temple, as a worshipper. He had then been found acceptable to God, as a result of which he was protected by the High Priest's ministrations (summarized by his breastplate), including the sacrifices he offered on behalf of all those who worshipped Yahweh and, more especially, Hiram had been protected by God's

195

unseen angelic host. But, said Ezekiel, when he (or his descendants) turned away from God they lost all that and, like Adam and Eve, had been cast out of that blissful state.[15]

Other Worshippers

It may well have been that Hiram remained faithful to his calling and his new faith all his life, and that the loss of the 'special relationship' between Israel and Tyre came after his death. We do not know about the timing of that tragedy, just that it eventually happened. Meanwhile other nations were following Hiram's lead and were coming to look and learn. Notice the international dimension to Solomon's work at the centre of the earth:

> *"[Solomon] had dominion over all the region on this side the river, from Tiphsah even to Azzah, over all the kings on this side the river: and he had peace on all sides round about him ... And there came of all people to hear the wisdom of Solomon, from all kings of the earth, which had heard of his wisdom ... Beside that he had of the merchantmen, and of the traffick of the spice merchants, and of all the kings of Arabia, and of the governors of the country ... So king Solomon exceeded all the kings of the earth for riches and for wisdom ... And he reigned over all the kings from the river even unto the land of the Philistines, and to the border of Egypt".[16]*

Solomon had established peace with a series of treaties with surrounding nations, some the result of peace treaties and some the product of peaceful alliances. The former resulted in kings and ambassadors coming to pay tribute year by year, which meant an annual visit to Jerusalem, where they continued to be impressed by all aspects of the King's lifestyle:

> *"King Solomon exceeded all the kings of the earth for riches and for wisdom. And all the earth sought to Solomon, to hear his wisdom, which God had put in his heart. And they brought every man his present, vessels of silver, and vessels of gold, and garments, and armour, and spices, horses, and mules, a rate year by year"* (1 Kings 10:23-25).

Queen of Sheba

The best known of these foreign potentates is, of course, the Queen of Sheba and her meeting with Solomon has been the subject of much speculation and tittle-tattle through the ages, in a way which prefigures the imaginings of the 21st century tabloid press. It is said that she was Solomon's lover; that she was the bride for whom he composed the Song of Songs; that the love-child born of their union was either Nebuchadnezzar or Menelik 1, the founder of Ethiopia.[17] These speculations come about because of a failure to perceive the essentially religious nature of their encounter, which is typical of what was also happening with other foreign rulers.

Solomon's navy, comprising Jews and Gentiles, had been out and about and the Queen of Sheba, probably ruling in the land we now know as Yemen,[18] got to hear about Solomon's wisdom and his kingly glory. So she came to see for herself and to test out his supposed insight and expertise. But, as the inspired writer of 1 Kings is careful to emphasise, hers was to be a voyage of religious discovery:

> *"When the queen of Sheba heard of the fame of Solomon concerning the name of the LORD, she came to prove him with hard questions ... and when she was come to Solomon, she communed with him of all that was in her heart. And Solomon told her all her questions: there was not any thing hid from the king, which he told her not. And when the queen of Sheba had seen all Solomon's wisdom, and the house that he had built ... and his ascent by which he went up unto the house of the LORD; there was no more spirit in her. And she said to the king, It was a true report that I heard in mine own land of thy acts and of thy wisdom ... Happy are thy men, happy are these thy servants, which stand continually before thee, and that hear thy wisdom. Blessed be the LORD thy God, which delighted in thee, to set thee on the throne of Israel: because the LORD loved Israel for ever, therefore made he thee king, to do judgment and justice"* (1 Kings 10:1-10).

This was no sexual pursuit; for her it was a deeply significant spiritual encounter. No doubt they talked about

197

many things that trouble monarchs, including issues of government and diplomacy.[19] But the deep things of her heart would have included intensely personal issues and the outcome was a declared faith in Yahweh, the God of Israel.[20] Notice that Solomon showed her the Temple, including the *"ascent by which he went up unto the house of the LORD"*. Some versions suggest instead that she witnessed *"the burnt offerings he made at the temple of the LORD"* (1 Kings 10:5 NIV).[21] Whether the Hebrew word in question refers to the stairs which permitted Solomon access to the chamber above the Most Holy Place, a colonnade which he had constructed from the Palace,[22] or the sacrifices offered in the Temple Courtyard, by the King or on his behalf, it is clear that the Queen was allowed into the Temple precincts to witness Divine worship. Truly this was now a house of prayer for all nations, just as God had always intended it should be.

Upper Chamber

When looking at the architecture of the temple, the possibility emerged[23] that there could have been a chamber above the Most Holy Place, which might have given the king a measure of privileged access, especially if it gave him a view into the Holy Place. The three-storey high chambers around the Temple are carefully described in the specification. The joists for these chambers were not to be built into the Temple but rested upon ledges or rebatements,[24] for the Temple wall got progressively thinner as it rose in height, which must have given it a rather buttress-like appearance, until the chambers were added.[25] There were stairways that led from one chamber to the next, and if there was indeed a room above the Most Holy Place, *"the ascent by which (Solomon) went up unto the house of the LORD"* might well have taken him (and perhaps them, if the Queen accompanied him) through these apartments into the very heart of the Temple, to a Royal Oratory, or royal chamber.[26]

Details are given about chains that were hung near the Vail and the folding doors that separated the Holy and Most Holy Places, and illustrators are at a loss to know where they might have hung. The Scripture says: *"he made a partition by the chains of gold before the oracle; and he overlaid it with gold"* (1 Kings 6:21). If there would otherwise have been an opening above the Vail, perhaps these chains hung across that area in such a way that they hid from priestly view the inhabitants of the Chamber, but still afforded the King and his companions a view of what was going on. If this is so, and we cannot be certain, it shows that the kings of Israel were regarded as having a special relationship with God, and were given access into His presence in a quite special way.[27]

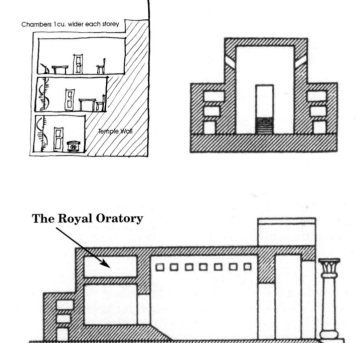

Cross-sections, showing the likely configuration of the Priestly and Storage Chambers alongside the Temple and the possible location of the Royal Oratory, above the Holy Place.

199

An alternative to this is that there was an entry for the King into the courtyard, perhaps even to the brazen scaffold, which was re-positioned near to the pillars of the Porch. If so, what had been a temporary expedient for Solomon might have become a permanent fixture, upon which seats had been set, rather like a royal box in the theatre.[28]

Queen of the South

If there is any remaining doubt about the unnamed Queen's response to the invitation to worship the God of Israel, and to become a believer, those doubts are dispelled by the words of the Lord Jesus. Reproving his adversaries, he once told them that:

"The queen of the south shall rise up in the judgment with this generation, and shall condemn it: for she came from the uttermost parts of the earth to hear the wisdom of Solomon; and, behold, a greater than Solomon is here" (Matthew 12:42).

Jesus was saying that the Queen of Sheba will be there at the judgement because she had come to hear Solomon and had been informed about God's purpose, and the implication is that she remained faithful to her new-found faith and will rise to greet a King much greater than Solomon. So the message is clear to us as well. If kings and queens came to marvel at all that was happening in Jerusalem, in Solomon's time, and to wonder at his kingly glory, how much more should we, in these last days, long to be present in Jerusalem to behold the glory of *"the King of kings and Lord of lords"*.

It's difficult to know exactly when these visitors came to meet with Solomon and to learn from him about the God of Israel. It seems the Queen came after the Temple was finished, and when it was in service, in which case this was in the second half of Solomon's reign. But there may have been a steady stream of people coming to see what was afoot, including during the building construction. And when Solomon began to widen his alliances by inter-marriage, no doubt other royal families and their retinues also came to observe, question and learn.

So everything was still going well for Solomon. All he had to do was to ensure that the international attention he was getting, and all the prosperity that resulted from his super-star status, did not turn his head, and win over his fickle heart.

NOTES

[1] See pages 103-108.

[2] See the substantial differences in the quantities of wheat, barley, oil and wine mentioned in 1 Kings 5:11 and 2 Chronicles 2:10.

[3] Hiram advanced Solomon 120 talents of gold (about 4 tons: 1 Kings 9:14). This vast wealth is not without parallel in the ancient world. See Allan R Millard *"Does the Bible Exaggerate King Solomon's Golden Wealth?"* (BAR 15.3 (1989)), summarised in Kaiser, pgs.280–282.

[4] So Edersheim, Vol. v, pg.103.

[5] According to AB, *"The LXX of 1 Kings 9:13 renders the MT kᵃbōl ("Cabul") as Gk Opion ("border"), implying that the original Hebrew was ("border") or that the translator interpreted it as such."* But also that *"Josephus explained that [Cabul] means "unpleasant" in Phoenician (Ant.8.5.3), and in the Talmud (b. Šabb. 54b) it is explained as "unfruitful".*

[6] See Kitchen, pg.114.

[7] *"'Brother'* may, in such an instance, be a covenant term (note that Hiram was on friendly terms with David, 1 Kings 5:15)", Victor P Hamilton, *"New International Dictionary of Old Testament Theology and Exegesis"*, 1:348.

[8] There has been a lot of scholarly debate about exactly where this Ezion-Geber seaport was on the Gulf of Eilat. According to a Phoenician historian, Hiram sent 800 camels loaded with timber to Ezion-Geber for the building of ten ships. Kaiser, pgs.277-280, gives a summary of the present state of play whereby the offshore island of Jezirat Fauran seems to offer the most natural protected anchorage.

[9] "Eden" is an apposite description of the Temple, which was

adorned with flowers of gold, with alternating palm trees and cherubim. Once again men walked with heavenly beings, albeit ones carved out of cedar wood.

[10] These are 9 of the 12 stones found in the High Priest's breastplate; the LXX lists all 12. Hiram was covered by the mediatorial work of God's high priest, ministered by prayer, sacrifice and offering.

[11] He was God's new creation in Jerusalem (Psalm 87:5), *"born again"* into a right relationship with Yahweh.

[12] He was sheltered by God's angels, which angelic protection and blessing was symbolised by the outstretched wings of the cherubim in the Temple. Hiram's men had helped make those; but God had an army of unseen "living creatures", that cared for His people.

[13] He was able to present sacrifices, for the priests to offer on his behalf at the brazen altar.

[14] The most helpful rendering of this verse, in line with the proffered interpretation, is that of *"The Amplified Bible"* – *"you sinned; therefore I cast you out as a profane thing from the mountain of God, and the guardian cherub drove you out from the midst of the stones of fire"*.

[15] See the above footnotes, appended to the Scriptural passage, for a further explanation. For a similar, though not identical, interpretation of this Scripture, see Bro. Ron Abel's *"Wrested Scriptures"*, 1st Edition, pages 170-172. Note that the reference to the Temple as "Eden, the garden of God, reinforces the symbolic identification of the Holy and Most Holy places, suggested on pages 130-133.

[16] 1 Kings 4:24,34; 10:15; 2 Chronicles 9:26.

[17] See D J Wiseman, pg.129,130, who considers these mere legends.

[18] *"The land whose queen visited Solomon (1 Ki. 10:1ff.; 2 Ch. 9:1ff.) was in all probability the home of the Sabaeans in SW Arabia. J. A. Montgomery (ICC, Kings, 1951, pp. 215f.) contends that the Sabaeans were still in N Arabia in the 10th century B.C. although they controlled the trade routes from S Arabia. On the other hand, Bright, p. 215, while recognizing that the Sabaeans were originally camel nomads, affirms,*

with greater probability, that by Solomon's time they had settled in the E area of what is modern Yemen" (D A Hubbard, *"New Bible Dictionary"*). See also Kitchen, pg.116, *"Sheba is universally admitted to be the same name as the place-name commonly transcribed 'Saba' that denotes a community and kingdom in ancient Yemen in southwest Arabia".*

[19] *"A major purpose of her costly (1 Ki. 10:10) yet successful (1 Ki. 10:13) visit may have been to negotiate a trade-agreement with Solomon, whose control of the trade routes jeopardized the income which the Sabaeans were accustomed to receive from the caravans which crossed their territory—an income on which Sheba (or better Saba) was dependent despite considerable achievement in agriculture due to favourable rainfall and an effective irrigation system"* (Hubbard, op. cit.)

[20] Bro. Ashton, *"Chronicles of the Kings"*, pg.122, also refers to 2 Chronicles 9:8, where the Queen recognises that the Kingdom over which Solomon reigned was, in fact, God's Kingdom, not Solomon's.

[21] So RVmg; NJB; REB *"Whole-offerings"*, though see 2 Chronicles 9:4, "stairs".

[22] See the diagram on pg.173 for a possible route; Wiseman (pg.130) suggests that this could have been the stairway leading up to the Temple, and suggests that: *"This walkway might later have been that known as 'Solomon's Colonnade' (John 25:3; Acts 3:11)".*

[23] See pgs.118-121.

[24] It may be that this restriction was designed to show that God was not to be "used" by His people, for the Temple was sacred and should be respected as such; or it could have been a safeguard to ensure that even if the floor loading of the Chambers was excessive, they would not put the structure of the temple at risk. Either way there are spiritual lessons to be gained, and it is interesting to know that a similar prohibition exists with Ezekiel's Temple (Ezek. 41:6).

[25] There may be an allusion to that buttress-like characteristic in 1 Timothy 3:15, where the ecclesia is termed *"a pillar and buttress of the truth"* (Kelly, *The Pastoral Epistles,* pg.86). It is the ecclesia's function to uphold (pillar) and support (buttress) the truth, despite the godlessness of the world

in which we live.

[26] Farrar, pg.93, notes that when the Tabernacle was brought from Gibeon with its furnishings, the Rabbis believed that it was "put in a room at the top of the Holiest". Perhaps the Lampstand, Table of Shewbread and Altar of Incense were the furnishings of the King's Chamber, above the Most Holy Place.

[27] Shaw Caldecott, pgs.261-273, describes an imaginary scene in which a King enters this 'Royal Oratory', which he thinks was at the front of the Temple (see page 121). He suggests that the approach was by a winding stair, and says this: *"It must have been a work of extraordinary difficulty, in the infancy of architecture, to build a perpendicular flight of stone steps, without other supports than were given by the angle of two walls, to a height of over a hundred feet ... It was the final marvel of the 'ascent by which he went up into the House of the LORD' (1 Kings 10:5) that left no more spirit in the Queen of Sheba"*. He further suggests that this Oratory was the place where Hezekiah came after hearing about the hostile words of Rabshakeh and where Ahab came (2 Chron. 28:24) after he had shut the front doors of the Temple. Bro. H. A. Whittaker also thinks there was a Royal Oratory, in *"Hezekiah the Great"*, CMPA (1985), pg.19, though he does not say where he thinks it was located.

[28] That is Farrar's preferred view, pg.111. He cites in support 2 Kings 11:14; 16:18; 23:3 and 2 Chronicles 6:13.

20

Ever-Expanding Horizons

THE Queen of Sheba brought more than questions when she came from Yemen to learn about Solomon. Notice what the record says about the arrangements associated with her visit, something that seems to be typical of what was happening with other monarchs as well:

> "She came to Jerusalem with a very great train, with camels that bare spices, and very much gold, and precious stones: and when she was come to Solomon, she communed with him of all that was in her heart ... And she gave the king an hundred and twenty talents of gold, and of spices very great store, and precious stones: there came no more such abundance of spices as these which the queen of Sheba gave to king Solomon ... And all the earth sought to Solomon, to hear his wisdom, which God had put in his heart. And they brought every man his present, vessels of silver, and vessels of gold, and garments, and armour, and spices, horses, and mules, a rate year by year" (1 Kings 10:2,10,24-25).

It was a foreshadowing of what will happen when some of the rulers of the world come to pay homage to the Lord Jesus Christ when he is enthroned in glory for, as the Psalmist says about the coming Kingdom, *"The kings of Tarshish and of the isles shall bring presents: the kings of Sheba and Seba shall offer gifts. Yea, all kings shall fall down before him: all nations shall serve him"* (Psalm 72:10,11).

Unparalleled Prosperity

What was Solomon doing with all these gifts and this enormous annual income – for these tributes were being paid "year by year"? And what was he doing with all the rest of the fortune that was being amassed? For gifts from visitors and tributes from subject nations were only the beginning. There were many other sources of income that contributed to the fulfilment of God's promise to the king, for He had said: *"I have also given thee that which thou hast not asked, both riches, and honour: so that there shall not be any among the kings like unto thee all thy days"* (1 Kings 3:13).

Solomon, and many in Israel, became enormously rich and prosperous because of many things, including:

- Tribute from subject nations (666 talents of gold, per annum);[1]

- Direct taxation, in the form of money, goods or unpaid labour;[2]

- Profit from the maritime business, conducted in partnership with Hiram;[3]

- Revenue from the control of the trade routes between Arabia and Mesopotamia;[4]

- Copper smelting and refining;[5]

- Profit from other trading enterprises, notably the sale of horses.

It was not money that was flowing into Solomon's coffers as a result of all this commercial activity, in the way that we might see national prosperity increasing today, with invisible earnings, an improved balance of payments, and suchlike. In ancient times a nation prospered by the physical transfer of commodities, like gold and silver. The Queen of Sheba, for example, brought or sent 120 talents of gold, which is about four tons in weight (the same amount that Hiram had advanced to Solomon).[6] Gold and silver, of course, could be used for adornment or decoration of the various buildings, but it could also be used to pay wages and buy other necessary commodities. But other things that were flowing into the country were of a more exotic and luxurious nature:

"The king had at sea a navy of Tharshish with the navy of Hiram: once in three years came the navy of Tharshish, bringing gold, and silver, ivory, and apes, and peacocks" (1 Kings 10:22).[7]

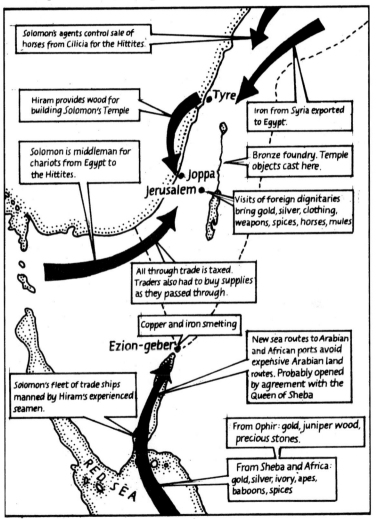

Solomon's agents control sale of horses from Cilicia for the Hittites.

Hiram provides wood for building Solomon's Temple

Solomon is middleman for chariots from Egypt to the Hittites.

Tyre

Iron from Syria exported to Egypt.

Bronze foundry. Temple objects cast here.

Joppa

Jerusalem

Visits of foreign dignitaries bring gold, silver, clothing, weapons, spices, horses, mules

All through trade is taxed. Traders also had to buy supplies as they passed through.

Copper and iron smelting

Ezion-geber

New sea routes to Arabian and African ports avoid expensive Arabian land routes. Probably opened by agreement with the Queen of Sheba

Solomon's fleet of trade ships manned by Hiram's experienced seamen.

From Ophir: gold, juniper wood, precious stones.

From Sheba and Africa: gold, silver, ivory, apes, baboons, spices

RED SEA

Riches and Honour
It may be difficult for us to conceive how a man as rich as
Solomon had become could want to get involved in such
commercial enterprises, just to increase his personal fortune and enlarge Israel's already substantial national
wealth. At first he needed all he could get to finance his
building work and pay for materials and manpower. But,
as he was to say in his own reflections upon such things:
*"the eye is not satisfied with seeing, nor the ear filled with
hearing" (Ecclesiastes 1:8)*. As we also discover, once we
start accumulating things it can be difficult to stop; more
can easily beget a desire for yet more, and then some more
again. It was like that with Solomon, or so it would seem.
Once he had accumulated a lot, he just couldn't stop accumulating.

One illustration may help to illustrate how the process
worked in practice. Solomon took an interest in horses and
chariots, whether for horse racing (the so-called "sport of
kings"), for defence purposes, or for both. At one stage he
had 1400 chariots, 12,000 horsemen and 4000 horses
spread around different cities, including Jerusalem.[8] Many
of those horses were imported from Egypt, and Israel was
well placed geographically to act as middle-man for
nations to the north, engaging in an early form of 10th
century arms-dealing. The record says that:

> *"Solomon had horses brought out of Egypt, and linen
> yarn: the king's merchants received the linen yarn at a
> price. And a chariot came up and went out of Egypt
> [was imported into Israel] for six hundred shekels of sil-
> ver, and an horse for an hundred and fifty: and so for
> all the kings of the Hittites, and for the kings of Syria,
> did they bring them out [export them] by their means" (1
> Kings 8:28,29).*

One writer comments about all this horse-dealing that,
*"since Solomon (controlled) the trade routes across his
extensive realm and since he was in a position to supply his
northern neighbours with these necessary commodities, he
turned the Egyptian horse-and-chariot industry into a
lucrative source of income for himself, as well as a means
of augmenting his military power."* [9] Evidently the Jewish

flair for business is not a recently-acquired skill.

Building Projects

But what was Solomon doing with all this wealth? How was it being used? In the early days, when the Temple was being built, much of it was needed to beautify God's House. For example, side-by-side with the mention of naval exploits is a direct mention of the Temple building and furnishing:

> *"The navy also of Hiram, that brought gold from Ophir, brought in from Ophir great plenty of almug[10] trees, and precious stones. And the king made of the almug trees pillars for the house of the LORD, and for the king's house, harps also and psalteries for singers: there came no such almug trees, nor were seen unto this day"* (1 Kings 10:11,12).

Once the House was finished, other building projects had commenced, and they too would have been resource demanding. To see the nature of all the building now taking place, we must remember to include the King's own comments in the Book of Ecclesiastes. For, whilst Kings and Chronicles detail Solomon's main strategic work in defending and consolidating the kingdom, in his personal account Solomon comes at all this from a quite different angle. First, the public works and those necessary for the defence of the realm:

● **The Temple Complex**

> *"Solomon was building his own house thirteen years, and he finished all his house. He built also the house of the forest of Lebanon ... And he made a porch of pillars ... Then he made a porch for the throne where he might judge, even the porch of judgment ... Solomon made also an house for Pharaoh's daughter, whom he had taken to wife"* (1 Kings 7:1-8).

● **Jerusalem**

> *"Solomon built Millo, and repaired the breaches of the city of David his father"* (11:27).[11]

209

● **Cities for Defence**

"Solomon built Gezer, and Bethhoron the nether, and Baalath, and Tadmor in the wilderness, in the land, and all the cities of store that Solomon had, and cities for his chariots, and cities for his horsemen, and that which Solomon desired to build in Jerusalem, and in Lebanon, and in all the land of his dominion" (9:15,17-19).

These defensive measures are an important indication that Solomon was only too well aware that his international visitors might decide to come back with their armies to help themselves to some of his riches. So, wise man that he was, he took precautions. The four cities specifically named in 1 Kings – Gezer, and Bethhoron the nether, and Baalath, and Tadmor in the wilderness – were strategically located on a trade route and served as a military facility. 2 Chronicles gives further details, showing that it was a very extensive building programme:

"The cities which Huram had restored to Solomon, Solomon built them, and caused the children of Israel to dwell there. And Solomon went to Hamathzobah, and prevailed against it. And he built Tadmor in the wilderness, and all the store cities, which he built in Hamath. Also he built Bethhoron the upper, and Bethhoron the nether, fenced cities, with walls, gates, and bars; and Baalath, and all the store cities that Solomon had, and all the chariot cities, and the cities of the horsemen, and all that Solomon desired to build in Jerusalem, and in Lebanon, and throughout all the land of his dominion" (2 Chronicles 8:2-6).

If this account is chronological, the restoration of those cities from Hiram would have been after the Temple and Palace construction had been completed,[12] and these other works might have followed on. So, much of this work could have taken place in the last 20 years of his reign, though some could have been taking place whilst the major building work was proceeding at Jerusalem, especially if it was work that was required to consolidate the kingdom or sup-

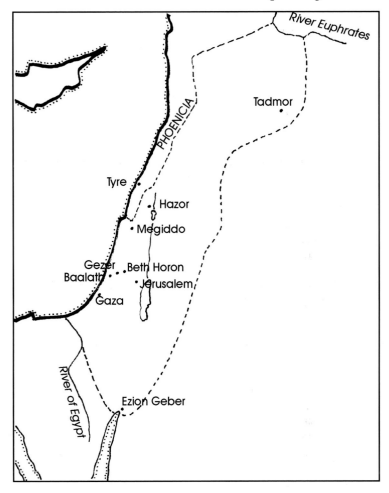

The four cities specifically named as Defence Cities are *"Gezer, and Bethhoron the nether, and Baalath, and Tadmor"*, but *"Hazor, and Megiddo, and Gezer"* are also specifically named (in 1 Kings 9:15) as ones where Solomon undertook building work.

port the extensive trading that was underway – the mention of *"store cities"* and *"chariot cities"* being relevant.[13]

The capture of Hamathzobah may refer to the two adjoining countries of Hamath and Zobah, the former of which is the more northern and had previously sent tribute to King David (2 Samuel 8:3-10). This is the only offensive battle recorded as having taken place in Solomon's reign, though there may have been others, and Tadmor would seem to have been built following victory in the north to secure that border, for it provided a natural defence to the north east.[14]

In addition to these named cites, three others are explicitly mentioned: *"Hazor, and Megiddo, and Gezer"* (1 Kings 9:15), though we are not told what works were done there. In recent years there has been some difference of opinion among archaeologists about which stratum belongs to which period of history, as the historicity of the Bible has again come under attack. But a few years ago there was considerable agreement that the six-chambered gateways found at Gezer, Hazor and Megiddo were designed by the same architect.

It seems that these features are characteristic of Solomon's extensive building or rebuilding work, and whilst the stables at Megiddo are now generally accepted as Ahab's, it is thought that they were built on top of earlier ones constructed in Solomon's reign.[15]

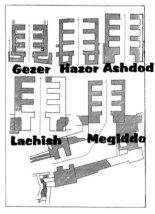

Gezer Hazor Ashdod

Lachish   Megiddo

Similar Gateways in various cities which Solomon fortified

Plastered benches lined each of the gateway chambers, which were probably used as guard rooms and the foundations went down more than 6 feet deep.

Personal Projects

In addition to his supervision or oversight of these large public works, King Solomon was personally engaged in domestic and horticultural projects:

- *"I made me great works;*
- *I builded me houses;*
- *I planted me vineyards:*
- *I made me gardens and orchards, and I planted trees in them of all kind of fruits:*[16]
- *I made me pools of water,*[17] *to water therewith the wood that bringeth forth trees"* (Ecclesiastes 2:4-6).

Solomon's observation about all this building work in Ecclesiastes is very well known. When he stood back and contemplated the satisfaction he had thus obtained, *"I looked on all the works that my hands had wrought, and on the labour that I had laboured to do: and, behold, all was vanity and vexation of spirit, and there was no profit under the sun"* (2:11).

Solomon's inspired writing "Ecclesiastes" is a thesis about the meaning of human existence, written in a very intriguing way. It is outside the scope of this book to examine it in any detail, but one aspect merits attention. Starting from absolute basics – like a man who finds himself alive and tries to make sense of the marvel of his existence – the King reasons himself to the conclusion that nothing makes any sense if there is nothing more to life than this life. The logical outcome, which is reached several times as the argument unfolds (not only at the end of the thesis), is that God alone gives meaning and purpose to human existence. Unless He exists, and is in control, Solomon says that there is no point to anything. Life is not worth living without God.

We may be inclined to wonder why Solomon should start from this premise, given his upbringing, Biblical education and his life-long awareness of the hand of God in his life.[18] Was he losing faith when he wrote the book? He was not, for this is inspired Scripture! The Book shows how Solomon witnessed to people who had no knowledge about God's revealed purpose. You only have to recall the continual encounters the King had with foreign kings and potentates to make sense of this approach.

They came from a wide variety of different countries and religious upbringings, and Solomon needed a way into their mindset which would not immediately alienate them, but which would give him a chance to sweep away their worldly assumptions and preconceptions. He wanted them to think things through from absolute basics and start their religious lives all over again, this time worshipping the one true God: Yahweh, the God of Israel. So, *"Ecclesiastes"* is a God-given revelation which incidentally illustrates Solomon's teaching methods, when he was talking to the Queen of Sheba and others, and answered their *"hard questions"* [19] about life, in all its aspects.

Done Everything!

As part of the description of his own spiritual pilgrimage, Solomon was able to explain that he had tried absolutely everything life had to offer. He lists a formidable catalogue of activities and pleasures, including: *"wisdom, ... madness and folly ... mirth ... pleasure ... laughter ... wine ... great works ... servants and maidens ... great possessions of great and small cattle ... silver and gold, and the peculiar treasure of kings ... singers and women singers, and the delights of the sons of men, as musical instruments, and that of all sorts"* (1:17-2:8).

Summing up that aspect of his enquiry into life, Solomon concludes that:

> *"I was great, and increased more than all that were before me in Jerusalem:*[20] *also my wisdom remained with me. And whatsoever mine eyes desired I kept not from them, I withheld not my heart from any joy; for my heart rejoiced in all my labour: and this was my portion of all my labour"* (2:9-10).

His wisdom remained with him – by which he means that he never lost the faculty for objective thought and was able to make a measured and rational assessment of everything he experienced. Solomon claims that he wasn't carried away, nor was he unduly influenced, by all these things with which he experimented. He kept his head. Or at least, when he paused for thought, he says that he was able to appraise what he had accomplished, in the light of eternity. When he came to himself, it was his practice to ask in a cold and calculating way: "What is the long-term benefit of all that?" He was forced to answer that: "It has no such benefit; it is all empty, frustrating, and futile!" Or, in his own words:

"I have seen all the works that are done under the sun; and, behold, all is vanity and vexation of spirit" (1:14).

Choose Wisdom

Writing for us, as well as for Gentile rulers, under the guidance of the Spirit, Solomon explains over and over, both in "Ecclesiastes" and in the section of "The Book of Proverbs" that he wrote, that if we follow the way of Wisdom, first and foremost, all the other things we need in life will come as well.[21] Yet, there may seem to be a problem here. How could a man as wise as Solomon – who was given a special gift of wisdom by God – point this out to us and yet go astray himself? Is there a difference between the wisdom Solomon was given and the sort of wisdom we need for everyday discipleship? And could he say one thing under the guidance of the Spirit, yet do something different himself?

There are special types of wisdom that God bestowed at various times for particular purposes.[22] Pre-eminently God had given Solomon the wisdom to govern, perceive, administer, construct and reveal. This sort of special wisdom included that which Solomon had when he was inspired by God to write Proverbs, Ecclesiastes and the Song of Solomon, and that Divine insight afforded him when he was shown the plans and specifications of the Temple God wanted built in Jerusalem.

When Solomon urged the merits of Wisdom, rather than Folly, he was not advocating that ordinary people should seek after his sort of special wisdom, revelation or ability. That, after all, was a special gift from God. Instead he was urging his immediate and eventual readers to live wisely, in accordance with the revealed will of God, and to

215

manifest the fruits of wisdom in their everyday conduct and behaviour. That was the choice he, too, had to make for himself. Despite having special gifts of Wisdom and a God-given insight, he still had to make the right choices in his daily life if he was to become a king in the Kingdom of God on earth, with the Lord Jesus ruling on David's throne. So, the material benefits and blessings that had come his way were not without their spiritual purpose. They posed for him the challenge we too face. What did he really value? Where did his heart really lie – with the things of this world, or with the things of God?

How would Solomon cope with the challenges presented by the increasing affluence that was being experienced by himself, his court and his nation? Could he keep his head while all around were losing theirs? That is the challenge for us too in our affluent and self-satisfying age.

NOTES

[1] 1 Kings 10:14. 666 talents was over 20 tons of gold per annum. Kitchen, pg.133,134 makes some helpful comments about wealth in the ancient world in general, to show that these figures are by no means excessive. Tyre paid 150 talents of gold to Assyria in c.730 B.C.; and when Alexander the Great conquered Persia, he abstracted 7,000 tons of gold from that Empire. So there was a lot of it about!

[2] The non-Israelite inhabitants of the land were almost made slaves (1 Kings 9:20,21), and the Israelite inhabitants had to make some contribution of labour for the construction of the Temple (1 Kings 5:13-18).

[3] 1 Kings 9:26-28; 10:22; 2 Chronicles 8:17-18; 9:21.

[4] *"Solomon's control of the frontier districts of Zobab, Damascus, Hauran, Ammon, Moab and Edom meant that he monopolized the entire caravan trade between Arabia and Mesopotamia from the Red Sea to Palmyra ('Tadmor,' 2 Chron. 8:4), an oasis 140 miles northeast of Damascus, which he built (I Kings 9:18) . By thus exercising control over virtually all the trade routes both to the east and to the west of the*

Jordan, the Israelite monarch was able substantially to increase the revenue flowing into the royal coffers by exacting tolls from the merchants passing through his territories (I Kings 10:15)", Unger, *"Archaeology and the Old Testament"*, pg.222.

[5] An interesting variant on our usual view about the ships of Tarshish is as follows: *"Ezion-geber (Elath), his manufacturing centre and sea-port on the Gulf of Aqabah, was a main base of his trading activities. From here his fleet manned by Phoenicians (the Israelites apparently had neither love for nor knowledge of the sea) sailed to Ophir carrying smelted copper. The phrase 'ships of Tarshish' is probably to be translated 'refinery ships', i.e. ships equipped to carry smelted ore. In return, these ships brought back splendid cargo"*, D A Hubbard, *"New Bible Dictionary"*, pg.1203. However, Wiseman, pg.133, prefers the interpretation that these were large ocean-going vessels.

[6] See pages 191-194.

[7] Wordsworth, vol iii, pg.45: *"His navy brought apes and peacocks to Jerusalem every three years. And why were they brought to Jerusalem? Probably to gratify curiosity; to amuse the people by the gambols and tricks and grimaces of the one, and by the splendour and pageantry and painted plumage of the other; and perhaps to while away the time of the strange women who were brought in those ships of Solomon, and to whom 'Solomon clave in love,' instead of cleaving to the LORD (xi.2), and who 'turned away his heart from serving the LORD to go after other gods.'"*

[8] 1 Kings 4:26; 10:26-29; 2 Chronicles 1:14-17; 9:25,28.

[9] Unger, op. cit. pg. 224. Kitchen, pg.115, explains that military necessity demanded that Egypt breed her own chariot horses in the second and early first millennia and he cites supporting evidence in Egypt of extensive stabling and appropriate records. Of the chariots he says *"At 600 shekels from Egypt and retailed by Solomon to northern rulers (Arameans and [Neo]-Hittites), these are clearly richly adorned 'Rolls Royce' models for fellow kings, not simply lightweight runabouts of wood and leather"*.

[10] *"Almug"* is thought to be Indian red sandalwood (Pterocarpus santalinus). See E N Hepper, *"Encyclopaedia of*

SOLOMON – WISE AND FOOLISH

Bible Plants", 1992, pg.158.

[11] *"Millo"* which means *"fill"* is thought to refer to the work of stone terracing in Jerusalem to level the sloping site. As the Temple and Palace were to the north of the City of David, Solomon would also have had to extend the city walls to enclose them, as well as repairing the existing ones (see 1 Kings 9:15).

[12] See page 193.

[13] Garstang, pgs.339,340, describes the fortification of the cities that are mentioned as a master-stoke which: *"left Solomon in control of the great high road which ran through his kingdom by way of Gezer, Megiddo, and Hazor, the importance of which was incalculable from the commercial standpoint as it was the only arterial road between Egypt and Syria, and had numerous ramifications".*

[14] Wood, *"Israel's United Monarchy"*, pg.324.

[15] See BAR 25:02 (March/April 1999) *"Excavating Hazor: Solomon's City Rises from the Ashes";* and Amnon Ben-Tor and Yigael Yadin, *"Hazor"*, 1975, pgs.187-223. Kitchen comments, pg.150, as follows: *"The net result for Hazor, Megiddo and Gezer is that cast-iron certainty over attribution of particular remains to the time (e.g.) of Solomon is not strictly possible ... but they come closer to reality and can be retained as a sensible working hypothesis."*

[16] These gardens may have been outside Jerusalem, which was quite a small city at this time, even with Solomon's enlargement to the north. But there does appear to have been a garden near the palace, later known as *"the king's garden"* (2 Kings 25:4), at the junction of the valleys of Hinnom and Kedron (Stanley, pg.197).

[17] *"The pools of water used to irrigate his young trees may be the traditional pools of Solomon which are located several miles southwest of Jerusalem in the Valley of Artas. There, according to Robinson ... 'Huge reservoirs built of squared stones and bearing marks of the highest antiquity were set in a steep part of the valley' "*, W C Kaiser, *"Ecclesiastes"*, 1979, pg.56.

[18] For example, God had appeared to him twice.

¹⁹ 2 Chronicles 9:1.

²⁰ This comment is sometimes thought to indicate that Solomon could not have written Ecclesiastes, because only David had reigned in Jerusalem before him. But there had been a series of kings through the ages, right back to Melchizedek, and including Adoni-Bezek (who might have been a king after the order of Melchizedek) and they had been wise and able rulers, because Jerusalem had remained safely in Jebusite hands despite Israel's conquest of the land round about the city. The fact that Solomon refers to those Gentile kings as well adds weight to his argument – he was better placed that anyone, Jew or Gentile, to make an assessment of the meaning of life.

²¹ Compare Jesus' words, *"Seek ye first the kingdom of God, and his righteousness; and all these things shall be added unto you"* (Matthew 6:33).

²² For example, Aholiab and Bezaleel were given Spirit gifts to enable them to build the Tabernacle; and the apostles were given similar gifts to establish the First Century ecclesias.

21

Living like a King

SOLOMON had everything he could possibly want – a Kingdom which was admired and respected; Kings and Queens coming to marvel at his achievements; riches in abundance; the love and loyalty of his subjects; and a good relationship with Almighty God, which had great promise for the future as well. What else could he need?

If only it was as simple as that! If only we could take stock of our own blessings, which are abundant, and then adjust our sights and expectations accordingly. If only we always wanted the things we need, and nothing else.

Solomon was just like us, only more so, because he had the opportunities that came the way of an Eastern monarch at a time when kingship could be despotic and unchallenged rule. People looked to the king with admiration and took him as their example; their role model. So he was in a position which had very great responsibility indeed – for the guidance of the nations around; the leadership of his own nation; the example given to his courtiers; and especially for the influence he had upon his own family. They would all take their lead from him and were bound to be hugely influenced by his decisions. And he was responsible, before God, for the decisions he took and the lifestyle he adopted, insofar as it would affect his spiritual life, and theirs. So are we.

"In all his glory"

We have seen the vast prosperity that King Solomon and many in Israel enjoyed at this time – it was the best time ever for the national economy, a real boom time. God had promised Solomon riches and they came in abundance. At first he used much of this national wealth for public building works, especially works designed to glorify God; then the money began to be spent on things which were designed to magnify the king – not so much the institution, more the individual. Solomon reigned in splendour:

> *"King Solomon made two hundred targets of beaten gold: six hundred shekels of gold went to one target. And he made three hundred shields of beaten gold; three pound of gold went to one shield: and the king put them in the house of the forest of Lebanon. Moreover the king made a great throne of ivory, and overlaid it with the best gold. The throne had six steps, and the top of the throne was round behind: and there were stays on either side on the place of the seat, and two lions stood beside the stays. And twelve lions stood there on the one side and on the other upon the six steps: there was not the like made in any kingdom"* (1 Kings 10:16-20).

This is a grand portrayal of a great King sitting in royal splendour upon his mighty and marvellous throne. Imagine what it was like when he processed about his courtyard, or went to the temple, surrounded by uniformed guards who were bearing golden shields, glittering in the sunlight. What would it have been like to wander among the shield-adorned columns of the House of the Forest of Lebanon, which emulated the splendour of pagan palaces in the countries around? [1]

The royal throne was probably inlaid with gold and ivory and was set on top of the six steps.[2] The lion was the tribal emblem of Judah (Genesis 49:9) and the twelve lions would probably have symbolised the twelve tribes of Israel, whilst the whole would have typified the *"Lion of the tribe of Judah"* (Revelation 5:5) and his glorious reign on David's ancient throne. Josephus says that:

> *"He also made himself a throne of prodigious bigness, of ivory, constructed as a seat of justice, and having six steps to it; on every one of which stood, on each end of the step, two lions, two other lions standing above also; but at the*

sitting place of the throne, hands came out, and received the king; and when he sat backward, he rested on half a bullock, that looked towards his back; but still all was fastened together with gold".[3]

If the historian was preserving a Jewish tradition, and there is some doubt about this as he had a colourful imagination, the combination of the Lion and the Ox (or bullock) would have made a powerful statement about rulership and service. For, as David had come to understand, the ruler must first prove able to rule himself (2 Samuel 23:3). And for all its extravagance and luxurious appearance, we should never forget that Solomon was God's appointed King: he sat upon *"the throne of the LORD"* over Israel (1 Chronicles 29:23). What mattered was the man who sat upon this exalted throne, and the standard of justice that he dispensed, not the throne itself. That was what set him apart from the thrones of other rulers round about.

"He will take ..."

When the people had asked for a king, so they could be like the other nations, Samuel warned them in no uncertain terms that it would cost them dearly. Kings, he said, were an expensive commodity and one particular phrase is repeated several times:

> *"This will be the manner of the king that shall reign over you: **He will take** your sons, and appoint them for himself, for his chariots, and to be his horsemen ... And he will take your daughters to be confectionaries, and to be cooks, and to be bakers. And he will take your fields, and your vineyards, and your oliveyards, even the best of them, and give them to his servants. And he will take the tenth of your seed, and of your vineyards, and give to his officers, and to his servants ... And he will take your menservants ... and put them to his work. He will take the tenth of your sheep: and ye shall be his servants. And ye shall cry out in that day because of your king which ye shall have chosen you; and the LORD will not hear you in that day"* (1 Samuel 8:11-18).

Now Israel was finding out just what Samuel meant, for the court and courtiers lived and ate in style. Luxury was the order of the day, with no expense spared. We have seen, from his agreement with Hiram for the loan of 120 talents of gold, that Solomon was quite capable of living beyond his means, as some of us are too. But *he* had the advantage of being able to balance his personal budget by increasing taxation or some new fiscal arrangement.

The detail in Scripture of all this splendour helps us to understand what life was like in Solomon's court, but it leaves one vital question unanswered: "What was all this doing to Solomon and to those with him?" That is something we all have to ask ourselves, in view of our own self-indulgent and extremely comfortable circumstances, if that is the lifestyle we too enjoy.

"They were eating and drinking ..."

When considering the administrative changes Solomon introduced, with boundaries which crossed the tribal territories, we noted that one reason was the need to keep the King's court supplied with food all year round. It wasn't that he was a huge eater, like Henry VIII, tossing chicken bones in every direction; he had a huge retinue of followers and he entertained lavishly, including overseas visitors who came to marvel at his wisdom and his works.

> *"Solomon's provision for one day was thirty measures of fine flour, and threescore measures of meal, ten fat oxen, and twenty oxen out of the pastures, and an hundred sheep, beside harts, and roebucks, and fallowdeer, and fatted fowl"* (1 Kings 4:22,23).

This level of consumption, year after year, was bound in time to be seen as a burden the common people had to bear. Remember that they were also subject to compulsory service on the labour gangs which were building the public works (1 King 5:13f.), which meant four months work every year; whether it was paid or unpaid we are not told. Israel benefited from all this peace and prosperity, of course. We are told that: *"Judah and Israel were many, as the sand which is by the sea in multitude, eating and drinking, and making merry"* (1 Kings 4:20). But we also know, from subsequent events in Rehoboam's reign, that a lot of resistance built up.[4] For, while ordinary folk, like us, were working hard to make the necessary provision, the King and his court were enjoying a very luxurious lifestyle indeed.[5]

> *"All king Solomon's drinking vessels were of gold, and all the vessels of the house of the forest of Lebanon were of pure gold; none were of silver: it was nothing account-ed of in the days of Solomon"* (1 Kings 10:16-21).

Some of us might be a bit fussy about the cups we like to drink out of, perhaps preferring 'a nice china cup'. But Solomon and his courtiers didn't like to drink out of silver cups; that was too common for them. Only gold was good enough! That speaks volumes: they had definitely acquired a taste for the good life, and it was very good indeed.

Some estimates suggest that it would have taken thirty or forty thousand people to consume that amount of food and drink each day,[6] which would give another idea of the extent of Solomon's court and the number of 'hangers-on' there were. But, whilst all this detail is there to make a particular point about Solomon, it also poses a challenge for us. How much of our income and affluence do we use for ourselves, so that we can enjoy the best things of life? And what influence do our possessions, like nice clothes, smart houses, and suchlike, have on the sort of people we are before God, and towards one another?

The Kingdom of God

Solomon was God's appointed king; the people he ruled over were God's people and the law he administered was God's law, and he was also subject to that law. Was this affluence permissible and sensible; or was it vastly over-done? When God granted Solomon the gift of wisdom, He also promised him riches and honour:

> *"I have given thee (1) a wise and an understanding heart; so that there was none like thee before thee, nei-ther after thee shall any arise like unto thee. And I have also given thee that which thou hast not asked, both (2) riches, and (3) honour: so that there shall not be any among the kings like unto thee all thy days. And (4) if thou wilt walk in my ways, to keep my statutes and my*

commandments, as thy father David did walk, then I will lengthen thy days" (1 Kings 3:12-14).

Notice that gifts (2) and (3) would come from God whether Solomon walked in God's ways or not. Obedience to God's law was not required for prosperity; indeed, it could be seen as a challenge to Solomon. But if he exercised wisdom (which was the first gift) he would be able to ensure that affluence and public acclaim did not go to his head. It's a point that he makes forcibly in the Book of Proverbs when he contrasts wisdom with anything else that might appear to have lasting value, making an obvious reference back to God's promises in that dream at Gibeon:

"Happy is the man that findeth (1) wisdom, and the man that getteth understanding. For the merchandise of it is better than the merchandise of (2) silver, and the gain thereof than fine gold. She is more precious than rubies: and all the things thou canst desire are not to be compared unto her. (4) Length of days is in her right hand; and in her left hand riches and (3) honour" (Proverbs 3:13-16).

It was a matter of keeping that order of priorities: wisdom and understanding were the first priority, for they could keep everything else in check. Obedience to God's law would bring its own reward, both in this life and in the life to come. God had richly endowed him in many ways. Would Solomon use those talents and endowments in a way that glorified God, or would he lapse into self indulgence? It's the very same challenge that faces us every day.

The King's Law

God's law contained a specific provision to which the appointed king was to be subject. He was to beware certain dangers which had been warned about long before there were appointed kings. This was what Moses had recorded for the benefit of all future monarchs:

"Thou shalt in any wise set him king over thee, whom the LORD thy God shall choose: one from among thy

brethren shalt thou set king over thee: thou mayest not set a stranger over thee, which is not thy brother. But (1) he shall not multiply horses to himself, nor (2) cause the people to return to Egypt, to the end that he should multiply horses:[7] forasmuch as the LORD hath said unto you, Ye shall henceforth return no more that way. (3) Neither shall he multiply wives to himself, that his heart turn not away: (4) neither shall he greatly multiply to himself silver and gold" (Deuteronomy 17:15-17).

These forbidden things were the very things Solomon now proceeded to do, enthusiastically. As we have seen earlier:

(1) *he became very active in the horse business – both as an end-user and as a trader;[8]*

(2) *he married an Egyptian wife who came complete with a peace treaty with that very people; and then he proceeded;*

(3) *to collect many other wives and concubines;*

(4) *in the process further multiplying silver and gold.*

Notice the key expression – repeated three times. He must guard *"himself"* with all diligence; self-indulgence can be the path to spiritual ruin. Doing things for Israel, God's nation, was one thing. Doing them to satisfy the flesh was a very different, and desperately dangerous, thing.

Then, as now, the danger was that he would be unable to resist the temptations of life: *"the lust of the flesh, and the lust of the eyes, and the pride of life" (1 John 2:16).*[9] Moses understood these dangers. For, having warned any future king about the dangers of accumulating things for himself, rather than for the nation as a whole, he added:

"(The book of the law) shall be with (the king), and he shall read therein all the days of his life: that he may learn to fear the LORD his God, to keep all the words of this law and these statutes, to do them: that his heart be not lifted up above his brethren" (Deuteronomy 17:19).

First things First

It was a lesson that Solomon had taken to heart for, wise man that he was, he once counselled us: *"Keep thy heart with all diligence; for out of it are the issues of life"* (Proverbs 4:23). But could he keep his spiritual balance, surrounded as he was with such a glamorous lifestyle? Could the pursuit of wisdom prevail over everything else; or would it be forced into second place?

Reflecting the way things were going, the inspired writers of Kings and Chronicles make a subtle but telling comment when describing the luxuries of Solomon's court:

"So king Solomon exceeded all the kings of the earth for (2) riches and for (1) wisdom. And all the earth sought to Solomon, to hear his wisdom, which God had put in his heart" (1 Kings 10:23,24);

"And king Solomon passed all the kings of the earth in (2) riches and (1) wisdom. And all the kings of the earth sought the presence of Solomon, to hear his wisdom, that God had put in his heart" (2 Chronicles 9:22,23).

This careful repetition in both accounts points to the fact that things had come to a critical point in Solomon's spiritual life. Could he keep his wisdom, or would other things get the better of him?

NOTES

[1]See Kitchen, pg.127-129, for information about other, shield-festooned, palaces in Egypt, Phoenicia and Urartu. Stanley, pgs.194-200 takes such an imaginary tour, drawing heavily upon the descriptions of Solomon in the Song of Songs.

[2] Students of numerology will observe that for all its splendour, this was the throne of a man (it had 6 steps, not 7).

[3] *"The Works of Josephus"* (*Antiquities* 8.140).

[4] Bright, pg.221, suggests that the monthly food provision from each new territory "placed a terrific strain on districts averaging 100,000 people apiece", although Kitchen, pg.133, calculates that the whole year's need of barley would only require about 13 square kilometres (or 5 square miles) of pro-

ductive land. He shows that similar amounts of food were consumed at nearby courts. Even so, there is no doubting the resentment that all this eventually caused (1 Kings 12:4).

[5] Garstang, pg.335: *"The essentially personal nature of the narrative, moreover, though truly reflecting Solomon's character and policy, almost excludes fresh light upon the social conditions and life of the people, towards whose welfare Solomon was, in fact, apathetic ... It is indeed to be inferred that during his reign social conditions were retrograde, and that the community as a whole had little chance of sharing in Solomon's personal prosperity or profiting from his various importations."* Farrar, pg.127: *"The results of this wide commerce which so dazzled Solomon's contemporaries were far more showy than solid. If it enriched the king, it by no means seems to have enriched the people. Even the king must have been liable to heavy losses, and his gains, whatever they may have been, were neutralized by the overwhelming expenses necessary to maintain the splendour and luxury of a Court arranged upon a scale too ambitious for the resources of his little kingdom. Every branch of the trade seems either to have ceased or languished at the death of Solomon or even earlier."*

[6] Quoted by W C Kaiser Jnr., *"Ecclesiastes – Total Life"*, pg.56.

[7] King David was careful to ride upon a mule (1 Kings 1:33) though both Absalom and Adonijah had horses, so by David's time horses were being used for warfare and for personal transport, at least by princes (Yigael Yadin, *"The Art of Warfare in Biblical Lands"*, 1963, pg.285). Solomon, however, had 4000 horses, which indicates a huge expansion (see 2 Chronicles 9:25; 1 Kings 4:26, where the KJV is incorrect – modern versions read 4,000, not 40,000).

[8] See page 208.

[9] The apostle John adds, *"...And the world passeth away, and the lust thereof: but he that doeth the will of God abideth for ever"* and that was very true for Solomon. All that he had accumulated was destined to pass away very rapidly indeed, for at his death all this wealth would attract the nations around who would come to help themselves, if they could.

22

Solomon's Women

SOLOMON had plenty of people around him who were anxious to share his extravagant life style, and he had a wife. He had married whilst still quite a young man, yet nothing is said about that wife until Rehoboam ascends the throne, when we learn that:

"Rehoboam the son of Solomon reigned in Judah. Rehoboam was forty and one years old when he began to reign, and he reigned seventeen years in Jerusalem ... And his mother's name was Naamah an Ammonitess" (1 Kings 14:21)[1]

Solomon reigned for forty years, so Rehoboam had been born already at the time of Solomon's coronation, even though the new king was still only twenty years old, or even younger. We know nothing about the circumstances of the courtship or marriage, unless these are depicted in the Song of Solomon, a poetic sojourn in which a young man searches for his true love. Such an exploration is, however, outside the scope of this book.

Naamah is only otherwise mentioned in 1 Kings 14:31 (when King Rehoboam died) and 2 Chronicles 12:13 (the parallel account). The fact that she is mentioned twice in 1 Kings 14 might indicate the important effect she had on Rehoboam, and it might point to the fact that she was also alive when he died. If so she would have been quite aged by then (her married age + at least 41 years + 17 years):

"Rehoboam was forty and one years old when he began to reign ... And his mother's name was Naamah an

Ammonitess ... And Rehoboam slept with his fathers, and was buried with his fathers in the city of David. And his mother's name was Naamah an Ammonitess" (vv 21,31).

Solomon Marries Again

We would like to know much more about Solomon and Naamah, and to get her reaction when Solomon married again, and again; but we know nothing more, at least nothing more from the historical accounts. What we are told is that the king also married an Egyptian princess, and that this marriage took place early on in his reign. That information is given up-front, before the building of the Temple had commenced (in the fourth year of his reign), and we are told where she lived in Jerusalem before the completion of the Temple (in his eleventh year), after which a separate Palace was constructed for her (completed in his 24th year).[2] The marriage itself is mentioned in the Divine record without critical comment, even perhaps with approval:

> *"Solomon made affinity with Pharaoh king of Egypt, and took Pharaoh's daughter, and brought her into the city of David, until he had made an end of building his own house, and the house of the LORD, and the wall of Jerusalem round about ... And Solomon loved the LORD, walking in the statutes of David his father: only he sacrificed and burnt incense in high places"* (1 Kings 3:1-3).

Being sensitive to Israelite feelings, Solomon kept her outside the City of David and then built her a separate palace. There may have been some political logic to this, in that he needed to show nearby, and powerful, Egypt that he was paying Pharaoh's daughter proper respect. But it could also be that this new wife – perhaps his second after Naamah – was somewhat disapproving of her new husband's increasingly extravagant lifestyle, and that Solomon solved that dilemma by letting her lead her own life, somewhat independent of his own.[3]

Egyptian Pharaoh

According to Jewish tradition, based upon the Biblical

230

record,[4] it is said that she became a Jewish proselyte. If so, she was the exception to the general rule. But who exactly was she and what advantage did Solomon, and Israel, get from a marriage alliance of this sort? It is suggested by commentators that it was unusual for Egyptian pharaohs to allow arranged marriages with other royal houses, which was once the case when Egypt was a much mightier power. Kitchen, a leading Egyptologist, is dismissive of these outdated comments, observing that:

"Solomon lived not in the fourteenth century but in the tenth! Times had changed; no vast empires now existed; the old Egyptian royal lines had long since been replaced by 'new men' not tied to the ways of four hundred years before – any more than (in Britain) subjects of Elizabeth II are tied to the full cultural norms obtaining under Elizabeth I, four centuries before. The entirely unjustified denials by Old Testament scholars notwithstanding, the following facts are clear. No New Kingdom pharaoh is ever known to have given a daughter to either a foreigner or a commoner ... In stark contrast, the period of the Twenty-First– Twenty-Third Dynasties is precisely when we do find kings' daughters being married off to commoners and foreigners ... Various Twenty-Second Dynasty kings married off their daughters to commoners (higher priesthood, viziers, etc.) – practices entirely unheard of four centuries earlier! Thus there is no problem in Siamun giving a daughter to a foreign ruler (especially if he himself were of Libyan blood) at this time, and biblical scholars will have to accept that fact; Amenophis III's old-style prejudice way back in 1357 is irrelevant to 'modern' 967!" ("On the Reliability of the Old Testament", pg.111).

Although an attempt has been made to recast the chronology of Egypt, unhelpfully in my view, Kitchen gives sound reasons why the Pharaoh in question is Siamun of the Twenty-First Dynasty, who reigned in Egypt from 979/978 B.C. to 960/945 and who would thus have been contemporary with the first ten years of Solomon's reign (971/970 to 961/960 B.C.). A triumphal scene from this king's reign shows, to Kitchen's satisfaction at least, that he alone of the Twenty-First Dynasty kings made a successful incursion to the north of Egypt. Heading north would lead the Pharaoh first to Philistine territory and then to Gezer (the city that was later given to Solomon as a marriage dowry). He speculates why such a raid might have been made by Egyptian forces, in conjunction with Solomon's army, to subdue the Philistines and to secure the trading route, and his suggestions seem very plausible.[5]

There are, of course, other suggestions about which Pharaoh it was and why he would have been interested in an alliance.[6] But any displacement of the established chronology needs to take account of the facts that:

- Solomon was very careful to observe all the necessary protocols which befitted such an important alliance, including building his Egyptian queen a palace of her own, and did nothing at first to show her any disrespect;

- A very different state of affairs existed between Egypt and Israel in the latter part of Solomon's reign, when Egypt willingly gave refuge to Jeroboam (1 Kings 11:40);

- The Pharaoh who gave such refuge is named as *"Shishak"*, better known to Egyptologists as "Shoshenq I", who reigned in Egypt from 945 to 924 B.C. (Solomon's reign ended in 930 B.C.).

More Alliances

If the established chronological structure is sound, as it seems to be, then Solomon's freedom of movement would have increased in relation to Egypt after the death of Pharaoh Siamun (in Solomon's tenth or eleventh year). The alliance was clearly important to Israel, for it is mentioned many times (1 Kings 3:1; 7:8; 9:16,24; 11:1; 2 Chronicles 8:11) and it may have given Solomon the idea that it would further secure his other national boundaries if he extended the practice and established further marriage alliances, for that is what he now did:

"But king Solomon loved many strange women, together with the daughter of Pharaoh, women of the Moabites, Ammonites, Edomites, Zidonians, and Hittites: of the nations concerning which the LORD said unto the chil-

dren of Israel, Ye shall not go in to them, neither shall they come in unto you: for surely they will turn away your heart after their gods: Solomon clave unto these in love. And he had seven hundred wives, princesses, and three hundred concubines ..." (1 Kings 11:1-3).

Like some other men of faith, David had about fifteen wives – eight who are named and "more wives" and "concubines" who are unnamed.[7] Whilst it was accepted that the Divine ideal was one man for one woman, and vice versa, some compromise appears to have been allowed in these early times. The wisdom of the ideal, however, becomes clearly apparent as wives multiply and people pay the price for thinking they know better than God.[8] It is as if God allows them enough rope with which to hang themselves, which they promptly do!

Whilst there was no express criticism concerning Solomon's marriage to the Egyptian princess, the record is now more specific. God had told the nation in general, not just their kings, that they should not inter-marry into heathen nations (Exodus 34:11-16 and Deuteronomy 7:1-4). And the kings had been told expressly: *"Neither shall he multiply wives to himself, that his heart turn not away"* (Deuteronomy 17:17, which is clearly alluded to in the 1 Kings 11 passage). Many things came together in what was now happening to show how unwise this was:

- There were only a few nations with which he might have wanted to secure alliances which could have directly benefited the nation, Egypt being the principal one. Most of the other nations mentioned were in Solomon's Empire, having been subdued by David and they were paying tribute (the Hittites and the Zidonians[9] would have been the exceptions).

- The Hittites and the Zidonians were, however, Canaanites; and the Exodus and Deuteronomy proscription was specifically about that class of person.

Intermarriage of this sort was not only against the letter of the Mosaic Law, it was a contravention of the spirit of that law, which gave sound reasons why such alliances were prohibited: because they would lead to a clash of loyalties which could lead someone away from God. The same principle survives into the New Testament, although the specific legislation no longer applies. Marrying out of the faith can lead us astray, as it did Solomon.

Being a man who had become accustomed to excess, Solomon now collected more wives than any of his predecessors – it seems that he had become that sort of a king! The record says that he eventually collected *"seven hundred wives, princesses, and three hundred concubines"* although it is sometimes suggested that a scribal error may have crept in, and that he had a somewhat smaller collection.[10] Whether or not that is the case, he had more than enough.[11]

It may have been a case that the eye was not satisfied with seeing (Ecclesiastes 1:8). Perhaps he saw, he wanted, and he possessed; and there was no-one to stop him because he was the king. But he, of all men, should have realised the danger of accumulating possessions and problems to himself. For he had said, in his saner moments:

> *"Lust not after her beauty in thine heart; neither let her take thee with her eyelids. For by means of a whorish woman a man is brought to a piece of bread: and the adulteress will hunt for the precious life. Can a man take fire in his bosom, and his clothes not be burned?"* (Proverbs 6:25-27).

It came down to this: Was Solomon able to multiply horses, riches and wives *"to himself"* in absolute defiance of the law that prohibited this very thing, and still maintain his faith and his spiritual integrity. Who was wiser? The king, or the God who had appointed him as king?

NOTES

[1]Edersheim,vol. V, pg. 63, suggests that Rehoboam was only 21 when he acceded to the throne, and thus suggests that Pharaoh's daughter was, in fact, Solomon's first wife. This is an entirely speculative suggestion, without any manuscript

support, but he cites 2 Chronicles 13:7 to suggest that Rehoboam was *"young and tenderhearted"* when he made the wrong decision. Sadly there are 41 year-olds who are still at that stage of immaturity.

[2] 1 Kings 9:24 and 2 Chronicles 8:11.

[3] Notice how the Scripture distinguishes between her and the other wives: *"King Solomon loved many strange women, together with the daughter of Pharaoh ... Solomon clave unto these in love".* It is difficult to know quite what the distinction is intended to convey. Perhaps it was her rank and importance that merited such a distinction; but it may have been that she was spiritually superior to the rest, because she clave to the LORD God of Israel.

[4] In 1 Kings 11:1-7 the false gods are listed, but there is no mention of Egyptian worship being introduced. However the Talmud says that *"when Solomon married the daughter of Pharaoh she brought to him a thousand different kinds of musical instruments, and taught him the chants to the various idols"* (Shabbath, f. 56, 2). So it is difficult to be sure about her religious persuasion.

[5] *"In summary, the two pieces of data (Siamun's relief; the passage in 1 Kings 9:16-17) make good political sense when set together, in the context of a possible alliance of Egypt (Siamun) and Israel (Solomon). If (for example) the Philistines had impeded, or overcharged tolls on, transit traffic through their terrain (or along their coast) that affected both Egypt and Israel, then the two may have colluded to end the menace by allying against and subduing Philistia. Siamun will have launched a strong police action through Gaza, sending one force up to Ascalon and Ashdod, with his main force going over via Gath and Ekron up to Gezer, to link up with a Hebrew force making a diversionary move on the north. Out of their success, Siamun could establish suzerainty over Philistia (levying tribute on its rich cities), while Solomon would gain the important border post of Gezer. If this occurred about the third year of Solomon (ca. 967), then Siamun would have enjoyed his triumph for only seven or eight years; the Philistines would have regained their full independence at his death in 960 or 959. But the Hebrew rulers retained Gezer permanently"* (Kitchen, pg.110).

[6] David Rohl, *"A Test of Time"*, 1995, pg.185, who seeks to establish a new Egyptian chronology, thinks the Pharaoh who made the alliance with Solomon was King Haremheb. Immanuel Velikovsky, *"Ages in Chaos"*, pg.139, suggests a quite different time displacement, and thinks it was Thutmose III. Kitchen, pg.109, is dismissive of all these ideas.

[7] 1 Chronicles 3:9 and 14:3.

[8] David had many problems because of the family struggles that ensued between rival factions in the palace and Solomon had much cause to ruminate on his own bad judgement in this respect.

[9] There is a Jewish tradition that Solomon married a daughter of Hiram, King of Tyre.

[10] Farrar, pg.141, observes that the largest harem recorded in the ancient world was that of Darius Codomannus who had one wife and 329 concubines. He observes that Solomon had a much smaller kingdom, with far fewer surrounding neighbours, and that the palace or palaces in Jerusalem were not big enough to contain all these wives. On the basis of Song of Songs 6:8, he suggests that perhaps Solomon had 70 wives (not 700). De Vaux, pg.115, gives details of large numbers of wives and concubines in heathen kingdoms, as does Wood, pg.329. Heaton, pg.93, adds *"It is the reign of Amenophis III which provides convincing parallels. According to the Amarna letters, he ordered from the king of Gezer forty 'beautiful women' at forty silver shekels each and, in addition, as he lost no time in announcing to the kingdom at large, three hundred and seventeen women accompanied from Mitanni the princess who came to join his harim. Queen Tiy, however, was his 'great royal spouse' and, like the Pharaoh's daughter at Solomon's court, enjoyed the privilege of a private palace".*

[11] Keil, pg.169: *"These are in any case round numbers, that is to say, numbers which simply approximate to the reality, and are not to be understood as affirming that Solomon had all these wives and concubines at the same time, but as including all the women who were received into his harem during the whole of his reign, whereas the sixty queens and eighty concubines mentioned in Song of Sol. 6:8 are to be understood as having been present in the court at one time".*

23
Solomon's Heart Attack

MOSES had spelled out the danger in the clearest possible terms and had prescribed the God-given remedy. The danger was that an excess of various things could lure someone away from God. Lust, when it had conceived, could bring forth sin and sin, when it was full-grown, could result in spiritual death.[1] It would not be God who did the temptation; but if a person set his or her sights on things that came within range, the outcome could take them away from God.

That was always the peril of idolatry. The idol was nothing, except what it represented in the mind of the idol-worshipper. Once persuaded that it could bring good luck, fortune or favour, the worshipper no longer saw it as a 'thing' but as a representation of something else. It was the 'something else' that the people of Israel had to beware all through their national existence; for the quest for something other than God meant they were no longer focused upon the God who was in fact the source of all their daily blessings.[2]

The Cause and the Cure
When Moses warned about the perils of kingship, his concern was that power over people could result in the king losing control of himself. That is why the words *"to himself"* are repeated so tellingly in Deuteronomy 17:15-17, words that we have already examined. Solomon's mistake was exactly that: to appropriate things to himself that he could have devoted to the well-being of the nation and the greater glory of God. That would, of course, have taken

great self-discipline and a willingness to be quite different from heathen kings, who exulted in self-glorification.

We are only too well aware in our own lives that often we could manage with less, but we are more content with that bit extra. So, as in all Scripture, Solomon's experience challenges us to be sure that we are making the right choice with the benefits and blessings that come our way. Moses warned all Israel's kings specifically about horses, wives and riches – a sort of ancient equivalent of today's "wine, women and song". He might, said Moses, lose his heart to them, and not to God.[3] But there was also a solution, for Moses said:

> *"... Neither shall he multiply wives to himself, that his heart turn not away: neither shall he greatly multiply to himself silver and gold. And it shall be, when he sitteth upon the throne of his kingdom, that he shall write him a copy of this law in a book out of that which is before the priests the Levites: and it shall be with him, and he shall read therein all the days of his life: that he may learn to fear the LORD his God, to keep all the words of this law and these statutes, to do them: that his heart be not lifted up above his brethren, and that he turn not aside from the commandment, to the right hand, or to the left: to the end that he may prolong his days in his kingdom, he, and his children, in the midst of Israel"* (Deuteronomy 17:17-20).

Heart Disease

God always knows best, for us as much as for Solomon. If we want to live like kings and priests, both now as well as in God's coming kingdom, we have to be every bit as vigilant. We must keep our hearts with all diligence, making sure that we centre our affections and desires wholly upon God, His kingdom and his righteousness. Like David of old, we must ensure that the things that have to do with His salvation and His glory are *"all my salvation, and all my desire"* (2 Samuel 23:5).

Solomon forgot those parting words of David as he made his own way in life. Perhaps he began to believe all the nice things that visiting potentates said about him, or

238

the luxuries of life just got to him. He lived excessively and might have begun to believe his own publicity. However it happened, he began to lose his grip on the main challenge of life – that of making his calling and election sure.[4] He lost his heart. For, says the Divine record:

"King Solomon loved many strange women ... of the nations concerning which the LORD said unto the children of Israel, Ye shall not go in to them, neither shall they come in unto you: for surely they will turn away your heart after their gods: Solomon clave unto these in love. And he had seven hundred wives, princesses, and three hundred concubines: and his wives turned away his heart. For it came to pass, when Solomon was old, that his wives turned away his heart after other gods: and his heart was not perfect with the LORD his God, as was the heart of David his father ... And the LORD was angry with Solomon, because his heart was turned from the LORD God of Israel, which had appeared unto him twice" (1 Kings 11:1-9).

Notice that it is not simply the breach of the commandments concerning marriage that offended Almighty God. Those commandments were explicit concerning the seven nations who occupied the land Israel went in to possess;[5] but the principle was crystal clear. As later reformers, like Nehemiah, insisted – inter-marriage with the heathen was, and is, an offence to God. It leads to divided loyalties and God, who wants to win our wholehearted love, and who loves us more than we can tell, knows what is best for us. So we had better take notice: Solomon did not. He thought he knew better; but look what it led to. He lost his heart; maybe even his grasp on eternal life.

It is not as if Solomon didn't know better. He had a lot to say about the importance of ensuring our love for God was unsullied and undivided. Our most precious possession, Solomon often implies, is our heart – the centre of both our understanding and our affection. Look at just a few of the precepts he urged his "children" to follow, that they might enjoy the blessings of a life with God:

"When wisdom entereth into thine heart, and knowledge is pleasant unto thy soul; discretion shall preserve thee, understanding shall keep thee … to deliver thee from the strange woman" (Proverbs 2:10-16);

"Trust in the LORD with all thine heart; and lean not unto thine own understanding. In all thy ways acknowledge him, and he shall direct thy paths" (3:5,6);

"Keep thy heart with all diligence; for out of it are the issues of life … That thou mayest regard discretion, and that thy lips may keep knowledge. For the lips of a strange woman drop as an honeycomb, and her mouth is smoother than oil: but her end is bitter as wormwood, sharp as a two-edged sword. Her feet go down to death" (4:23–5:5);

"For the commandment is a lamp; and the law is light; and reproofs of instruction are the way of life: to keep thee from the evil woman, from the flattery of the tongue of a strange woman. Lust not after her beauty in thine heart; neither let her take thee with her eyelids. For by means of a whorish woman a man is brought to a piece of bread: and the adulteress will hunt for the precious life" (6:23–26).

Notice that in this last piece of Divinely-given advice, Solomon is directing us to the very cure than Moses had recommended: obedience to God's commandments; walking in the light of revealed truth rather than in the darkness of ignorance; being kept in the Way of Life by the influence and guidance of what God has revealed.

Wisdom or Folly?

Not for the first time in this study, we have occasion to be puzzled about how it was that Solomon could see things so clearly at one time in his life, but get into such a muddle when he sought to apply that knowledge to his own situation. At least, we would be puzzled if our own experience wasn't just the same. Like us, Solomon knew what he ought to do, but he didn't, or couldn't, do it himself. As the apostle Paul later said of himself:

"I am carnal, sold under sin. For that which I do I allow not: for what I would, that do I not; but what I hate, that do I … For the good that I would I do not: but the evil which I would not, that I do … I find then a law, that, when I would do good, evil is present with me. For I delight in the law of God after the inward man: but I see another law in my members, warring against the law of my mind, and bringing me into captivity to the law of sin which is in my members" (Romans 7:14–23).

Paul's solution was to live *"the life of the Spirit"*, as he explains in the next chapter of Romans, and to allow the influence of that change to permeate everything he would thereafter do. He wanted to live in Christ, and for Christ to live in him. Solomon's advice to us is just the same, though the language he uses is of course different. It is intriguing to note that if we bring both those forms of expression together, the one illuminates and explains the other. For the *"life of the Spirit"* is the life of *"Wisdom"*, a life spent wisely, following and practising the precepts of Almighty God.

The Way of Wisdom

Writing for us, under guidance of the Spirit, Solomon explains that if we choose wisdom from God, first and foremost, then all the other things we need in life will be added to us.[6] Terms change between the Testaments, but the required lifestyle does not. God bestowed special kinds of Wisdom at various times: Solomon was given wisdom to govern, perceive, administer, construct and reveal. This sort of special wisdom included that which came when Solomon was inspired by God to write his part of the Book of Proverbs, Ecclesiastes and the Song of Solomon. And he was given some sort of Divine insight when building the Temple in Jerusalem, just as some of the builders were Spirit-endowed. That sort of wisdom can, exceptionally, be conveyed to us even through unbelieving people like Balaam; it does not transform or convert the messenger, unless he too heeds it and seeks to follow it.

When he advocated the merits of wisdom, rather than folly, Solomon was not suggesting that ordinary people, like us, should seek after his sort of special wisdom, revelation or ability. That was a special gift from God, given to whom He will. Instead, the king was urging his immediate hearers, or eventual readers, to live wisely, in accordance with the revealed will of God, and to manifest the fruit of wisdom in their everyday conduct and behaviour. He says that he had written some of his proverbs so that we might:

> *"Know wisdom and instruction ... perceive the words of understanding ... receive the instruction of wisdom, justice, and judgment, and equity; to give subtilty to the simple, to the young man knowledge and discretion. A wise man will hear, and will increase learning; and a man of understanding shall attain unto wise counsels: to understand a proverb, and the interpretation; the words of the wise, and their dark sayings. The fear of the LORD is the beginning of knowledge: but fools despise wisdom and instruction"* (Proverbs 1:2-7).

We are to learn from Solomon and then live as he instructs – developing the fruit of Divine wisdom by living in the fear of God. As he argues the advantages and blessings that will come from this course of action, the King pictures Wisdom as a woman whom we should choose as our closest companion through life, someone who should accompany each of us along life's path. For, he says, if we live according to her prompting, and let her into our life, we shall:

> *"walk in the way of good men, and keep the paths of the righteous"* (Proverbs 2:20);

> *"find favour and good understanding in the sight of God and man"* (3:4);

> *"walk in thy way safely, and thy foot shall not stumble ... not be afraid: yea, thou shalt lie down, and thy sleep shall be sweet ... for the LORD shall be thy confidence, and shall keep thy foot from being taken"* (3:23-26);

> *"(wisdom) shall bring thee to honour, when thou dost embrace her. She shall give to thine head an ornament of grace: a crown of glory shall she deliver to thee. Hear,*

242

O my son, and receive my sayings; and the years of thy life shall be many" (4:8-10).

Do you notice the New Testament parallel to all of this? What are we encouraged to do if we are to enter into such a blessed and contented state with God? In the language of the New Testament, we must *"receive the Spirit"; "walk in the Spirit"; be "led of the Spirit"; "sow to the Spirit";* develop the *"fruit of the Spirit"; "live in the Spirit"*.[7] For what the Old Testament calls the way of Wisdom, the New Testament calls the way of the Spirit, and the language Solomon uses about choosing Wisdom is later used in much the same way about the Spirit.[8] This is a helpful parallel to bear in mind, especially having regard to all the controversy there has been about what "life in the Spirit" really means.

According to wise King Solomon, who wrote by inspiration: to live according to the Spirit is to live according to the dictates of Divine Wisdom; and to walk in that way we must first be instructed accordingly, from the Word of God. If we choose to follow that path through life, like him, we shall eventually receive riches, honour and length of days. The difference is that Solomon received those blessings immediately, and they were only worldly ones. For the saints of God, the prospect before them is an eternal inheritance – comprising the riches of God, the honour and glory of His Kingdom, and nothing less than the gift of everlasting life.

The Way of Folly

But we can go wrong and stray from the narrow way that leads to life, and so could King Solomon. The impulses of his flesh got the better of him, as they can of us. We are certainly in no position to sit in judgement, or even point a reproving finger. There, but for the grace of God, we go too. The *"evil woman"* of folly is always watching her opportunity to lure the simple to her house, where death lurks in the cellar (Proverbs 5:25-27).

Solomon had been softened by the luxurious lifestyle he had allowed himself. Things had got out of hand and one thing led to another. Commenting upon this time in

SOLOMON – WISE AND FOOLISH

Solomon's life, one writer said:

"Two deadly evils lurked behind the superficial brilliancy, and wrought incredible harm to king and people – (1) the curse of polygamy and (2) the curse of despotism. The primitive simplicity of the monarchy was nobler, though less showy, than this iridescence (sic) of moral stagnancy and luxurious decline. There must have been many who watched with unfavourable eyes the displacement of national simplicity by alien magnificence ... It is clear from the Book of Deuteronomy that he was doing in every direction the very things which were least in accordance with the true ideal of kingly power among the Chosen People. Three things had been specially forbidden to the theocratic sovereign, and all these three things Solomon conspicuously did. If we judged by that passage alone we should think that Solomon was held up as the example of everything which a king ought not to be." [9]

No details are given about precisely how the new phase of Solomon's life began: when he began to multiply wives to himself. It could have started after the death of Pharaoh Siamun; but it might have been the understood thing between sovereigns that a few extra ancillary wives or concubines were fine, provided the wife-in-chief was treated with proper respect (which Solomon was careful to do). The trouble was twofold:

1. The process of wife collecting escalated. If we drop our guard and begin to satisfy fleshly desires, there is no knowing where that might lead. It led Solomon to accumulate a house full of women and to get a lot of heartache. But not at first, or he would no doubt have stopped the process sooner than he did.

2. His wives won over his heart for, the record says: *"Solomon clave unto these in love"* (1 Kings 11:2). This expression goes right back to the Garden of Eden, when Adam clave to his wife, but it also carries strong connotations of faithfulness and loyalty. God's people should *"cleave"* to Him, first and foremost; He is to be the primary recipient of their love. [10] Such was Solomon's defection from his true purpose in life – to love God

244

with all his heart – that Scripture records that: *"his heart was not perfect with the LORD his God, as was the heart of David his father"* (1 Kings 11:4).

One wife must have led to another, and then another. Solomon's heart-sickness might have been impelled by a deep desire to find true love – perhaps to recapture something he had once enjoyed in balmier days. Or he may have been affected by many desires, all mixed up inside him: the desire for power, prestige, companionship, affection, notoriety. Who can say for sure what led him on? He had once described the confusion of the human condition in the memorable phrase, *"the plague of his own heart"* (1 Kings 8:38,39). Now he was experiencing it himself.

What would God do about it, if anything? Leave him to his fate, undisturbed? And what, in his saner moments, did Solomon think about this new direction for his life? Where would it lead; and could he recover his composure and his confidence in God? Was there any way of turning back, or had he gone too far down the slippery slope of sin?

NOTES

[1] James 1:13-15.

[2] Wordsworth, pg.44, has a typically robust comment: *"The first step downward in Solomon's career seems to have been this; he did not regard his wealth and power and magnificence, and extent of dominion, as gifts of God. He did not consecrate them, as he had done in the earlier part of his reign, to the service of God, and to His glory. As his wealth increased, his love of splendour increased with it. He seems to have been dazzled by the brilliance of the silver and gold which blazed around him, and to have been enamoured of earthly magnificence, and to have doted on earthly delights; his parks, his paradises, his gardens, his palaces, and pavilions. These things enfeebled his moral health; his spiritual vigour was enervated by luxury and voluptuousness."*

[3] Loving God with all our heart is a key theme in Deuteronomy (see Deuteronomy 4:9,29,39; 5:29; 6:5-6;

SOLOMON – WISE AND FOOLISH

10:12,16; 11:13; 26:16; 30:2,6,10).

[4] 2 Peter 1:10 – the challenge for every generation, Solomon included.

[5] See Deuteronomy 7:1-4.

[6] Compare Jesus' words, *"Seek ye first the kingdom of God, and his righteousness; and all these things shall be added unto you"* (Matthew 6:33).

[7] Galatians 3:2,14; 5:16,18,22,25; 6:8.

[8] *"Behold (says Wisdom), I will pour out my spirit unto you, I will make known my words unto you"* (Proverbs 1:23); *"When wisdom entereth into thine heart, and knowledge is pleasant unto thy soul" (2:10); "Let not mercy and truth forsake thee: bind them about thy neck; write them upon the table of thine heart" (3:3)*. There is, however, an important difference in the way in which the New Testament believer perceives the Wisdom or Spirit of God; it is no longer *personified* (as in Proverbs chapters 8 & 9). It is *personalised*; for now it is embodied in the Lord Jesus Christ (see, for example, 1 Corinthians 1:24).

[9] Farrar, pg.140.

[10] *"Dābaq* also carries the sense of clinging to someone in affection and loyalty. Man is to cleave to his wife (Gen 2:24). Ruth clave to Naomi (Ruth 1:14). The men of Judah clave to David their king during Sheba's rebellion (II Sam 20:2). Shechem loved Dinah and clave to her (Gen 34:3) and Solomon clave in love to his wives (I Kgs 11:2). Most importantly, the Israelites are to cleave to the Lord in affection and loyalty (Deut 10:20; 11:22; 13:4; 30:20; Josh 22:5; 23:8) if his blessing is to be theirs. In Jer 13:11 it is said that the Lord caused the Israelites to cleave to him, and Hezekiah is approved because he clave to the Lord. In these verses parallel words and phrases that describe this proper attitude to the Lord are: fear, serve, love, obey, swear by his name, walk in his ways, and keep his commandments" (TWOT).

24
From Bad to Worse

SOLOMON did everything a king had been told not to do. The warnings in Deuteronomy chapter 17 are the very things that are mentioned in 1 Kings 11:1-4. Riches, possessions or wives could intervene between a king and his God so as to win his heart away; and now it had happened to Solomon, just as forecast. Whether that separation from Yahweh was an immediate development or a change that gradually took place in his religious affections, the end result was the same. The various wives brought their gods with them and it seems that Solomon pandered to their individual needs and wants, including their religious preferences. Thus he introduced the worship of foreign gods.

Flee Idolatry!

Solomon did not abandon God; what he did was to relax his attitude towards the worship of idols and the practice of false religion. He still worshipped the God of Israel, the true and only God, for we are told that:

- *"His wives turned away his heart after other gods: and his heart was not perfect with the LORD his God, as was the heart of David his father"* (11:4);

- He *"went after Ashtoreth the goddess of the Zidonians, and after Milcom the abomination of the Ammonites"* (11:5);

- He *"went not fully after the LORD, as did David his father"* (11:6);

SOLOMON – WISE AND FOOLISH

- *"And the* LORD *was angry with Solomon, because his heart was turned from the* LORD *God of Israel"* (11:9).[1]

Probably he still kept the three great feasts, as he had done earlier in his reign (1 Kings 9:25), but he also tolerated the worship of other gods, even if he did not serve them. And the expression that he *"went after"* Ashtoreth and Milcom clearly indicates that he at least acquiesced and more likely practised idol worship.[2] Yet the emphasis in this passage is not upon what Solomon did, but upon what he did not do. He did not keep his heart perfect; he did not fully follow the LORD; he did not keep his heart (his passions and desires) fully focused upon his God. He was not his father's son; in this respect he was not a man after God's own heart.

Although he had been doing well, now that he was old he began to fail (1 Kings 11:4), and that is a salutary lesson for all of us, for we too are getting older. Solomon gave his heart away to something else; and that 'something else' was really nothing at all. That could be just like us as well. So many of the things we work for, strive to achieve, or love to do are really of no lasting significance; judged in the light of eternity, they too are nothing! We are being asked to give our total commitment in obedience to and love of God: not just part of our lives but all we have to give. Everything we do and everything we have should be given to God as part of a wholly dedicated life.

God doesn't want the left-over bits of our lives: He wants the best we have to give. And the more He gives us, the more He expects us to give back. Solomon had been given so much by God and God was perfectly entitled to expect his whole-hearted worship and life-long service: *"For unto whomsoever much is given, of him shall be much required"* (Luke 12:48). But how had Solomon's defences slipped to such an extent that in his later life he became so self-indulgent and so self-obsessed? One writer offers this assessment:

"The fact that this backsliding is said to have taken place when he was old, whereas he could not have been more, and was probably less, than sixty years old even when he

248

*died, seems to show that the force of his will was much bro-
ken by enervating self-indulgence. Like Samson, he had
become too weak to withstand the constant pressure of fem-
inine importunity. But besides this we must allow for the
sort of latitudinarianism and sense of political expediency
which must of necessity have been introduced into such a
mind as that of Solomon by incessant intercourse with heathen dynasts, and the ambition to imitate their ways ...
The least, surely, which could have been expected was that
the rites of heathendom for these alien queens should only
have been permitted in the most private manner, and with
the least offensive forms. So far was this from being the
case, though Solomon probably continued his three great
annual visits to the Temple, he not only tolerated, but
encouraged, and that openly, the exercise of heathen rites in
close neighbourhood to the Temple which he might well
seem to have built in vain. We are able to mark in this
respect a distinct degeneracy. At first he had been uneasy
at the mere presence of Pharaoh's daughter in the City of
David because it had been hallowed by the presence of the
Ark of God. For her he seems to have built no temples. In
all probability she died early, for after the completion of the
palace we hear of her no more. But for the sake of his other
wives he lent to idolatry the sanction not only of tolerance,
not only of acquiescence, but of direct participation in the
most revolting forms of superstition."* [3]

Public Reaction

When Solomon was drifting away from true religion, what
was happening to the rest of the nation? Where were the
priests and Levites, who were meant to be a balancing
force in the Kingdom? [4] And what did the people in general think about what was going on, especially as this addi-
tional building work was being undertaken at their
expense, through taxation? There are all sorts of possibili-
ties about the public reaction to this new religious development. Perhaps:

● The people were so impressed by the economic prosperity Solomon's reign had brought them that they
were prepared to tolerate anything, even a change of
religion;

SOLOMON – WISE AND FOOLISH

- It was seen as a purely private development – worship for the foreign wives only – and that this was tolerated because they were important diplomatically;

- The change was a deeply unpopular development which Solomon forced through by exercising his sovereign power, regardless of opposition.

Which was it? The indication is that the drift to idolatry was not that unpopular, indeed, that it was quite well received. Solomon's wives were allowed to worship idols, in close proximity to Jerusalem, and, even after Solomon's days, the practice lingered for very many years. So, it could not have been that objectionable to people or they would have removed all trace of this "defilement" as soon as Solomon was dead. Consider what all this involved:

> "Solomon went after Ashtoreth the goddess of the Zidonians,[5] and after Milcom the abomination of the Ammonites. And Solomon did evil in the sight of the LORD, and went not fully after the LORD, as did David his father. Then did Solomon build an high place for Chemosh, the abomination of Moab, in the hill that is before Jerusalem, and for Molech, the abomination of the children of Ammon. And likewise did he for all his strange wives, which burnt incense and sacrificed unto their gods" (1 Kings 11:3-8).

We are not told that Solomon built shrines, or "high places" in Jerusalem itself, but in "the hill that is before Jerusalem". This is the Mount of Olives, to the east of Jerusalem, for more information is given about all this 300 years later. In the time of King Josiah (640-609 BC), when he purged the idolatrous sites at which Israel had persistently worshipped, it is recorded that this place of Solomon's idolatry was also ceremonially defiled. The young king's reformation began in the Temple, when the idolatrous rubbish that had accumulated there was thrown out. Then, with the assistance of priests from Judah, he attacked the place just outside Jerusalem where Molech had once been worshipped, before they moved across the valley to clear the Mount of Olives:

250

"(Josiah) defiled Topheth, which is in the valley of the children of Hinnom, that no man might make his son or his daughter to pass through the fire to Molech ... And the altars that were on the top of the upper chamber of Ahaz, which the kings of Judah had made, and the altars which Manasseh had made in the two courts of the house of the LORD, did the king beat down, and brake them down from thence, and cast the dust of them into the brook Kidron. **And the high places that were before Jerusalem, which were on the right hand of the mount of corruption, which Solomon the king of Israel had builded for Ashtoreth the abomination of the Zidonians, and for Chemosh the abomination of the Moabites, and for Milcom the abomination of the children of Ammon, did the king defile.** *And he brake in pieces the images, and cut down the groves, and filled their places with the bones of men. Moreover the altar that was at Bethel, and the high place which Jeroboam the son of Nebat, who made Israel to sin, had made he brake down, and burned the high place"* (2 Kings 23:10-15).

What an epitaph! For Solomon's name to appear in later Bible history linked to Jeroboam the son of Nebat! Of all the things Solomon might have wanted to leave as a legacy, such as a secure and stable state which was well regarded by its neighbours; what he left was a defiling and abominable site alongside the Temple he had been privileged to construct for God. He left a choice for Israel. Either they could worship the true and living God or the false gods of the nations around. And what a paradox it was!

The Temple was a treasure house of riches and artefacts which had been visited by many, if not all, of the kings from round about. If it was to remain unspoiled and intact, it was vital that God's people remained faithful to their calling; for the God who had allowed them to place His name in their midst was a jealous God, and He could easily change the arrangements, with a little help from the Egyptians, Syrians, Assyrians or Chaldeans!

SOLOMON – WISE AND FOOLISH

No-gods

Notice that the same four false gods are listed in the 2 Kings 23 passage just as they appear in the 1 Kings 11 account (Molech, Ashtoreth, Chemosh and Milcom) and it appears that remnants of their worship had lingered in this place for the last 300 years, ever since Solomon introduced them. Consequently this site, the southern peak of the Mount of Olives, was known as *"The Mount of Offence"* from early Christian times.[6] And, in the Divine record, Solomon's name became conjoined with those of *"Ahaz"*, *"Manasseh"* and *"Jeroboam the son of Nebat, who made Israel to sin"*, a very sorry epilogue indeed for someone who had been so ardent and zealous a Temple builder and Kingdom maker.

To give us a better insight into Solomon's descent into idolatry, it may be helpful to outline what we now know about the three or four no-gods in whose name Solomon had shrines or altars built just outside the city of David.

False god	Nation	Other Scriptural Refs
Molech, Milcom	Ammon	Leviticus 18:21; 20:2-5; Jeremiah 32:35; Amos 5:26; Acts 7:43

Worship associated with sacrifice of children in the fire, though such is not specifically mentioned as happening in Israel until Ahaz (2 Kings 16:3) and Manasseh (2 Kings 21:6)[7]

Ashtoreth	Zidon	Judges 2:13; 10:6; 1 Sam. 7:3,4; 12:10; 31:10 (plural: "Ashtaroth")

Canaanite goddess, also known as Astarte, a consort of Baal – the Canaanite storm and fertility god.

Chemosh	Moab	Numbers 21:29; Judges 11:24; Jeremiah 48:7,13,46

National deity of Moabites, also associated with infant sacrifice (2 Kings 3:27). Thought to be a sun god and a god of war.

Not only had the law warned against multiple marriages for God's king, and prohibited intermarriage with the Canaanites,[8] but women from Moab and Ammon were specifically excluded from the congregation of the LORD, even for ten generations (Deuteronomy 23:3). And the worship of false gods was utterly forbidden, as expressed in the very first two of the Ten Commandments:

"Thou shalt have no other gods before me. Thou shalt not make unto thee any graven image, or any likeness of any thing that is in heaven above, or that is in the earth beneath, or that is in the water under the earth: thou shalt not bow down thyself to them, nor serve them" (Exodus 20:3,4).

Solomon was setting these laws aside with impunity and was introducing the most abhorrent things into the kingdom. At this distance from the events, it is difficult to be certain about what was entailed at that time in the religious practices of the Ammonites, Moabites and Zidonians. But their religious practices were far removed from the purity and holiness of the true worship of the LORD. When you consider the accounts given in later Latin and Greek writers,[9] you certainly get an idea of where this sort of profane worship could end up.

In later times, the image of Moloch was said to be a human figure with a bull's head and outstretched arms, ready to receive the children destined for sacrifice. The image of metal was heated red hot by a fire kindled within, and the children laid on its arms rolled off into the fiery pit below. In order to drown the cries of the victims, flutes were played, and drums were beaten; and mothers stood by without tears or sobs, to give the impression of the voluntary character of the offering.

It seems amazing to think that Solomon could ever have introduced such heinous acts into Israel, and perhaps things were not as horrendous or barbaric at that time. But it certainly became like that, in the days of Ahaz and Manasseh; so it could have been that bad from the start. And it lost Solomon the kingdom for his descendants, for God was later to declare:

SOLOMON – WISE AND FOOLISH

"Behold, I will rend the kingdom out of the hand of Solomon ... Because that they have forsaken me, and have worshipped Ashtoreth the goddess of the Zidonians, Chemosh the god of the Moabites, and Milcom¹⁰ the god of the children of Ammon, and have not walked in my ways, to do that which is right in mine eyes, and to keep my statutes and my judgments, as did David his father" (1 Kings 11:31-33).

Losing his Grip

There is a real irony in all this, for when the king was pondering the meaning and purpose of life, in the Book of Ecclesiastes, one of the things that depressed Solomon was the fact that he could not control the quality or fate of the person who would succeed him in life.

"I hated all my labour which I had taken under the sun: because" he said, *"I should leave it unto the man that shall be after me. And who knoweth whether he shall be a wise man or a fool? Yet shall he have rule over all my labour wherein I have laboured, and wherein I have shewed myself wise under the sun. This is also vanity"* (Ecclesiastes 2:18,19).

So he had a lot of advice to offer to his son (or sons) in the Book of Proverbs, about how he should keep the law of God close at hand, bind it on his heart, always follow its precepts, and suchlike.[11] But there is no guidance to be found there whereby a father should be careful to set a good example, or to ensure that he does not go astray, and imperil his son or children in the process. That never seems to have occurred to Solomon as a possibility,[12] except for one wry comment that *"A foolish son is the calamity of his father"* (19:13).[13]

As it worked out, his own poor example was very likely to lead Rehoboam, his chosen successor, astray and his idolatry would lose his son the very kingdom Solomon had done so much to extend and beautify. It is one thing lamenting about those things over which we can have no control. The moral is that we should do our utmost to exercise the best possible control over those matters that are capable of being influenced and directed for good, both for ourselves and for those who come after us.

The problem was, of course, that Solomon lost his heart, and so was losing his grip on all aspects of life. In his later life, the things that Solomon had seen so clearly were now obscure. What had been so "black and white" had become a series of shades of gray, or so it would appear. Remember what the record says.

"It came to pass, when Solomon was old, that his wives turned away his heart ... and his heart was not perfect with the LORD his God ... and Solomon did evil in the sight of the LORD, and went not fully after the LORD" (1 Kings 11:4-6).

This record is given us, without any watering down of the attitude God had towards Solomon, so that we can properly learn what God expects of us, in our training to become "kings and priests". He demands no less than our wholehearted response to His gracious offer of salvation. It is as though Yahweh Himself says to each of us, *"My son"* (or *"my daughter"*) *"give me thine heart, and let thine eyes observe my ways"* (Proverbs 23:26). What God expected of Solomon, He expects of each one of us.

We have got to remain alert to those demands all through our lives. For it was *"when Solomon was old"* that he let go of God's hand and set off in his own direction. Once again, he forgot his own, Spirit-guided injunction: *"There is a way which seemeth right unto a man, but the end thereof are the ways of death"* (Proverbs 14:12). Solomon shows us that it's never too late to go astray, and we must make sure that we do not lose our grip. As the apostle Paul counsels:

"Let him that thinketh he standeth take heed lest he fall" (1 Corinthians 10:12).

All Mixed Up

It was not merely that Solomon allowed idol worship in Jerusalem, or that he facilitated it. Both those things would have been bad enough. The record says that: *"Solomon went after Ashtoreth the goddess of the Zidonians, and after Milcom the abomination of the*

255

SOLOMON – WISE AND FOOLISH

Ammonites. And Solomon did evil in the sight of the LORD, and went not fully after the LORD" (1 Kings 11:4-6).

Can you spot the key piece of information, which also explains how Solomon got away with the introduction of idolatry? It was the very problem that beset Israel for the rest of their national existence, until the exile got idolatry right out of their system. The king worshipped or facilitated the worship of Ashtaroth and Milcom *as well as* Yahweh, the God of Israel. No doubt he applied his famous powers of logical argument to explain that as God is LORD of all, and idols are nothing in themselves, the worship of any god is, in fact, the worship of the only God who actually exists; or he used some such piece of sophistry.

The result was that for generations afterwards God's people forgot God's unique and sole status. They confused the difference between the true and the false and thereafter kept lapsing back into old and wrong ways. Describing the state of Jerusalem in the days of Ezekiel – when there was an idol in the Temple court, seventy elders were worshipping animal motifs inscribed on the walls, women were mourning for the god Tammuz and twenty-five men were seen worshipping the sun, one writer observes:

"Syncretism – the mixing of elements from several religions – is one of the easiest paths to follow. Would-be believers can hedge their bets and keep all the gods happy. Yet the God of Israel is a jealous God. There can be no other contenders for a person's worship and devotion. In our multi-faith, pluralistic societies this emphasis needs to be made and is often misunderstood. Yet our compromising is no less abhorrent to God than the pagan practices here described".[14]

We have got to be just as careful that we don't mix things up. Bits and pieces of what other denominations believe can easily get picked up by us, including when we read their publications, unless we read with care and discrimination. Their religious practices and traditions can get absorbed into our worship, for no other reason than they appeal to us. And the attitudes and priorities of worldly thinking are always a potent influence, because

256

we are naturally inclined in that direction. All these, and many other things, can gradually water down or quite alter the things that we believe. So, whilst we need to move with the times, to present the gospel in the most attractive and topical way, we must beware of mixing things up and thus losing our way with God, as Solomon did.

Any Regrets?

Heading off on his own, into uncharted territory, do you think Solomon had any regrets about this new spiritual adventure upon which he was embarking? For, he was deliberately leaving behind the guidance of God, and doing his own thing, as many people do today. Do you think that at any time he looked back wistfully to happier and better days? And did God do anything about it, to make the king think again, and turn again to Him?

NOTES

[1] Farrar, pg.143: *"There is a curious piece of casuistry in the Talmud: 'Whoever says that Solomon sinned is decidedly wrong ... His wives turned away his heart to walk after other gods, but he did not go ... But what of 1 Kings xi.7? He intended to build a high place for Chemosh, but did not build it' (Shabbath, f. 55.56; comp. Sanhedrin f. 55.56). All that can be said for Solomon is that he is not stated personally to have 'served' other gods."*

[2] Rawlinson, pg.548, says that the expression always signifies actual idolatry (Deut.11:28; 13:2; 28:14). Keil, pg.170, offers this understanding: *"According to v. 7, the idolatry here condemned consisted in the fact that he built altars to the deities of all his foreign wives, upon which they offered incense and sacrifice to their idols. It is not stated that he himself also offered sacrifice to these idols. But even the building of altars for idols was a participation in idolatry which was irreconcilable with true fidelity to the Lord".* Edersheim, vol v, pg111, says: *"Whenever the Jewish kings were personally guilty of idolatry, the Hebrew word avad, 'served,' is used. Comp. 1 Kings 16:31; 22:53; 2 Kings 16:3; 21:2-6,20-22. Jewish tradi-*

tion also emphatically asserts (Shab. 56 b.) that Solomon was not personally guilty of idolatry".

[3] Farrar, pg.143.

[4] Farrar, pg.152: *"We hear of no single word of priestly protest. The Priesthood seems to have sunk into the torpor of ceremonialism under the patronizing dominance of the king. Doubtless they burned with perfect precision "the two kidneys and the fat,' and went through the whole round of rites which belonged to all that was then known of the Levitic ordinances. But they seem to have been content with this strenuous idleness of perpetual functions which they mistook for work. There is not the faintest sign that they exercised, or tried to exercise, any sort of moral or spiritual influence, or even that they offered so much as a barren protest when they saw the counter-smoke of incense rising from idolatrous altars on the opprobrious hill. Nothing could have stemmed the rolling tide of national corruption but the bold and independent voice of prophecy".*

[5] There is a real paradox here. If it is true that Hiram became a believer in the God of Israel (see Chapter 19, above), then Solomon's toleration of the worship of a Zidonian god would have sent quite the wrong message to Hiram and his subjects.

[6] Keil, pg.171. More details are given in SBD: *"Next to the central summit, on the southern side, is a hill remarkable only for the fact that it contains the 'singular catacomb' known as the 'Tombs of the Prophets,' probably in allusion to the words of Christ. Matt. 23:29. 3. The most southern portion of the Mount of Olives is that usually known as the 'Mount of Offence'. It rises next to that last mentioned. The title 'Mount of Offence,' or 'Scandal,' was bestowed on the supposition that it is the 'Mount of Corruption' on which Solomon erected the high places for the gods of his foreign wives. 2 Kings 23:13; 1 Kings 11:7. The southern summit is considerably lower than the centre one."*

[7] If Leviticus 18 is a description of the forbidden practices of the Canaanites, who were then in the land, it would appear that the practice of offering children in sacrifice by fire was already established, even if it did not feature in Israel's worship of Molech until later reigns – to give Solomon every pos-

sible benefit of the doubt.

[8] Although the Canaanites were specified (Exodus 34:16; Deuteronomy 7:1-3), because they were the immediate danger, the prohibition was later understood to have applied more generally to partners from other nations (Ezra 9:2ff; Nehemiah 13:23).

[9] These details which Diodorus Siculus gives in his History of the Carthaginian *"Kronos"* or *"Moloch"* are taken from an article in ISBE.

[10] It seems evident from the absence of *"Molech"* in this reiteration that Milcom and Molech were one and the same, or perhaps only variations of the same false god.

[11] See Proverbs chapters 1-7, which are all addressed to *"my son"*, though that term has a wider meaning as well (referring to all who want to become members of Solomon's spiritual family) and 10:1; 13:1; 17:25; 19:13,26; 23:13-15,22; 28:7.

[12] There is such guidance elsewhere in Scripture, for example in Ephesians 6:4 and Colossians 3:21.

[13] *"Solomon did evil in the sight of the LORD, and went not fully after the LORD, as did David his father"* (1 Kings 11:6).

[14] John McGregor in *"The New Bible Commentary"*, IVP, Editor. D. A. Carson, etc.

25

It's Never Too Late

G OD never stands idly by when His people are in need. Solomon had prayed that God would intervene when Israel was in trouble and had catalogued the sort of things he feared might do them harm: defeat, drought, famine, pestilence, warfare, captivity and exile. In each case, he asked God to help them when they prayed *"towards this place"* – the Temple he had been privileged to erect for God. And he had recognised that there was a more subtle danger still, one that could attack Israel whilst they were still free men, with plenty to eat and drink, free from pestilence, at peace and at rest. In his saner moments he had recognised the danger of losing one's heart to other things:

> *"What prayer and supplication soever be made by any man, or by all thy people Israel, which shall know every man the plague of his own heart, and spread forth his hands toward this house: then hear thou in heaven thy dwelling place, and forgive, and do, and give to every man according to his ways, whose heart thou knowest; (for thou, even thou only, knowest the hearts of all the children of men;) that they may fear thee all the days that they live in the land which thou gavest unto our fathers"* (1 Kings 8:38-40).

God's Answer

Now it was his own heart that was lost and that was plagued: he had given his heart away. But did he know that things were no longer right between him and his God?

Did Solomon realise that he had strayed away from God's Law and that he was at risk of losing everything? And if so, was he sorry: did he care? He knew all right, and very soon he had much cause to regret his chosen course of action:

"The LORD was angry with Solomon, because his heart was turned from the LORD God of Israel, which had appeared unto him twice, and had commanded him concerning this thing, that he should not go after other gods: but he kept not that which the LORD commanded. Wherefore the LORD said unto Solomon, Forasmuch as this is done of thee, and thou hast not kept my covenant and my statutes, which I have commanded thee, I will surely rend the kingdom from thee, and will give it to thy servant. Notwithstanding in thy days I will not do it for David thy father's sake: but I will rend it out of the hand of thy son. Howbeit I will not rend away all the kingdom; but will give one tribe to thy son for David my servant's sake, and for Jerusalem's sake which I have chosen" (1 Kings 11:9-13).

God had appeared to him twice before (at the start of his reign and then in his 24th year) but now it would seem it was God's prophet who delivered this rebuke and the prediction concerning the defection of the ten tribes. Later in the chapter, Ahijah the Shilonite is the prophet who tells Jeroboam the very same thing (11:29-32), so it would seem that it was he who challenged Solomon. We are not told about Solomon's reaction, whether he was impressed, shocked, untouched, or whatever. Instead the record concentrates on something else, a second encouraging feature.

God had not left Solomon alone when he got into spiritual difficulties. He had told His king that He was angry and had warned him what He was going to do about it. God takes a keen interest in His children and wants the best for all of us. His Word is the means whereby *we* can hear His counsel and obtain guidance when *our* steps falter and fail. Now God took action to try to make Solomon think again. He deliberately placed obstacles in Solomon's way to make his wayward subject think again.

SOLOMON – WISE AND FOOLISH

God's Action Plan

God never gives up when confronted by opposition, especially when the problem is one that could lead to the loss of a son whom He loves. He loved Solomon as He loves us and seeing that things were going awry in Solomon's life, and angry that His king was introducing idolatry into His Kingdom, God sent Solomon some trouble and tribulation to disturb the peace and plenty that had prevailed for so many years. He unleashed a three-pronged attack into Solomon's life, having first sent a clear declaration of intent which, no doubt, served as an opportunity for Solomon to repent and mend his ways.

Such is God's foreknowledge that even when Solomon was praying for God to *"hearken ... to the supplication of thy servant, and of thy people Israel, when they shall pray toward this place: and hear thou in heaven thy dwelling place: and when thou hearest, forgive"*, God knew how His servant would be placed less than 20 years on and now He was chastening him; for God had not abandoned him. As Solomon himself said, we should: *"despise not the chastening of the LORD; neither be weary of his correction: for whom the LORD loveth he correcteth; even as a father the son in whom he delighteth. Happy is the man that findeth wisdom, and the man that getteth understanding"* (Proverbs 3:11-13).

God's action plan involved three different adversaries: (1) Hadad the Edomite; (2) Rezon the son of Eliadah and (3) Jeroboam the Son of Nebat. He had warned Solomon earlier in his reign that:

> *"If ye shall at all turn from following me, ye or your children, and will not keep my commandments and my statutes which I have set before you, but go and serve other gods, and worship them then will I cut off Israel out of the land which I have given them; and this house, which I have hallowed for my name, will I cast out of my sight; and Israel shall be a proverb and a byword among all people: and at this house, which is high, every one that passeth by it shall be astonished, and shall hiss; and they shall say, Why hath the LORD done thus unto this land, and to this house? And they shall*

answer, Because they forsook the LORD their God, who brought forth their fathers out of the land of Egypt, and have taken hold upon other gods, and have worshipped them, and served them: therefore hath the LORD brought upon them all this evil" (1 Kings 9:6-9).

Now God was bringing that *"evil"* or trouble upon Israel, not in the time of Solomon's children but, sadly, during his own reign. God would *"stir up"* Solomon's adversaries (1 Kings 11:14,23) and they would be a problem to him. In this way God continues to work in the lives of His people, through the circumstances of our everyday lives. It is part of the work of heaven that goes on all the time, unseen and unknown to us, which helps make us the people that God wants us to be.[1]

God's Adversaries
Who were these enemies of Solomon who were stirred up by God, for His purposes? Let's consider them one by one.

● Hadad the Edomite
Hadad was of Edom's royal line and had been taken to Egypt, while still a young lad, when David invaded Edom and put their fighting men to the sword.[2] Having settled in Egypt, Hadad was eventually married to the sister of Pharaoh's queen Tahpenes (1 Kings 11:20) and bare a son named Genubath who was brought up in the royal household. Evidently the Pharaoh treated Hadad like his own son and wanted him to stay in Egypt. Yet, when the opportunity came, at the death of David and Joab, which would have been early in Solomon's reign, he was keen to return to Edom, ready it would seem to take any opportunity to regain Edom's full independence by opposing Solomon and being his adversary.

Whenever it was during Solomon's reign that Hadad returned from Egypt, and the account is not specific about that, he seems to have caused little difficulty until towards the end of Solomon's forty years. For we are told that Solomon *"had peace on all sides round about him"* (1 Kings 4:24); and the naval venture was launched successfully, and without opposition, *"on the shore of the Red Sea, in the land of Edom"* (9:26). The Septuagint has an addition which says that Hadad and Rezron (enemy number two) combined: that the two worked together against Solomon, with Hadad becoming king in part of Syria. But this extra information is regarded by scholars as unlikely. It might have been inserted to try to account for the fact that Hadad was also the name of later Syrian kings, eleven successive kings in all.[3]

● **Rezon the son of Eliadah**

Rezon caused Solomon trouble further north. One of David's most decisive battles had been against Hadarezer, king of Zobah (2 Samuel 10:16-19; 1 Chronicles 19:18). But Rezon, one of the Syrian captains, had broken away from the service of the king of Zobah and he and a bunch of like-minded guerrillas had captured Damascus and made that their power base.

> *"God stirred him up another adversary, Rezon the son of Eliadah, which fled from his lord Hadadezer king of Zobah: and he gathered men unto him, and became captain over a band, when David slew them of Zobah: and they went to Damascus, and dwelt therein, and reigned in Damascus. And he was an adversary to Israel all the days of Solomon, beside the mischief that Hadad did: and he abhorred Israel, and reigned over Syria"* (1 Kings 11:23-25).

It seems that to some extent Rezon was a problem all through Solomon's reign, by guerrilla attacks, rather than open warfare.[4] His activity seems to have increased as Solomon drifted away from God.[5]

● **Jeroboam the son of Nebat**

Jeroboam was an adversary made of even sterner stuff than the first two. He *"lifted up his hand against the king"* (11:27) – which appears to mean that he attempted a rebellion of some sort. An industrious and energetic young man, Jeroboam had been entrusted by Solomon to oversee some building work in Jerusalem, and had apparently disagreed about some aspect of what he was then asked to do.

> *"Jeroboam the son of Nebat, an Ephrathite of Zereda, Solomon's servant, whose mother's name was Zeruah, a*

widow woman, even he lifted up his hand against the king. And this was the cause that he lifted up his hand against the king: Solomon built Millo, and repaired the breaches of the city of David his father. And the man Jeroboam was a mighty man of valour: and Solomon seeing the young man that he was industrious, he made him ruler over all the charge of the house of Joseph" (1 Kings 11:26-28).

Quite a bit of information is given in that passage about the initial disagreement between Solomon and the young Jeroboam. Notice that he was an Ephrathite (of the tribe of Ephraim) and that he had been engaged in building work in the City of David, the original city settlement which Solomon had expanded northwards. He was probably working to bridge the ravine which separated Zion from Moriah and Ophel, the future Tyropoeon. That work brought the Temple mountain within the city walls, enabling the fortification of the city of David to be completed.[6]

Undertaking this project, Jeroboam showed himself to be a very able and energetic man, which led Solomon to place him in charge of all the heavy work of the house of Joseph. It must have been while occupying this post that he attempted a rebellion against Solomon and it seems that it was because of the appointment of the Ephraimites to such heavy work that Jeroboam initiated a rebellion,[7] presumably together with his fellow tribesmen.[8]

Jeroboam was forced to leave Jerusalem but not without someone giving him a parting gift, although this encounter may have preceded his departure. The prophet Ahijah stopped Jeroboam to tell him that God was going to make him ruler over 10 of the 12 tribes and gave him ten pieces of a ripped-up mantle. He repeated the substance of what God had said to Solomon, this time encouraging Jeroboam to live in a way that was well pleasing to God:

"Thus saith the LORD, the God of Israel, Behold, I will rend the kingdom out of the hand of Solomon, and will give ten tribes to thee … Because that they have forsaken me, and have … not walked in my ways … I will take

265

the kingdom ... and will give it unto thee, even ten tribes ... and thou shalt reign according to all that thy soul desireth, and shalt be king over Israel. And it shall be, if thou wilt hearken unto all that I command thee, and wilt walk in my ways, and do that is right in my sight, to keep my statutes and my commandments, as David my servant did; that I will be with thee, and build thee a sure house, as I built for David, and will give Israel unto thee. And I will for this afflict the seed of David, but not for ever" (1 Kings 11:29-39).

Ahijah highlighted God's displeasure with Solomon, including rehearsing details of his idolatry, following Ashtoreth, Chemosh and Milcom, and again made the contrast between David's faithful following and Solomon's neglect. But it was also clear that God knew Jeroboam's innermost feelings and desires: what his soul desired and how he wanted to be king over the Northern tribes (11:37). Notwithstanding His foreknowledge of what Jeroboam would do, *"to make Israel to sin"*,[9] God's prophet now offered Jeroboam the opportunity to rule over the Northern tribes in covenant relationship with God, the same covenant promises that God had earlier made to David (2 Samuel 7:11). What an opportunity that was for this young man to rule for God, both in the near future and in the long term, in the Kingdom of God. Sadly, the plague of his own heart would prove too strong for him, too, as it was doing for Solomon.

Flight into Egypt

Aware of Jeroboam's rebellious intents, and perhaps Ahijah's prediction, Solomon tried to have him killed (1 Kings 11:40), forcing Jeroboam to flee to Egypt, where he stayed until after Solomon's death. The record says that he was given refuge by *"Shishak king of Egypt"* a monarch who is known in secular history as Shoshenq I, founder of the Twenty Second Dynasty in Egypt, a pharaoh who was of Libyan ancestry and reigned 945-924 BC.[10] There had been a lot of Libyan migration into Egypt and it has been suggested that by the end of the New Kingdom the Egyptian army was almost entirely made up of Libyan mercenaries. Prior to his reign, Shoshenq I had been the

Commander-in-Chief of that army, and he was the nephew of king Osorkon the Elder, who was also a Libyan and whose reign preceded the Twenty-First Dynasty, while his own son was married to Psusennes II's daughter Maatkara. So, Shoshenq I's rise to power was not wholly unexpected. But it did mark a significant change in Egypt's foreign policy. For, *"after more than a century of passivity on the part of Egyptian rulers, Sheshonq I intervened aggressively in the politics of the Levant to reassert pharaonic prestige there."* [11]

It should be clear, then, that Jeroboam's flight to Egypt would have been a welcome development so far as the new pharaoh was concerned. He would have brought inside information about Solomon's administration and the internal politics of the country, including about the disaffection of the Northern tribes, and this would have suited Sheshonq's future intentions very well. He was content to bide his time and to support Jeroboam as his protégé but, when the time was right, he took action. After Solomon's death and the fragmentation of the kingdom, Shesonq invaded Judah and took away as booty both the wealth of the Temple and the adjoining palaces. And it seems that he also invaded Israel at that time, perhaps to bring his protégé to heel, possibly because Jeroboam had reneged on the deal that he would, as King of Israel, pay tribute to Egypt.[12]

Solomon's Response

How did Solomon respond to these three adversaries through whom God brought pressure to bear? Was he responsive and, as a chastened and reproved older man, did he surrender to the will of God and reform his ways? The record in 1 Kings, having told us that Solomon tried to kill Jeroboam, concludes like this:

"And the rest of the acts of Solomon, and all that he did, and his wisdom, are they not written in the book of the acts of Solomon? And the time that Solomon reigned in Jerusalem over all Israel was forty years. And Solomon slept with his fathers, and was buried in the city of David his father: and Rehoboam his son reigned in his stead" (11:41-43).

No mention is made of his reaction or response, and it is the same in the Chronicles record, which neither mentions Solomon's idolatry nor the remedial action that God had taken. There is of course a good reason for this. Scripture gives us an opportunity to identify with its characters and then poses a challenge to each of us. How would we have reacted? How do we react to the varying circumstance of our own lives? What are we willing to do to change our ways and to come nearer to God? It's never too late for us.

NOTES

[1] Bro. Robert Roberts, *"Ways of Providence"*, pg.155 (6th Edition): *"Concerning these, we are informed (I. Kings xi.) that the Lord 'stirred them up'. The statement is an illustration of the subject in hand. The men themselves were not aware that the Lord 'stirred them up.' They simply found themselves the subject of a propensity to be active and enterprising in the promotion of their own interest in an antagonism to Solomon. They were instruments in the hands of God for the punishment of Solomon. The application of all these cases to our own times will be obvious. God has not changed. He has not abandoned the earth. By the hand of the Lord Jesus and the angels, He is working out a work in it, both as regards nations and individuals, Jews and Gentiles. It matters not that we cannot see the divine hand in visible operation."*

[2] 1 Kings 11:14-22; for the invasion by David, see 2 Samuel 8:13,14 and 1 Chronicles 18:12,13.

[3] Rawlinson, pg.549, says that Hadad was a royal title, rather like Pharaoh, which was the Syriac name for "The Sun". Farrar, pg.55, refers however to a variant reading of the LXX whereby Hadad became king *"in the land of Edom"*. He says there is confusion in the original text.

[4] Keil, pg.176: *"Rezon, on the other hand, really obtained possession of the rule over Damascus. Whether at the beginning or not till the end of Solomon's reign cannot be determined, since all that is clearly stated is that he was Solomon's adversary during the whole of his reign, and attempted to revolt from him from the very beginning. If, however, he made him-*

self king of Damascus in the earliest years of his reign, he cannot have maintained his sway very long, since Solomon afterwards built or fortified Tadmor in the desert, which he could not have done if he had not been lord over Damascus, as the caravan road from Gilead to Tadmor (Palmyra) went past Damascus".

[5] Rawlinson, pg.550, arranges the succession of the Damascus kings as follows: Hadad-Ezer (Hadad I), contemporary of David; Rezon (usurper), contemporary of Solomon; Hezion (Hadad II), contemporary of Rehoboam; Tabrimon (Hadad III), contemporary of Abijam; Ben-hadad (Hadad IV), contemporary of Asa.

[6] Keil, pg.177.

[7] Edersheim, vol v, pg.116, captures the feeling of resentment that was building up in Israel as one public work followed another.

[8] Edersheim, vol v, pg.116: *"His tribesmen, as a matter of course, came to know him as their chief and leader, while in daily close intercourse he would learn their grievances and sentiments. In such circumstances the result which followed was natural. The bold, strong, and ambitious Ephraimite, 'ruler over all the burden of the house of Joseph,' became the leader of the popular movement against Solomon".* ABD: *"In addition, it has been suggested that Solomon's cession of North Israelite towns (1 Kgs 9:10–13) to the Phoenician king Hiram was the 'last straw' which precipitated Jeroboam's revolt"* (Halpern 1974: 528).

[9] 1 Kings 14:16 is the first of 18 occurrences; that catchphrase is associated with Jeroboam from the time of his apostasy onwards.

[10] There are some variations on this date. For example, Morris Bierbrier, *"The Late New Kingdom in Egypt (c.1300-664 B.C.)"*, 1975, dated Shoshenq I's accession "between 945-940 B.C."

[11] Ian Shaw, *"The Oxford History of Ancient Egypt"*, OUP, 2000, pg.335.

[12] See Kitchen, pgs.32-34.

26

Solomon's Epitaph

THE search for any trace of regret in the Divine account is complicated by one thing about which we cannot be certain. From the time that his lapse into idolatry is described in Scripture (in 1 Kings 11:4-8), there is no record of anything more that Solomon said. God's words, through His prophet, about Solomon and about His future intention, are contained there; but if Solomon had anything to say we are not told what it was.

New Testament Witness

Nothing is said about his final deeds or thoughts and there is no assessment given about his eternal prospects. He gets, for example, no commendatory mention in Hebrews chapter 11, which would have been an important indication of his final state of mind. The Lord Jesus refers to Solomon twice. Once, when he refers to the coming of the Queen of Sheba, and once when he comments about his kingly splendour. Both mentions endorse the historical record, but the point of both is that the Lord's glory far surpassed that of the earthly magnificence to which Solomon aspired:

> *"The queen of the south shall rise up in the judgment with this generation, and shall condemn it: for she came from the uttermost parts of the earth to hear the wisdom of Solomon; and,* **behold, a greater than Solomon is here**" (Matthew 12:42).

> *"Consider the lilies of the field, how they grow; they toil not, neither do they spin:and yet I say unto you, That*

***even Solomon in all his glory was not arrayed like
one of these.*** *Wherefore, if God so clothe the grass of the
field, which to day is, and to morrow is cast into the
oven, shall he not much more clothe you, O ye of little
faith?* (Matthew 6:28-30).

Those two references, and the parallel accounts in
Luke's record of the gospel, are all that we are told about
Solomon in the New Testament, except for Stephen's
observation that: *"Solomon built him an house"* (Acts
7:47), and that is followed by the immediate comment that
God did not want a house, as such, but a broken and a contrite heart, not a stiff-necked and uncircumcised one
(7:51).

Old Testament Comment

After the historical record of Kings and Chronicles, and
setting aside those passages where reference is made without comment to Solomon's descendants or to the temple
arrangements that he and King David put in place, there
is only one other significant mention of him, with comment. When Nehemiah was remonstrating with the people
of Jerusalem who had returned from exile, he made the
following comparison:

*"I contended with them, and cursed them, and smote
certain of them, and plucked off their hair, and made
them swear by God, saying, Ye shall not give your
daughters unto their sons, nor take their daughters unto
your sons, or for yourselves.* ***Did not Solomon king of
Israel sin by these things? Yet among many
nations was there no king like him, who was
beloved of his God, and God made him king over
all Israel: nevertheless even him did outlandish
women cause to sin.*** *Shall we then hearken unto you
to do all this great evil, to transgress against our God in
marrying strange wives?"* (Nehemiah 13:25-27).

Nehemiah leaves us with the very same impression
that we get from the Book of Kings, if not from Chronicles,
that in his old age Solomon lost his heart and might therefore have lost his prospect of eternal life. As such that
stands as a dire warning to all of us: *"Wherefore let him*

that thinketh he standeth take heed lest he fall" (1 Corinthians 10:12).

A Few Regrets?

In the absence of any certain comment elsewhere in Scripture, are there any indications at all that Solomon might have showed some regret towards the end of his life, or that he turned back to God before it was too late? There may be some and it is for each reader to make of them what he or she will.

We cannot know precisely when Solomon wrote the Book of Ecclesiastes, or those Proverbs which bear his name. It may well be that he kept on writing them all through his life and speaking them as occasion allowed, including when he was giving judgement in civil or criminal cases. If so, we may be able to glean something of his attitudes and aspirations at this last stage of his life.

Solomon was well acquainted with women for nearly 1000 of them were known to him, both wives and concubines. But did they bring him happiness, or lasting affection? It would seem not. For these are some of the things he had to say about wives, and women in general, and there seems to be real regret and sadness in some of these observations:

"I find more bitter than death the woman, whose heart is snares and nets, and her hands as bands: whoso pleaseth God shall escape from her; but the sinner shall be taken by her. Behold, this have I found, saith the preacher, counting one by one, to find out the account: which yet my soul seeketh, but I find not: one man among a thousand have I found; but a woman among all those have I not found" (Ecclesiastes 7:26-28);

"Live joyfully with the wife whom thou lovest all the days of the life of thy vanity, which he hath given thee under the sun, all the days of thy vanity: for that is thy portion in this life, and in thy labour which thou takest under the sun" (9:9);

"A virtuous woman is a crown to her husband: but she

that maketh ashamed is as rottenness in his bones"
(Proverbs 12:4);

"Whoso findeth a wife findeth a good thing, and
obtaineth favour of the LORD" (18:22);

"The contentions of a wife are a continual dropping.
House and riches are the inheritance of fathers: and a
prudent wife is from the LORD" (19:13,14);

"It is better to dwell in a corner of the housetop, than
with a brawling woman in a wide house ... It is better to
dwell in the corner of the housetop, than with a brawl-
ing woman and in a wide house ... A continual drop-
ping in a very rainy day and a contentious woman are
alike" (21:9, 25:24, 27:15).

Lost Love?

One further piece of advice Solomon gave may be significant. Counselling his son (or any who wanted to follow
after him in the ways of God), he seems to be saying that it
is better to love one woman ardently than to spread your
affection hopelessly. Could it be that he once had such a
true love and then spent the rest of his life trying to recapture that ardent and spiritual partnership. For, he says, to
those who were to come after, ourselves included:

"Let thy fountain be blessed: and rejoice with the wife of
thy youth. Let her be as the loving hind and pleasant
roe; let her breasts satisfy thee at all times; and be thou
ravished always with her love" (Proverbs 5:18,19).

Perhaps Solomon once knew true love, only to lose it.
Seeking to recapture those early passions and feelings, he
indulged in excess – seeking love, he found instead women
whose hearts were like snares and nets, and their hands
as bands; contentious and brawling women, who made his
life a misery, even in a house as large as the palace at
Jerusalem. They were, as Nehemiah puts it, *"outlandish*
women". Given that they were a prime cause in luring
him away from God, there does seem to be more than a
tinge of regret in these writings. Perhaps Solomon did

come to deeply regret the course his later life had taken.

Conclusion of the Matter

We have considered the three courses of action that God took to show Solomon that He was angry with the way things had gone and that He was seeking to turn a foolish old king from his headlong rush towards destruction. Solomon was both wise and foolish: he knew the value of wisdom, but he was not always able to walk in wisdom's way. Now he was going downhill towards the grave.

There remains one possibility that he was prevailed upon to take heed of God's warnings and return to God's way. If Ecclesiastes was written at the end of Solomon's life, then it would indicate that he turned again to the true worship of the God of his fathers. For that book contains an assessment of all the vicissitudes of life, and concludes that fearing God is the one and only thing that leads to eventual satisfaction: it is the only way to long-term profit and eternal satisfaction.

This is not the place to examine that book at length, but there are some indications that it was written by a man in his later life. For example, he encourages people to follow God while they are still young, talks a lot about death and the state of the dead, portrays old age as though he had personal experience (notably in chapter 12). And, here and there, as he turns his gaze heaven-ward, he make observations that could indicate that he had learned his own lesson about the God who alone was worthy of worship.

"Be not rash with thy mouth, and let not thine heart be hasty to utter any thing before God: for God is in heaven, and thou upon earth: therefore let thy words be few ... When thou vowest a vow unto God, defer not to pay it; for he hath no pleasure in fools: pay that which thou hast vowed. Better is it that thou shouldest not vow, than that thou shouldest vow and not pay. Suffer not thy mouth to cause thy flesh to sin; neither say thou before the angel, that it was an error: wherefore should God be angry at thy voice, and destroy the work of thine hands?" (Ecclesiastes 5:2-6);

Solomon's Epitaph

"In the day of prosperity be joyful, but in the day of adversity consider: God also hath set the one over against the other, to the end that man should find nothing after him ... It is good that thou shouldest take hold of this; yea, also from this withdraw not thine hand: for he that feareth God shall come forth of them all" (7:14-18);

"Let us hear the conclusion of the whole matter: Fear God, and keep his commandments: for this is the whole duty of man. For God shall bring every work into judgment, with every secret thing, whether it be good, or whether it be evil" (12:13,14).

God will most certainly *"bring every work into judgement"*, Solomon's works as well as our own. Every knee will bow before the *"greater than Solomon"*, to declare him Lord and, until then, none of us can know the outcome of our own lives, far less of Solomon's. The key issue is always to: *"Examine yourselves, whether ye be in the faith; prove your own selves. Know ye not your own selves ...?"* (2 Corinthians 13:5).

The Last Word
One writer summed up Solomon's life in the following terms, writing off all his future prospects:

"No more is told of him than that, at the close of a reign of forty years, he 'slept with his fathers, and was buried in the city of David his father.' So far as we know, in that death-chamber no words of earnest, loving entreaty to serve Jehovah were spoken to his successor, such as David had uttered; no joyous testimony here as regarded the past, nor yet strong faith and hope as concerned the future, such as had brightened the last hours of David. It is to us a silent death-chamber in which King Solomon lay. No bright sunset here, to be followed by a yet more glorious morning. He had done more than any king to denationalise Israel. And on the morrow of his death: rebellion within the land; outside its borders – Edom and Syria ready to spring to arms, Egypt under Shishak gathering up its might; and only a Rehoboam to hold the rudder of the State in the rising storm" (Edersheim, V, pg.119).

Another offers this analysis, which looks not just at the man but at his legacy so far as the nation and the world is concerned:

"The downfall of such a man as Solomon was a tragedy of the first magnitude, for it involved the ruin and devastation of the land and the people for three thousand years, and the deferment of deliverance and blessing for all the nations of the earth. Everything has doubtless been according to the counsel and foreknowledge of God (Acts 2.23); but this does not lessen the guilt of sinful men" (Fereday, pg.103).

We may wish to take a more sympathetic approach to the king's fate, perhaps hoping for the best for him as well as for ourselves. He undoubtedly changed the structure and attitude of the nation, in part for good. But, in the final analysis, what matters is not what we *do* in this life but what we *are*: the sort of people we have become. It is a sad outcome if we gain high prestige and power in this life, but lose out in the life that is to come.

Note the words of the Lord Jesus, who first commented upon Solomon's glory, and then offered some timely advice. We can do no better than end with the Lord's words for, like Solomon, we can be both wise and foolish. We need to ensure that wisdom gets, and keeps, the upper hand.

"Consider the lilies how they grow: they toil not, they spin not; and yet I say unto you, that Solomon in all his glory was not arrayed like one of these ... And seek not ye what ye shall eat, or what ye shall drink, neither be ye of doubtful mind. For your Father knoweth that ye have need of these things. ***But rather seek ye the kingdom of God; and all these things shall be added unto you. Fear not, little flock; for it is your Father's good pleasure to give you the kingdom"*** (Luke 12:27-32).